THE CIVIL WAR
AND THE SUMMER OF 2020

RECONSTRUCTING AMERICA
Andrew L. Slap, series editor

The Civil War and the Summer of 2020

Hilary N. Green and
Andrew L. Slap, Editors

Foreword by
Andre E. Johnson

Fordham University Press
New York 2024

Copyright © 2024 Fordham University Press

All rights reserved. No part of this publication may be reproduced, stored in a retrieval system, or transmitted in any form or by any means—electronic, mechanical, photocopy, recording, or any other—except for brief quotations in printed reviews, without the prior permission of the publisher.

Fordham University Press has no responsibility for the persistence or accuracy of URLs for external or third-party Internet websites referred to in this publication and does not guarantee that any content on such websites is, or will remain, accurate or appropriate.

Fordham University Press also publishes its books in a variety of electronic formats. Some content that appears in print may not be available in electronic books.

Visit us online at www.fordhampress.com.

Library of Congress Cataloging-in-Publication Data available online at https://catalog.loc.gov.

Printed in the United States of America

26 25 24   5 4 3 2 1

First edition

Dedicated to those who died of COVID-19 and at the hands of police violence during the summer of 2020

Contents

Foreword. Telling the Story: George Floyd and the Legacy of Black Truth
Andre E. Johnson   xiii

Preface   xxi

Introduction
Hilary N. Green | 1

VIOLENCE

1   White Supremacy, the American Militia, and the Legacy of the Civil War Era
Barbara A. Gannon | 13

2   African Americans and Native Americans in North Carolina During the Summer of 2020: The Struggle for People of Color to Find a Shared Civil War–Era Memory
Jaime Amanda Martinez | 20

3   Witnessing Ned Scott's Coffin: Spectacular Police Violence in the Age of Emancipation
John Bardes | 28

4   Abaline Miller and the Struggle for Justice against the Employer Police State after Slavery
William Horne | 38

RESISTANCE

5   From Eagle Buttons to Face Masks: The Dangers of Expressing Racial Equality
    Emmanuel Dabney | 49

6   "Give Me My Rights": Patriotism and Protest Among Black Civil War Soldiers and Black Lives Matter Activists
    Jonathan Lande | 57

7   A Lens Through Which We Can View Society: Sports and Race in America
    Daryl A. Carter | 66

8   Slave Agency, the Emancipation Monument, and History's Reckoning
    Karen Cook Bell | 74

9   Fighting for Black Humanity: Political Action of Post-Emancipation Black Christians
    Nicole Myers Turner | 81

10 Jim Crow Then, Jim Crow Now: Police Violence, Tort Law, and Black Resistance in the Twentieth and Twenty-First Centuries
    Myisha S. Eatmon | 90

11 "How wonderful a country": Black Lives Matter and the Long History of Aboriginal Resistance
    Samuel Watts | 97

MEMORY

12 Carpetbagging the Colfax Riot Marker
    LeeAnna Keith | 107

13 "Moving History": The Life and Afterlife of Louisville's Confederate Monument
Anne E. Marshall | 113

14 Goodbye, Calhoun. What's Next?: The Future of Charleston's Commemorative Landscape
Adam H. Domby | 122

15 "Back at Bragg": Civil War Memory and the US Army
Beau Cleland | 131

16 There's still no balm in Gilead: The Fatal Costs of Traumatic Memory
Scott Hancock | 140

Acknowledgments 151
List of Contributors 153
Index 157

Foreword

*Telling the Story: George Floyd
and the Legacy of Black Truth*

Andre E. Johnson

A year after the murder of George Floyd, an AP reporter interviewed me for a story about the case of George Floyd and how video, taken by either witnesses or police body cameras, is being quickly shared and used to dispute initial police accounts. He wanted to talk about how this visual information could affect police reform measures and why such videos were powerful, especially when they disprove information from police. Up until then, he had operated from a belief that the initial police reports were always true. Then, at least for this reporter, the murder of George Floyd changed his steadfast belief in how police operate. Before Darnella Frazier uploaded the video that shocked and horrified the world, the Minneapolis Police Department put out an initial statement that read, "Man Dies After Medical Incident During Police Interaction."[1] According to the report, Floyd had "physically resisted" arrest:

> Two officers arrived and located the suspect, a male believed to be in his 40s, in his car. He was ordered to step from his car. After he got out, he physically resisted officers. Officers were able to get the suspect into handcuffs and noted he appeared to be suffering medical distress. Officers called for an ambulance. He was transported to Hennepin County Medical Center by ambulance where he died a short time later.[2]

The blatant lie by the Police Department in its initial report to the media prompted the AP reporter to do some digging, and what he found was shocking, at least to him. He noticed that this was not the first incident of police lying in their initial reports involving fatal police encounters. He found other cases in which police misled the public or outright lied about an incident of abuse. When he interviewed me, he seemed excited that these videos existed to refute lies peddled by the police. He asked me whether I thought change might happen now that these videos existed. I had to gently remind him that this was not the first time we have had video evidence and that despite body cameras, there was still, in many cases, no one held accountable for the death of a Black person at the hands of police. Furthermore, I shared that while some see these videos as our saviors in fighting racial injustice, the sharing of Black death has its own set of problems. However, I had to concede that if it had not been for Frazier's bravery in recording that video and uploading it for the world to see, Derek Chauvin would likely still be on the police force, training officers.

Why did it take Frazier's video for us to "believe"? Why not just take the testimony of the people who begged the police to stop killing George Floyd? Why not believe them? Maybe the answer lies in the fact that America has had a hard time believing Black people. Black truth has always been problematic. Black truth has always been questioned and viewed as inaccurate. It is almost as if truth and Blackness cannot coincide—that Black truth is somehow tainted because of the conditions in which Black folks find themselves. For a long period in this country, courts would not receive Black testimony and Black people could not testify in any case against a white person. Black people could not serve on many juries, and many times, the only way that Black people found themselves in courtrooms was as defendants.

But Black people kept sharing Black truth with all who would listen. Before the advent of cellphones, many would turn to newspapers to record abuses that Black people suffered at the hands of racists. One such person was Bishop Henry McNeal Turner. Born "free" in New Berry Courthouse, South Carolina, in 1834, Turner was an autodidact who always aspired to be more. Early in his life, he had a dream in which he saw himself speaking to thousands of people and helping members of his race. His rhetorical training started at the feet of his grandmother, who taught him the art of storytelling, and the itinerant preachers who used to travel around preaching the word of God. As a child, Turner used to mimic the preachers he heard as his friends served as ecstatic congregants in his backyard church. When friends were not available, animals served as Turner's audience.

Turner's father died early in his childhood, and when his mother remarried, the family moved to Abbeville, South Carolina. There Turner started to work for a group of attorneys who noticed his quick wit, sharp mind, and astounding memory. They took it upon themselves to further his educational pursuits by teaching him the classics, sciences, and even theology. He had always wanted a formal education, but the state of South Carolina did not allow African Americans to attend a school or for others to teach them how to read and/or write. Turner would later call this moment an answer to his prayers.

Turner would later accept his call to preach at the age of nineteen in the Methodist Episcopal Church. Three years later, he married Eliza Ann Peacher of Columbia, South Carolina. She would be instrumental in his early days of preaching as Turner served as an itinerant preacher for the denomination. However, despite preaching to both Black and white audiences and his success on the revival circuit, Turner quickly became disillusioned with the Methodist Church because, although licensed to preach, he could never be ordained or become a bishop. During a serendipitous trip to New Orleans, Turner met Willis H. Revels, who would introduce him to the African Methodist Episcopal Church (AME). Turner would later join the church and find himself assigned to churches in Baltimore and Washington.

It was here that Turner's public career took off. He not only served as pastor of Israel AME Church in Washington, but he also served as a regular correspondent for the *Christian Recorder* newspaper. Several newspapers featured his sermons, and he hosted many senators and other members of Congress in his church. He also became a supporter of the Union during the Civil War. Many of his sermons aimed at encouraging his congregants to support in some way the Union effort. Turner also led efforts to recruit members for the First Regiment United States Colored Troops.

For his hard work and support of the cause, President Abraham Lincoln appointed him chaplain of the group, making him the first African American named chaplain of any branch of the US military.

During this time, Turner preached integrated revivals, commanded audiences with senators, congressional leaders, and presidents, and became a popular correspondent for the *Christian Recorder* newspaper. He also became a state Constitutional delegate and a state representative. He would eventually become the presiding elder of Georgia for his church and eventually bishop. Along with these accomplishments, Turner was the first African American postmaster general (in Georgia), offered bills in the Georgia House of Representatives giving all women the right to vote, promoted a bill to create an eight-hour workday, was the publication manager (1876–80) of the African Methodist Episcopal Church (AME), and ordained the first woman as an elder in the AME church—an ordination that the other bishops later rescinded.

Moreover, while doing all of this, Turner found time to start three newspapers—*Southern Recorder* (1887–89), *Voice of Missions* (1893–1900), and *The Voice of the People* (1901–4)—and serve as editor of all three; take four trips to Africa himself; establish the AME church in Africa; write numerous articles and essays for various newspapers; write Introductions to several books; preach and lecture all over the country; and carry out his Episcopal duties. In short, if he lived today, many would call Turner a public intellectual or public theologian—and yes, given the copious amount of material Turner wrote, he would definitely be a blogger and active on social media.

After the war and Union victory, Turner returned south and involved himself in the politics of Reconstruction. Like many African Americans, Turner believed that Reconstruction would lay the foundation for equality. On January 1, 1866, as the keynote speaker for Emancipation Day services in Augusta, Georgia, Turner, at probably the height of his optimism, ended his speech with the charge to Blacks in the audience:

> Let us love the whites, and let by-gones be by-gones, neither taunt nor insult them for past grievances, respect them; honor them; work for them; but still let us be men. Let us show them we can be a people, respectable, virtuous, honest, and industrious, and soon their prejudice will melt away, and with God for our father, we will all be brothers.[3]

As America began the Reconstruction project, Turner quickly found out how tough it would be for white prejudice to melt away. On one trip to Alabama, Turner, in a letter published June 23, 1866, in the *Christian Recorder*, shared the story of the beating of Rev. Robert Alexander—a minister who wanted to preach and start a school in the area. "Four white citizens broke into his room at midnight," Turner wrote, "and beat and stabbed him until he appeared like a lump of curdled blood." When the women ran screaming to the Agent of the Freedmen's Bureau for help, saying, "Come and save our minister from being murdered," the Agent only replied, "I can't do anything for you" and "never got out of his bed." Turner closed the letter with a lament: "O God! where is our civilization? Is this Christendom, or is it hell? Pray for us."[4]

Turner, while a member of the Georgia House of Representatives, had an opportunity to participate in a joint committee to investigate the Georgia Penitentiary System. During Turner's investigation, he discovered that Black women not only were on chain gangs but also were "whipped on the butt in the presence of men" and made to relieve themselves in front of men. Then there was a story of a man known only as Aaron, whom prison guards whipped with a "double strap."[5]

"They stripped him stark naked and tied him with the shackles around the crosstie and then stretched him out with his belly down on the crossties. He fell off and was then whipped on the privates. As we were going home at night, he stopped and said, 'Good-bye, boys, I am going to die.' Aaron's torturer then said, 'If you want to die, I'll help you.' He then whipped him for about ten minutes, when he fell dead. He was buried just about day the next morning."[6] Even when prisoners became sick, they were subject to beatings. Turner learned of one such case when the doctor, instead of treating the man, killed him by bludgeoning him

FOREWORD   xvii

to death. There was no inquest held over the body, and a fellow prisoner had to make a box for the dead prisoner.[7]

Turner testified before Congress on November 3, 1871. When asked about the "lawless violence and outrages" perpetrated by the Ku Klux Klan, Turner talked about how "night prowlers" threatened his own life. "I am satisfied that on two or three occasions," Turner answered, "I may say in a dozen instances, if I had not secreted myself in houses at times, in the woods at other times, in a hollow log at another time, I would have been assassinated by a band of night-prowlers, or rovers, I will call them."[8]

When asked by a member of the committee if Turner had known of any people "injured" by "night marauders," Turner answered that he had seen "scores of them. I have seen men who had their backs lacerated. I have seen other men who had bullets in them; I have seen others who had their arms shot off, shot so badly that they had to be amputated; I have seen others with legs shot off. I have heard of any quantity of horrible deed."[9]

When asked how many murders had been committed in the state since the spring of 1868, Turner responded:

> We held a Southern States convention week before last in Columbia, South Carolina, at which place there were delegates from all the Southern States. We met together at the request of the committee on murders and outrages, and according to the best of our knowledge and belief it was estimated that since [R]econstruction between fifteen hundred and sixteen hundred had been perpetrated.[10]

When his interlocutor asked, "in the South?" Turner answered, "No, in the state of Georgia." When pressed on how many murders had happened in all the southern states since 1868, Turner responded that it had not been "less than twenty thousand." That number, Turner noted, was what delegates had agreed upon based on the reporting that each delegate made to the "murder and outrages" committee.[11]

In his many letters to the editor, Turner chronicled the state-sponsored violence perpetrated against African Americans. In one to the *Colored Tribune* published March 18, 1876, Turner wondered just how long African Americans could last in America. "I have just figured up the reported number of colored persons who have been brutally killed within the last twenty-five days in this State alone," Turner wrote, "and find the sum to be twenty-seven." Moreover, the twenty-seven Turner wrote could have been "augmented to thirty-seven if all the facts were known through the State" and "no white man has been or will be arrested if he kills forty Negroes."[12]

In another letter to the editor of the *Christian Recorder* newspaper dated January 4, 1883, Turner wrote that it had been estimated that the murders and outrages perpetrated upon Black people since 1867 were somewhere in the neighborhood of 200,000.[13] Quoting an article in the *New Orleans Christian Advocate*, Turner, in a letter to the editor dated February 22, 1883, wrote that "there is not a night that some colored person is not lynched in the State of Louisiana. . . . There is not a night, or a day either, the year round that our people are not most brutally murdered."[14]

In another editorial in the *Voice of Missions* newspaper, Turner, responding to his emigration critics, wrote that "times are growing worse, the Negro is becoming more degraded, our treatment more brutal, laws more inhuman[e] are being enacted, and not a single remedy is proposed, not a plan suggested, not an idea advanced for the betterment of our condition."[15]

After the Supreme Court ruled in *Plessy v. Ferguson* that separate could indeed be equal, Turner lamented the decision. Calling the court an "abominable conclave of Negro hating demons," he wrote, "I have absolutely no interest in the issues of the bloody, lynching nation, with its brutal Supreme Court in Washington City issuing decisions against my race which were never dreamed of in hell." He implicated both political parties—Democratic and Republican—and wrote, "Neither of them care[s] anything about the Negro" because, in Turner's estimation, neither party in Congress "ever open[ed] their mouths about the way my race is butchered, shot and burnt without law or civil rule." He continued his denunciation when he wrote, "This rotten country has no business being a nation anyway." He called the nation an "an organized mob," and for those who did not participate directly in "lawless murders, Jim Crow car discriminations and every other devilment against my race, [they] stand by and say 'well done' by their silence."[16]

Turner would eventually believe that emigration to Africa was the answer to most of the problems African Americans faced. However, while the majority of African Americans did not favor African emigration, Turner continued to bear witness to the atrocities that Black people suffered on a daily basis. He, along with Ida B. Wells, Frances Ellen Watkins Harper, and a host of others, continued to proclaim the truth about racialized violence to any who would hear it.

Turner's continued chronicling of Black death, coupled with his stinging critiques and indictments of both white people and the "scullion" class of Negro leadership, frustrated many. While many wanted to look the other way, Turner

FOREWORD   xix

kept the focus on the vile and wicked deaths of Black people across America. Turner warned that if nothing was done about the extrajudicial killings and racialized violence from white terrorists on Black bodies, people would just become accustomed to it—people would believe that since it is ubiquitous, it must just be the natural order of things.

The essays in this volume continue the tradition of bearing witness to Black truth. Despite governors and state legislatures around the country banning the teaching of this history, the Civil War and Reconstruction are pivotal points in the history of our nation. A true understanding of the tenor and times during that period will help us navigate the treacherous waters we face today. As we grapple with racialized violence, voter suppression, police brutality, white Christian nationalism, and much more in our own time, reading and hearing the voices of those who bore witness to share Black truth in their own perilous times should encourage us to do the same.

Notes

1. Andy Mannix, "Minneapolis Chief Cites 'Fluid' Situation for Troubling Misinformation released After George Floyd Death," *Minneapolis Star Tribune*, June 3, 2020, https://www.startribune.com/mpls-police-still-haven-t-explained-misinformation-after-floyd-s-death/570970152/.

2. John Elder, "Investigative Update on Critical Incident," Internet Archive, May 26, 2020, https://web.archive.org/web/20200526183652/https://www.insidempd.com/2020/05/26/man-dies-after-medical-incident-during-police-interaction/.

3. Henry McNeal Turner, "Emancipation Day Speech," in Andre E. Johnson, ed., *The Speeches of Henry McNeal Turner: The Press, The Platform, and the Pulpit* (Jackson: University of Mississippi Press, 2023), 41.

4. Henry McNeal Turner, "Starling Correspondence," *Christian Recorder*, June 23, 1866, The #HMTProject, http://www.thehenrymcnealturnerproject.org/2017/09/starling-correspondence-june-23-1866.html.

5. Joint Committee to Investigate the Georgia Penitentiaries: Testimony of Hubbard Cureton and James Maxwell as asked by Henry M. Turner, May 5, 1870, #TheHMTProject, http://www.thehenrymcnealturnerproject.org/2017/10/joint-committee-to-investigate-georgia.html.

6. "Joint Committee to Investigate the Georgia Penitentiaries."

7. "Joint Committee to Investigate the Georgia Penitentiaries."

8. Testimony of Henry M. Turner, November 3, 1871, Testimony Taken by the Joint Select Committee to Inquire into the Condition of Affairs of the Late Insurrectionary States. Georgia, vol. 7. (Washington: Government Printing Office, 1872), 1035.

9. "Testimony of Henry M. Turner," 1036.

10. "Testimony of Henry M. Turner," 1041–42.

11. "Testimony of Henry M. Turner," 1042.

12. Henry McNeal Turner, "Letter from Dr. Turner," *Colored Tribune* (Savannah, Georgia), March 18, 1876, The #HMTProject, http://www.thehenrymcnealturnerproject.org/2017/10/letter-from-dr-turner-march-18-1876.html.

13. Henry McNeal Turner, "Advisory Committee of African Colonization," in Andre E. Johnson, ed., *An African American Pastor Before and During the American Civil War, Volume 4: The Literary Archive of Henry McNeal Turner, 1880–1892* (Lewiston, NY: Mellen Press, 2015), 9.

14. Henry McNeal Turner, "The African Question," quoted in Johnson, *An African American Pastor Before and During the American Civil War, Volume 4*, 18.

15. "Why Don't You Go to Heaven!" *Voice of Missions*, June 1894.

16. Henry McNeal Turner quoted in *No Future in This Country: The Prophetic Pessimism of Bishop Henry McNeal Turner* (Jackson: University of Mississippi Press, 2020), 40–41.

Preface

George Floyd's murder in the summer of 2020 sparked a national reckoning for the United States that had been 400 years in the making. Millions of Americans took to the streets to protest both the murder and the centuries of systemic racism that already existed among European colonists but transformed with the arrival of the first African American slaves in 1619. The violence needed to enforce that systemic racism for all those years, from the slave driver's whip to state-sponsored police brutality, attracted the primary attention of the protesters. The resistance of the protesters echoed generations of African Americans' resisting the violence and the oppression of white supremacy. Their resistance to violence, though, soon spread to other aspects of systemic racism, including a cultural hegemony built on and reinforcing white supremacy. At the heart of this white supremacist culture is the memory of the Civil War era, when in 1861 8 million white Americans revolted against their country to try to safeguard their enslavement of 4 million African Americans. Despite these traitors' causing the death of more than 750,000 Americans in a four-year insurrection, in the decades afterward the United States chose to honor many of its leaders. These men who had led armies against their own country to preserve slavery and white supremacy had huge statues erected in their honor and schools and army bases named after them, and they were glorified in history books and movies. This volume seeks to show the intertwined and longstanding connections between systemic racism, violence, resistance, and the memory of the Civil War era in the United States that finally exploded in the summer of 2020.

The volume has three interconnected sections that build on one another. The first section, titled "Violence," explores systemic racism in the Civil War era and now, with essays on topics including slavery, policing, and slave patrols. The second section, titled "Resistance," shows how African Americans resisted the violence for the past two centuries in essays discussing matters including self-emancipation and African American soldiers. The last section, titled "Memory," investigates the ways Americans have remembered both this violence and resistance since the Civil War, including Confederate monuments and historical markers.

This volume is primarily for nonhistorians, so it is not a typical collection of academic essays. The goal is for the essays to be accessible and to represent a wide variety of perspectives. While all the essays draw on history and connect it to the present, many also share the personal experiences and feelings of the authors.

Diversity is an important and intentional aspect of this volume. We intentionally sought scholars of different genders and races, along with scholars spread among different levels of seniority. Other contributors have scholarly credentials but work outside university history departments.

While experiencing the tragedies of a global pandemic, the United States and the entire world went through the throes of a new Freedom Summer in 2020. This reckoning with institutional racism, enforced with violence and white supremacist memory, was centuries in the making and will take decades to dismantle fully.

The Civil War
and the Summer of 2020

Introduction

Hilary N. Green

You must accept them and accept them with love. For these innocent people have no other hope. They are, in effect, still trapped in a history which they do not understand; and until they understand it, they cannot be released from it.

—James Baldwin, *The Fire Next Time*[1]

We have to fight again on old battlefields but our confidence is greater, our vision is clearer, and our ultimate victory surer because of the contributions of a militant, passionate black giant left behind him.

—Martin Luther King Jr., "Honoring Dr. Du Bois"[2]

May 25, 2020, began as a typical day of the global COVID-19 pandemic. The number of infected individuals continued to spike as the mounting death toll approached a milestone of 100,000 American deaths. Globally, scientists worked toward creating a vaccine and slowing down a pandemic hemorrhaging lives in both wealthy and poor countries. Politically, an embattled US president sought re-election against a former senator and vice president who hoped his third attempt at the presidency would be successful. In Minneapolis, Minnesota, however, the cellphone footage of the arrest and subsequent death of an African American man cemented 2020 for reasons besides the pandemic as a year that scholars would discuss for generations. By evening, the day saw the introduction of another hashtag victim to the American lexicon but also the unleashing of a global racial reckoning.

On this day, Minneapolis police officer Derek Chauvin arrested George Floyd for using a counterfeit $20 bill while purchasing cigarettes at a convenience store. The arrest turned deadly. Chauvin, a white officer with a record of eighteen complaints filed against him, pinned the handcuffed, forty-six-year-old Floyd with his knee on his neck for almost nine minutes. Earning the citizen documentarian a 2021 Pulitzer Prize in the Special Citations and Awards category, Darnella Frazier's footage captured Floyd's words that he could not breathe and his final calls for his mother before dying.[3] The pleas of onlookers went unheard. The two other on-the-scene Minneapolis officers also failed to intercede. Frazier's recording of the incident, moreover, did not move Chauvin. Floyd died on the Minneapolis streets. The death of the father, son, and beloved community member prompted community action nationally and internationally.

As the Floyd family mourned, communities took to the streets. These nonviolent Black Lives Matter (BLM) protesters demanded police and criminal justice reform while adhering to COVID-safe practices. Nineteen-sixty-eight seemed like an apt comparison based on the police response to unarmed, racially diverse protesters. The assassinations of Martin Luther King Jr. and Robert F. Kennedy caused mass protests by those who mourned the civil rights activist and a major white ally who sought the presidency. If the Nobel Peace Prize–winning crusader of nonviolence and the major white civil rights ally for social change could be killed, how could ordinary Americans maintain any hope in a country plagued by police violence, a resurgent Ku Klux Klan, de-industrialization, urban decay exacerbated by urban renewal policies, and a global military conflict in southeast Asia? Communities of color felt under siege.[4] Even their athletic heroes were not exempt from the policing of their actions on and off the sports stage. Stripped of his boxing title, Muhammad Ali faced economic repercussions for his protests against the Vietnam War. The Olympic Project for Human Rights (OPHR) proposed boycotting the Summer Olympics but "elect[ed] instead to encourage athletes to protest as they saw fit." For raising their fists in the air with bowed heads, Tommie Smith and John Carlos lost their Olympic medals earned at the 1968 Summer Olympics held in Mexico City. These men also inspired a generation of athletes to use their platforms to fight for social justice.[5]

When white armed protesters demanded the re-opening of economies temporarily closed for public safety during the pandemic in early 2020, the hands-off and sympathetic police response drew attention to the varied application of law and order in the country. In contrast, the post–George Floyd BLM protesters encountered tear gas, rubber bullets, and mass arrests. At one rally in Kenosha, Wisconsin, Kyle Rittenhouse, a white Illinois youth, shot three protesters after police welcomed the civilian seeking to protect the city. Despite killing two protesters and seriously injuring another, he received bail until his Federal murder trial began. A jury later acquitted him. The different racialized and partisan police responses made visible the persisting racial legacy of the two Americas, "one black, one white—separate and unequal," discussed in the 1968 Kerner Commission Report. Despite progress made nationally, the COVID-19 pandemic compounded the unresolved issues of racism, income inequality, food and healthcare deserts, and policing.[6] Beyond the United States, BLM activists demanded an end of global policing practices targeting Black, Brown, Indigenous, and Aboriginal communities. From Minneapolis to Sydney, Australia, activists took to the streets and voiced their discontent in response to George Floyd's murder.[7]

As the long summer of 2020 continued, media coverage added other names of African American victims to accounts of police brutality occurring before and after Floyd's murder. Breonna Taylor, a medical worker, was killed during a police raid on her Louisville, Kentucky, apartment. The local protests turned national with allies demanding justice for her death in their respective communities. While Taylor's family received a multi-million-dollar settlement, her death did not prevent the police from killing a Louisville barbecue vendor who fed the homeless and peaceful protesters.[8] Three white men's pursuit and murder of Ahmaud Arbery when he jogged in a Glynn County, Georgia, neighborhood energized the African American running community, members of which brought attention to his death by sharing their "Running While Black" stories on social media and participating in memorial runs.[9] With each subsequent death and national reports of earlier cases such as that of Elijah McClain of Aurora, Colorado, American communities contemplated what could be done in terms of police reform. Combined with the COVID-19 death toll reaching Civil War–level casualty numbers, scholars began to wonder whether 1868 or the entire Civil War era would be a better comparison than the twentieth-century references for the police killings of African Americans and marginalized communities of color.[10]

The American Civil War and Reconstruction eras became increasingly relevant as the summer continued. After surviving impeachment proceedings, an unsympathetic and emboldened President Donald Trump used Federal resources to arrest and imprison nonviolent protesters seeking social justice. He took to social media. He derided BLM protesters as lawless anti-Americans while praising white open-the-COVID-economy protesters as patriotic Americans. He even used the US Park Service Police to clear a Black Lives Matter protest held at Lafayette Park for a photo op with Bible in hand in front of St. John's Episcopal Church in Washington, D.C. With every tweet and Fox News interview, the forty-fifth President seemed more like his impeached and white supremacist Reconstruction-era predecessor Andrew Johnson than either Lyndon B. Johnson or Richard Nixon. African Americans and communities of color did not have a place in his vison for the United States. Like his Reconstruction predecessor, Trump held a contempt for BLM activists and their allies that proved palatable. Echoes of Frederick Douglass's assessment of Johnson at Lincoln's second inauguration resonated for this author and other scholars of the Reconstruction era: "Whatever Andrew Johnson may be, he certainly is no friend of our race."[11]

The racial reckoning extended even to the Civil War commemorative landscape filled with monuments promoting a pro-Confederate historical interpretation. Communities began questioning these monuments erected during the height of political and cultural redemption of post-emancipation and Reconstruction gains. Monuments dedicated to Confederate generals as well as to Christopher Columbus, settler colonists, enslavers, and individuals connected to indigenous genocide fell. Media coverage capitalized on the fodder provided by protesters in Birmingham, Alabama, and elsewhere who dramatically toppled these stone reminders of the Civil War, racism, and perceived lack of inclusion in community decision making. However, the media failed to document the everyday democratic processes, resulting in their removal, or how 2020 represents another phase of monument removal initiated by the murder of nine African American Emanuel AME Church parishioners by Dylann Roof in Charleston, South Carolina, in 2015. Petitions, in-person hearings, and procedural votes by city and county commissioners do not make for television ratings, nor do they attract clicks in online message boards. George Floyd's murder resulted in more democracy rather than less. The placement of these largely southern monuments in front of courthouses had lent itself to the protests over police reform and became easy victories in the post-Floyd racial reckoning. Within a year, almost 300 monuments and memorials had been removed from courthouse lawns, public squares, and college campuses.[12]

The reassessment of the American cultural landscape prompted a real and rhetorical backlash. Social media fears of a possible July 4, 2020, protest attracted large numbers of AR-15–toting monument defenders at the Gettysburg National Military Park. Debates over statues of Presidents Abraham Lincoln and U.S. Grant, removals of two Federal Civil War–era monuments, and announcement of the Federal military installation renaming effort contributed to the toppling of the Rochester, New York, monument of the nineteenth-century African American leader Frederick Douglass.[13] The contested and unresolved Civil War memory wars came to bear on contemporary issues as "heritage not hate" supporters went on the defensive. President Trump further inflamed the latest iteration of the Civil War culture wars by issuing an Executive Order 13933 protecting monuments and memorials. This executive action became a template for other monument defenders globally. The UK Parliament debated legislation protecting controversial monuments from so-called "woke worthies and baying mobs."[14]

Turning his gaze to American education curriculum, President Trump also launched the 1776 Commission with a prominent Civil War historian in attendance. Executive Order 13958 tasked the group of nonhistorians and others with correcting "one-sided and divisive accounts [that] too often ignore or fail to properly honor and recollect the great legacy of the American national experience—our country's valiant and successful effort to shake off the curse of slavery and to use the lessons of that struggle to guide our work toward equal rights for all citizens in the present."[15] Without any professional historians serving on the assembled commission, the executive action attempted to delegitimize both The 1619 Project, led by Pulitzer Prize- and MacArthur Genius Grant–winning Nikole-Hannah Jones, and professional scholars who emphasize diverse understandings of the American past.[16] The Executive Order was announced a few days before Election Day, and the consequences were not clear at the time. Was this another political and cultural redemption like the 1876 presidential election contest between Rutherford B. Hayes and Samuel Tilden? Would the outcome of the November 2020 election fuel another reconciliation over race and Civil War memory as discussed by historians since David Blight published *Race and Reunion*? In this national reckoning, would African Americans and marginalized communities again be excluded as some white politicos demanded over the summer of 2020 events and post-election contestation of the results?[17]

The final 1776 Commission report suggested the latter. Consisting of a twenty-page report with four appendices, the report fulfilled the commission's charge. The members of the commission produced a "report summarizing the principles of the American founding and how those principles have shaped our country."[18] Instead, the final report reflected an ahistorical and whitewashed narrative of the nation's past, including the role of the Civil War era. Report writers cherry-picked quotations from Frederick Douglass and Abraham Lincoln. Despite the loss of lives, the report viewed resolution of the Civil War as occurring on the battlefield with the surrenders of Robert E. Lee and other Confederate generals in 1865. The report also framed the Reconstruction-era constitutional amendments as a mistake. This neo–Dunning School interpretation blamed Black authors and their allies' "theory of group rights" over the founding founders' values for the source of The 1619 Project, Critical Race Theory (CRT), and other "destructive theories that today divide our people and tear at the fabric of our country."[19]

And despite his failed coup d'état attempt on January 6, 2021, the self-professed Make America Great Again president initiated an educational propaganda campaign attacking the so-called anti–Critical Race Theory movement.[20] Although the teaching of CRT has been limited to legal and graduate school training, anti-CRT proponents lumped the teaching of the full American experience during the Civil War era and other eras, including nuanced understandings of the African American and other marginalized communities, as "CRT" and "woke curriculum" indoctrinating the students in K-12 classrooms and at colleges and universities. State legislators and sympathetic governors have used the 1776 Report framework for targeting books, faculty, and diversity programs.[21] The modern counter-revolution required myths and false histories taught in K-12 schools, colleges, and universities as W. E. B. Du Bois's last chapter of *Black Reconstruction* suggested. The twenty-first-century development of the "Propaganda of History" drew its playbook from the United Daughters of the Confederacy's textbook campaigns and even the complicity of some professional historians in the wake of Reconstruction's demise.[22]

The Civil War and its legacy offered an appropriate lens for understanding this tumultuous summer that became a long winter. It is difficult when the historian becomes the research whether through their scholarly pursuits coinciding with historical developments or by simply being a witness. The authors of the essays in this volume rise to the challenge of providing context of how the Civil War era sheds light on the summer of 2020 and vice versa, while demonstrating the ways that the personal is political. All wrestled with providing order to a seemingly chaotic epoch of recent history. Some essays are raw thoughts but provide a critical lens for understanding the diverse and overlapping events. Other essays serve as meditations on the much longer history of the formal and informal policing of Black bodies from the Civil War era to the present in the United States, African Diaspora, and Global South. While others show the blurring of lines between professional historian and therapist for reconciling the nation's burden of race, Lost Cause monuments and other enduring Civil War–era legacies.

Above all, the volume essays show how scholars of the Civil War era were not immune from the Summer of 2020 events. We coped with illness among ourselves and members of our beloved communities. We survived pandemic teaching and learned the difference between synchronous, asynchronous, and hybrid modes of teaching delivery. We educated others seeking understanding on the unresolved Civil War–era legacies on twenty-first-century lives, institutions, and communities. We helped communities and campuses attempting to reconcile their Confederate monumental landscape. We, too, collectively mourned the pandemic dead that approached, and sadly, might even surpass Civil War levels.

Instead of taking to the streets, we put our collective knowledge of the Civil War and Reconstruction scholarship to use and provide the necessary historical context and insights for understanding the long, hot summer of 2020. The essays are organized around the themes of violence, resistance, and memory. While the categories may seem simplistic, the various essays explore the real, rhetorical, and political violence witnessed, including white militias attempting to enforce public engagement at the Gettysburg National Military Park and police brutality. The Resistance essays consider not only BLM protests but also the global reverberations and counter-resistance to the perceived success by Black, Brown, Indigenous and other marginalized communities. Likewise, the concluding essays take a more nuanced view of memory, including diverse perspectives, politicized uses of memory, and the debates over the Confederate commemorative landscape. Ultimately, we attempt to move the needle toward repair without replicating the unfinished work of Reconstruction and persisting legacies of the Civil War era.

Notes

In assembling this volume, we have been privileged to work with a diverse array of scholars, each bringing his or her own nuanced perspectives to complex and provocative topics. We felt that it was critical to allow authors the freedom to use the racial and ethnic terms they deemed most appropriate for their essays. This freedom extends to the question of capitalization. The differences are not inconsistencies or errors but rather a reflection of the ongoing debates and evolving norms surrounding these terms.

1. James Baldwin, *The Fire Next Time* (1963; repr., New York: Vintage Books, 1991), 8.
2. Martin Luther King Jr., "Honoring Dr. Du Bois," in *The Radical King: Edited and Introduced by Cornel West*, edited by Cornel West (Boston: Beacon Press, 2015), 119–20.
3. Pulitzer Prize Board, Darnella Frazier, 2021 Pulitzer Prize Winner in Special Citations and Awards, https://www.pulitzer.org/winners/darnella-frazier.
4. Taylor Branch, *At Canaan's Edge: America in the King Years, 1965–1968* (New York: Simon and Schuster, 2006), 767–71; Terry H. Anderson, "1968: The End and the Beginning in the United States and Western Europe," *South Central Review* 16 (Spring 2020): 1–14; David Cunningham, "Understanding State Responses to Left- versus Right-Wing Threats: The FBI's Repression of the New Left and the Ku Klux Klan," *Social Science History* 27 (Fall 2003): 329–32, 341–49.
5. David K. Wiggins, "Vince Matthews, Wayne Collett, and the Forgotten Disruption in Munich," *Journal of African American History* 106 (Spring 2021): 281–83; Douglas Hartmann, *Race, Culture, and the Revolt of the Black Athlete: The 1968 Olympic Protests and Their Aftermath* (Chicago: University of Chicago Press, 2003), 93–166.
6. Nicholas Bogel-Burroughs, "Kyle Rittenhouse, Accused of Killing 2 in Kenosha, Freed on $2 Million Bail," *New York Times*, November 20, 2020; Julie Bosman, "Kyle Rittenhouse Was Found Not Guilty of Intentional Homicide and Four Other Charges,"

New York Times, November 19, 2021, https://www.nytimes.com/live/2021/11/19/us/kyle-rittenhouse-trial#kyle-rittenhouse-verdict; Fred R. Harris and Alan Curtis, eds. *Healing Our Divided Society: Investing in America Fifty Years After the Kerner Report* (Philadelphia: Temple University Press, 2018), 3–5, 76–97.

7. Luke Henriques-Gomes and Elias Visontay, "Australian Black Lives Matter Protests: Tens of Thousands Demand End to Indigenous Deaths in Custody," *The Guardian*, June 6, 2020, https://www.theguardian.com/australia-news/2020/jun/06/australian-black-lives-matter-protests-tens-of-thousands-demand-end-to-indigenous-deaths-in-custody.

8. Rukmini Callimachi, "Breonna Taylor's Family to Receive $12 Million Settlement from City of Louisville," *New York Times*, September 15, 2020; Lolis Eric Elie, "Louisville Barbeque Owner Killed in Police Shooting Fed a Food Desert," *New York Times*, June 5, 2020.

9. Kurt Streeter, "Running While Black: Our Readers Respond," *New York Times*, May 18, 2020.

10. Elise Schmelzer, "Elijah McClain Death: Aurora Police Didn't Have Legal Basis to Stop, Frisk, or Choke 23-year-old, Investigation Finds," *Denver Post*, February 22, 2021.

11. Paul Egan, "Trump Supports Michigan Protesters, Says Gov. Whitmer Should 'Give a Little,'" *Detroit Free Press*, May 1, 2020; Tom Gjelten, "Peaceful Protesters Tear-Gassed to Clear Way for Trump Church Photo-Op," NPR.org, June 1, 2020; Chris Cameron, "Judge Narrows Lawsuits Over Clearing of Protesters Before a Trump Photo Op," *New York Times*, June 21, 2020; Eric Foner, *Reconstruction: America's Unfinished Revolution, 1863–1877* (New York: Harper & Row, 1988), 179–84; Frederick Douglass, *Life and Times of Frederick Douglass, Written by Himself* (Boston: De Wolfe and Fiske Co., 1892), 442, accessed at Documenting the American South, https://docsouth.unc.edu/neh/dougl92/dougl92.html.

12. Karen L. Cox, *No Common Ground: Confederate Monuments and the Ongoing Fight for Racial Justice* (Chapel Hill: University of North Carolina Press, 2021), 149–74; Hilary Green, "Shifting Landscapes and the Monument Removal Craze, 2015–20," *Patterns of Prejudice*, 488–89.

13. Hilary N. Green, "Gettysburg and July 4, 2020: Four Historians Respond," *Muster*, July 20, 2020; Gregory Downs, "Toppling of the Ulysses Grant Statue Is No Way to Treat History," *San Francisco Chronicle*, June 25, 2020; Rebekah Bryer, "Yes, D.C.'s Emancipation Memorial Advances White Supremacy," *Washington Post*, June 25, 2020; "Boston Art Commission Votes Unanimously to Remove Emancipation Memorial," WBUR.org, July 2, 2020; Hope Hodge Seck, "Here's Congress' Detailed Plans to Get Rid of Confederate Base Names and Monuments," Military.com, December 4, 2020; Michael Gold, "Who Tore Down This Frederick Douglass Statue," *New York Times*, July 7, 2020.

14. Donald J. Trump, "Protecting American Monuments, Memorials, and Statues and Combating Recent Criminal Violence: A Presidential Document by the Executive of the President on July 2, 2020," *Federal Register*, July 2, 2020; Gareth Harris, "UK Government Announces New Laws to Protect Controversial Historic Monuments from 'Woke Worthies and Baying Mobs,'" *The Art Newspaper*, https://www.theartnewspaper.com/2021/01/18/uk-government-announces-new-laws-to-protect-controversial-historic-monuments-from-woke-worthies-and-baying-mobs.

INTRODUCTION 9

15. Donald J. Trump, Executive Order 13958, November 2, 2020.

16. Moriah Balingit and Laura Meckler, "Trump Alleges 'Left-wing Indoctrination' in Schools, Says He Will Create National Commission to Push More 'Pro-American' History," *Washington Post*, September 17, 2020; American Historical Association Council, "AHA Condemns Report of Advisory 1776 Commission (January 2021)," Historians.org, January 20, 2021.

17. David W. Blight, "The Reconstruction of America: Justice, Power, and the Civil War's Unfinished Business," *Foreign Affairs* (January/February 2021), https://www.foreignaffairs.com/articles/united-states/2020-12-08/reconstruction-america.

18. The President's Advisory 1776 Commission, *The 1776 Report*, January 2021, 1.

19. The President's Advisory 1776 Commission, *The 1776 Report*, January 2021, 12.

20. Nicholas Fandos and Emily Cochrane, "After Pro-Trump Mob Storms Capitol, Congress Confirms Biden's Win," *New York Times*, January 7, 2021.

21. Maya T. Prabhu and Ty Tagami, "Georgia Lawmakers Try to Identify Critical Race Theory in Schools," *The Atlantic Journal-Constitution*, January 25, 2022; Mike Gonzalez and James Quarles, "Why Georgia Schools Must Reject Critical Race Theory," The Heritage Foundation, March 14, 2022; Sharon Bernstein, "Georgia Becomes Latest U.S. State to Ban 'Divisive' Concepts in Teaching About Race," Reuters, April 28, 2022.

22. W. E. B. Du Bois, *Black Reconstruction in America, 1860–1880*, Introduction by David Levering Lewis (1935; repr. New York: The Free Press, 1992), 711–29; Karen L. Cox, *Dixie's Daughters: The United Daughters of the Confederacy and the Preservation of Confederate Culture* (Gainesville: University Press of Florida, 2003), 48–158; W. Fitzhugh Brundage, *The Southern Past: A Clash of Race and Memory* (Cambridge: Belknap Press of Harvard University Press, 2008), 27–54.

Violence

1

White Supremacy, the American Militia, and the Legacy of the Civil War Era

Barbara A. Gannon

It was an early July day when the militia came to defend Gettysburg, Pennsylvania, from invasion. Armed men waved flags, brandished weapons, and prepared for an assault. The Pennsylvania State Militia reported that it mobilized as "a deterrent against the enemy forces." Surprisingly, the year was not 1863 but 2020. The enemy was not the Confederate Army of Northern Virginia—the ANV of Civil War fame—but ANTIFA—a leftist anti-fascist group. ANTIFA maintains an astonishing level of secrecy; no evidence confirms its existence. In contrast, in 1863, the very real ANV descended on Gettysburg. Wisely, the official Pennsylvania State Militia either fled or surrendered to the superior Confederate forces. In 2020, armed, unofficial militia groups, waving both the US Stars and Stripes and the CSA Stars and Bars, made their stand. They surrounded a single man wearing a Black Lives Matter T-shirt visiting the cemetery wherein rest men who gave their last full measure of devotion for a new birth of freedom and the end of slavery.[1] The white militia men followed in the blood-stained footsteps of nineteenth-century militias and believed that their actions were fitting and proper. While this may seem ironic, the relationship between contemporary militias and white supremacy represents a legacy of the long Civil War era, which includes antebellum slavery and postwar Reconstruction.

Militias before the Civil War, particularly in slave states, played a crucial role in maintaining white supremacy. Not surprisingly, the slave states supported robust militia organizations to maintain control over their enslaved populations. While contemporary militias may share the same racial views and mission as their antebellum counterparts, the latter is not the former's antecedent. Instead, twenty-first-century militias and their members inherited the legacy of post-emancipation white paramilitaries, such as the Ku Klux Klan, that emerged during Reconstruction to control newly freed African American citizens. Reinforcing the desirability of using the militia construct, the Second Amendment sanctified militias' right to bear arms; likely the Founders understood the relationship between this right and the need to enforce white supremacy. Once federal and state governments rejected white Americans' efforts to exert race control, unofficial militias re-organized to re-establish white supremacy and to challenge governments that failed to maintain white rule. While modern militia members invoke early colonial and state groups' memory, modern militias inherited the white paramilitary organizations' Reconstruction legacy and their opposition to interracial governments. It is likely no coincidence that militia membership surged after the United States elected its first Black president. These paramilitaries won the nineteenth-century battle. The outcome of the twenty-first-century insurgency remains unknown.

Well before Reconstruction, even before the nation was formally conceived in slavery by the Constitution, white militias organized in local communities to assert control over people of color. By necessity, English settlers formed these militia units upon arrival in the New World because the world was neither new nor unoccupied. All white males of a certain age owed the community military service. Militia members supplied their weapons and ammunition and participated in musters during which they drilled with their company. These organizations ensured white rule in the West by removing or eliminating Native Americans or holding and punishing enslaved Black southerners. No one envisioned these organizations as challenging the colonial or, later, state governments that regulated these militias.

The United States also used full-time federal forces to perform similar functions; the antebellum "Trail of Tears" was organized by the US Army. The government stationed most federal forces out west in a counterinsurgency role to respond to Native Americans who challenged the racial status quo. Similarly, the militias stood by if needed to protect local communities with no federal forces to ensure white supremacy, either from a return of Native Americans to their own land; the Black Hawk War (1832), which mobilized Illinois militiaman Abraham Lincoln or to crush slave revolts; or Nat Turner's uprising of the enslaved in 1830s Virginia. Much of the impetus for antebellum southern militias came from fears that slaves were plotting violent rebellion.

Despite these concerns, violent resistance was rare; deterrence worked, but cavalry militias also maintained the type of routine brutality that held millions of men and women in slavery. White militiamen used cavalry units' mobility to search larger areas for escaping slaves—a slave patrol. If patrollers detained enslaved men and women who failed to produce paperwork that allowed them to be away from their slave quarters, the enslaved received fifteen lashes. Some of these men and women may have been escaping; most were visiting their spouses or children. If the patrol decided that the enslaved appeared "insolent," they received more than double that punishment—thirty-nine lashes. For decades before the war, the cavalry militia enforced racial control. After the war, the slave patrol's postwar incarnation, the Ku Klux Klan, demonstrated the relationship between the cavalry militia and white supremacy.

The ongoing need for a regular slave patrol explains why southern states organized more militia cavalry units than northern states. In an 1854 report to Jefferson Davis, then Secretary of War for the United States and later president of the Confederate States, slave states reported more than 200 cavalry militia companies. Americans faced no foreign enemy worthy of such a powerful cavalry force. Southerners had identified a domestic threat that they believed required these units—their own enslaved citizens. In contrast, the free states of New Jersey, Pennsylvania, and New York maintained no part-time cavalry units. To reinforce mounted troops, slave states, particularly in the Southeast, maintained well-organized infantry units. Virginia reported the most robust force: almost 116,000 men commanded by nearly 6,000 officers, organized in more than 1,300 militia infantry companies. Militia officials at the division, brigade, and regimental levels oversaw these units. North Carolina, South Carolina, and Alabama had fewer part-time soldiers available, but they maintained the same complex command structure and robust officer corps to command their militia units. Only the ever-present fear of an internal threat—slave insurrection—explains southern states' willingness to maintain military forces well in excess to any possible external threat.[2]

Even though northern states had larger populations and more military-age men, the free-state militias appeared moribund, with few exceptions. Pennsylvania identified about 13,000 officers and militiamen in its ranks, a small force given its large population. At least Pennsylvania reported; neither New York nor New Jersey documented any available militia. Even if northern states mustered militiamen, sometimes their units had few officers. Maine claimed more than 55,000 militiamen but identified one single officer for this force. Rhode Island did better, but 15,000 men needed more than 47 officers to lead their units. The free militias in western states seemed to be in slightly better condition. Wisconsin maintained more than 46,000 part-time soldiers under arms, and Illinois supported more than 170,000 militiamen. Western states may have been free, but they shared the southern states' need to assert racial control and expand white rule at the indigenous population's expense.[3]

Southern militia maintained well-organized militias partly because they had many more trained officers than did the northern states. Slave owners' sons attended the Virginia Military Institute (VMI), The Citadel, and other southern military institutions. Few of these men planned a military career; instead, military training reinforced the implicit and explicit use of violence to ensure racial control. When they returned home after graduation, they provided white militia units with trained leaders. When the Civil War came, these men and their militias re-organized as Confederate Army units. Slave states' militias' extensive peacetime experience largely explains the initial success of the wartime Confederate Army.

Overtime, the US Army overcame this military advantage and won the war that freed enslaved men and women. The Fifteenth Amendment enfranchised freedmen, who, together with white Republican allies, created multiracial state governments. To reassert racial control, white Americans formed extralegal paramilitary organizations, including the Ku Klux Klan, to undermine Republican Reconstruction governments that worked for Black political rights after the Civil War. Nineteenth-century terrorist paramilitaries used violence against Black Americans and their white allies. Ultimately, these groups defeated efforts to create multiracial democracies.

While the Klan represented the best-known such group, modern militias seem more like the "White Leagues" that operated in the open with a command structure and leadership that adapted military ranks. The federal government acted against the secretive Klan but was less able to fight the White Leagues. In 1874, one of the most powerful leagues managed to briefly overthrow the Louisiana Reconstruction government after the so-called Battle of Liberty Place. The Liberty Place monument to the Reconstruction paramilitaries that defeated the democratically elected government stood in New Orleans until 2017. The combination of paramilitary violence, northern indifference, and the disputed election of 1876 prompted the government to withdraw federal troops from Louisiana and elsewhere. As a result, the militia terror campaign succeeded. Democratic Party rule returned state governments' official militias to their traditional role of ensuring white supremacy in southern states; unofficial militias were no longer necessary.

As time passed, the militia as a military organization faded, and the National Guard took its place. Partly, the National Guard emerged to fill another need— that of labor control. Northern militia units failed to crush labor strikes, and the regular US Army stepped into this role. Professional soldiers despised this mission and preferred frontier duty, such as removing and eliminating Native

Americans. In its place, the National Guard emerged. State governors moved National Guard forces from one side of the state to the other to address labor disturbances to avoid using local militia forces sympathetic to the strikers. It was not until a few years after the Civil War centennial, and during the 1960s civil rights movement, that the National Guard returned to its older mission of restoring racial order. Part-time soldiers mobilized in the aftermath of what officials termed "race riots," including those that occurred in the aftermath of Martin Luther King Jr.'s assassination in 1968. Officials stopped using National Guard soldiers in 1970 when a group of them killed four unarmed white students at Ohio's Kent State University who were protesting the Vietnam War, violating deadly force's racialized boundary.

As time passed, the civil rights movement's gains ensured that state governments and the federal government could no longer officially support white supremacy. African American men and women occupied prominent public offices and, eventually, the presidency. Some white Americans viewed African American gains as their loss. Suddenly, the term *militia* re-emerged in the political landscape as part of a larger subset of anti-government paramilitaries. Scholars and others credit deadly federal police actions for inspiring these new self-proclaimed patriot groups, including the 1992 gunfight at Ruby Ridge, Idaho, which killed the wife and son of a man accused of firearm violations. One year later, federal agents stormed the Branch Davidian compound in Waco, Texas, an action that killed seventy men, women, and children. Two years later, a small group of right-wing domestic terrorists blew up the Alfred P. Murrah Federal Building in Oklahoma City, ostensibly to avenge what happened in Waco. A new era of paramilitary militias began in these smoking ruins.

The Southern Poverty Law Center and the Anti-Defamation League track these groups closely as part of their focus on right-wing extremist groups; their data supports a link between paramilitaries, militias, and multiracial rule. While the 1990s saw a dramatic spike in the growth of militias because of these tragedies and the 1993 assault weapons ban, the first eight years of the twenty-first century, during the presidency of George W. Bush, witnessed a dramatic decline in the number of extant paramilitary organizations. Given what we know about the relationship between race and militias, it should come as no surprise that when Barack Obama, the first Black president, assumed office in 2009, hundreds of paramilitary groups organized against the ultimate achievement of interracial democracy. These groups flourished during Obama's presidency and they continued to operate after Donald Trump's subsequent election; however, they changed their focus. Instead of challenging the federal government, which in their minds seemed to be in good hands under Trump, they targeted Democratic state and local governments that they believed challenged white supremacy. Finally, militias and other paramilitary groups embraced another role and emerged as gun-wielding counterprotesters opposing men and women of all races who demanded change, including racial justice.[4]

The modern turning point for these organizations reflects the link between the Civil War, racial justice, and gun-wielding paramilitaries. In 2017, torch-bearing white supremacists marched on the University of Virginia in Charlottesville to defend a Confederate General Robert E. Lee statue from those who wanted this artifact removed. Like their 1877 counterparts, some claimed to be militias and other "patriot" groups, but these armed and organized white men asserted their right to armed resistance based on the Second Amendment, also known as the militia clause. One of these modern militiamen struck with his car and killed Heather Heyer, a local white woman committed to racial justice and a multiracial society. In their new incarnation, these modern militias re-enact their Reconstruction forebears and target African Americans' white allies.

While Black lives and white allies' lives do not matter to these militias, neither do a number of other types of lives. Modern militias added Hispanics, particularly Mexicans, whom they view as illegitimate and undocumented, regardless of their legal status. In an impressive demonstration of multi-religious hatred, these groups view both Muslims and Jews as threats to a white racial order. The LGBTQ community, liberals, Democratic governments, and scientists have recently joined a long list of targets for militias and other paramilitary organizations.

The plot to kidnap Gretchen Whitmer, the Democratic governor of Michigan, in 2020 demonstrates the relationship between twenty-first-century militias and their nineteenth-century forbears. The only difference is that during Reconstruction, the white leagues attacked male Republican governors; today, paramilitaries targeted a female Democratic governor. In this case, members of a Michigan militia allegedly plotted to kidnap Governor Whitmer and put her "on trial" for "crimes against the Constitution." Her "crime": implementing actions to control the COVID-19 pandemic. Much like the paramilitaries of Liberty Place, these men purportedly planned to attack the state capitol. While this event seems to have little in common with the events in Reconstruction-era Louisiana, blue-state Democrats who represent the party of Obama, like their Republican forebears, govern in the militia's crosshairs.

In the centuries-old history of the American militia, much has changed, and some things have stayed the same. Militias still bear arms, though now a single militia member can carry a weapon capable of wiping out an entire colonial militia company gathered on the village green. Along with more firepower, modern militias have identified more enemies—African Americans, Hispanic Americans, Muslim Americans, Jewish Americans, and any type of American who disagrees with their views. Despite these apparent differences, these men and women shared a vision of America that links the oldest militias to the newest—a commitment to white supremacy based on well-armed, if not well-regulated, racism. In this world, Black lives do not matter. Why else would the militias come, 157 years later, to Gettysburg's rescue?

Notes

1. Shawn Boburg and Dalton Bennett, "Militias Flocked to Gettysburg to Foil a Supposed Antifa Flag Burning, an Apparent Hoax Created on Social Media," *Washington Post*, accessed July 15, 2020, https://www.washingtonpost.com/investigations/hundreds-of-armed-men-went-to-gettysburg-to-defend-it-from-a-phantom-antifa-flag-burner-created-on-social-media/2020/07/04/206ee4da-bb05-11ea-86d5-3b9b3863273b_story.html.

2. US Congress, Senate, *Report of the Secretary of War Communicating an Abstract of the Return of the Militia of all the States and Territories, with their Arms, Accoutrements, and Ammunition.* 33rd Cong., 1st sess., 1854, Ex. Doc. No. 30.

3. Ibid.

4. Southern Poverty Law Center, "Antigovernment Movement," accessed November 9, 2020, https://www.splcenter.org/fighting-hate/extremist-files/ideology/antigovernment; Anti-Defamation League, "The Militia Movement 2020," accessed November 9, 2020, https://www.adl.org/resources/backgrounders/the-militia-movement-2020.

2

African Americans and Native Americans in North Carolina During the Summer of 2020

The Struggle for People of Color to Find a Shared Civil War–Era Memory

Jaime Amanda Martinez

The violence of the Confederacy toward people of color is woven into the fabric of UNC Pembroke in ways that are fundamentally different from what you would encounter at any of the predominantly white institutions in North Carolina. The story of Henry Berry Lowry's 1865 war against county officials and the Home Guard lurks around every corner—battles waged in large part because these officials kept coming into the area and conscripting men to work on the Wilmington fortifications. Our campus buildings are named not for Confederate generals and slaveholders but instead for the Lumbee Indian men who founded the institution in the 1880s, men who had clear memories of the ways the Confederacy and its supporters had harmed their community. Yet in a state and nation dotted with markers to the Confederacy and increasingly eager to commemorate black participation in the Civil War, Native Americans' wartime experiences have been overlooked by academic and public historians alike. This erasure may explain some of the ongoing tensions between black and native communities in southeastern North Carolina. Thus in the summer of 2020, a few members of the Lumbee community took up a position adjacent to the Confederacy's most vocal modern-day defenders by opposing a Black Lives Matter march led by UNC Pembroke students.

The Civil War experience of many black and Lumbee men from Robeson County was one of exploitation by the Confederacy, as both groups were subject to impressment as laborers for Fort Fisher. Outside of Robeson County, and particularly in Marlboro County, South Carolina, it seems that Lumbee men were frequently deemed "white enough" to enlist in or be drafted into the Confederate Army. It is unclear whether these "enlistments" were the result of free choice or coercion, although the answer most likely varies with county jurisdiction and individual circumstances. For men impressed to build fortifications, the daily labor was grinding: Each three-man crew was expected to move approximately eight tons of dirt and sand every day, pitching it up to twelve feet from the bottom of the ditch to the top of the mound. War Department officials conceded that the standard soldier's ration was inadequate for this type of work but were unwilling or unable to supplement it. Impressed laborers slept in tents close to the breastworks, and when within sight of Union gunboats—as they usually were at Fort Fisher—they were not allowed to light fires. We have yet to uncover any comprehensive accounts of medical care (if any) provided to the labor force at Wilmington, approximate mortality rates, or where a cemetery might have been located. The engineers in charge of the Wilmington fortifications, so meticulous in their work and vocal in their demands for resources and manpower, apparently did not think it necessary to inform state or Confederate officials about the well-being of their black and native force.[1]

Some men may have died from impressment before they even left their homes. Ishrael Massie, speaking with a Works Progress Administration interviewer in 1937, recalled a violent clash between Confederate soldiers seeking to enforce an impressment quota and an enslaved man from his community. North Carolina Adjutant General Richard Gatlin did authorize his militia officers to use force when necessary to gather impressed laborers, although he recommended that they bring a large enough group of men to each farm to intimidate slaveholders and conscripted laborers without needing to resort to direct violence. Rounding these men up to build fortifications frequently involved overt physical violence, but Confederate and state officials also perpetrated cultural and psychological violence against free men of color by so forcefully appropriating their labor on behalf of the state.[2]

Under North Carolina's impressment laws, counties were expected to provide slave laborers to meet requests from the governor or Confederate officials, but they always had the option to substitute "free Negro men" instead. The law said nothing explicit about Native Americans.[3] And yet, local and state officials decided to subject native men—at least those not able to enlist or be drafted as white men—to the same labor conscription plan applied to free black men. To militia and Home Guard officers eager to meet their impressment quotas without inconveniencing Robeson County's slaveholders, Lumbee men must have seemed like the obvious solution. Until, of course, they fought back.

After the war, via oral histories, pension applications, and petitions to the Southern Claims Commission, dozens of Lumbee men described being forced to build fortifications near Wilmington, particularly in the last two winters of the conflict. They clearly resented being treated like slaves or even being subject to the same laws as free African Americans, since they sought to maintain a distinct identity within their communities. They also objected to these labor quotas on material grounds: The men who worked at Fort Fisher suffered from exposure and disease, while their families struggled to grow sufficient food in their absence. Many who were sent in 1863 and worked for upward of six months decided, while home on furlough, to hide in the local swamps when the Home Guard returned to enforce the next impressment quota. They shared their hiding places with runaway slaves and escaped Union soldiers from the nearby prisoner of war camp in Florence, South Carolina.[4]

Stories of impressment for Fort Fisher have been handed down through the generations by Lumbee families, but until recently they have been ignored or denied by those responsible for interpreting the Civil War experience in southeastern North Carolina. More broadly, mainstream Civil War historians seem to have largely forgotten that there were any Native American people living in the Southeast to participate in the Confederate war effort by either choice or force. An emerging body of Civil War scholarship discusses Native American people, and one common thread among that scholarship is the observation that native people, when they had a choice in how, or if, they participated in the war, chose to act in ways that they thought would support their own quest for national sovereignty, rather than out of support for or affinity with either the Union or the Confederacy. But this scholarship overwhelmingly focuses on Indian Territory and the far Western Theaters of the war.[5]

Among Lumbee communities, there were some who chose to enlist, others who were drafted as soldiers or forced to perform labor, and others who sought to stay out of it. By February 1865, with most of the able-bodied young men from Lumbee families in Robeson County either working on the Wilmington fortifications or hiding out in the swamps to avoid being sent there, food was scarce. Men began to emerge from the swamps to raid the smokehouses and corn cribs of the county's plantations; they also raided the courthouse for weapons and killed two men: a local planter and a Confederate conscription officer. The Home Guard shot Allen and William Lowry, a father and son on whose farm they found some of the stolen goods, just days before Sherman's columns marched through the county in early March 1865. Over the next seven years, Allen's son Henry Berry Lowry led a guerrilla uprising against local and state officials and wealthy community members connected to the Confederacy, the Democratic Party, or the Ku Klux Klan.[6]

While the Lowry Gang was proudly interracial, the restrictions and indignities of living in Jim Crow North Carolina drove wedges between the Lumbee, black, and poor white residents of Robeson County over the next few decades. Federal and state officials and even other native people applied one-drop rules and strict notions of blood quantum to deny Lumbee people their identity and status as Native Americans.[7] Segregated education was a particular point of conflict; Lumbee resistance to attending black schools helped create a three-tiered system of segregated education in North Carolina and the very university where I teach. UNC Pembroke is quick to announce its status as an historically native-serving institution *and* one of the most racially diverse colleges in the Southeast, but some people within the Lumbee community see the increasing numbers of white and particularly black students at the university over the past thirty years as a threat to its historic identity. Some express concern and confusion that, while the student bodies at the UNC system's historically black universities have remained predominantly African American, native students are now significantly outnumbered at the state's only public institution founded to serve Native Americans.[8]

On June 26, 2020, I watched with confusion and profound sadness the video footage that students and colleagues posted from a Black Lives Matter march in Pembroke. Though not officially a university event, the march was organized by members of the student government, started on campus, ended in front of a university building downtown, and was cleared and monitored by both campus and local police. The student organizers spent three weeks publicizing their march, presenting it as a show of support for a broader national movement rather than a response to any specific local event, and taking great care to emphasize their peaceful intent. But a few days before the march a counternarrative emerged on social media, one which insisted that the students were coming to destroy the town and that anyone who identified Pembroke as his or her actual or ancestral home should arrive prepared to defend it. The march itself involved an interracial group of students, staff, faculty, administrators, and community members who traversed the mile-and-a-half sidewalk that connects the campus to the center of town, stopping along the way for a prayer blessing from the minister of the Baptist Church across the street from the university. Downtown, a local storekeeper handed bottled water to the marchers as they gathered in front of the UNCP Entrepreneurship Center for speeches before returning to campus.[9]

Resistance to the Black Lives Matter march in Pembroke took many forms, according to the videos and photos shared on social media. The most aggressive was from a group that gathered across the street from the marchers' sidewalk; at least one member of this contingent brandished a rifle. Two men with an oversized Trump flag in the back of their pickup drove slowly, menacingly, up and down the street. Local police kept this group to their side of the street, although more than one marcher reported that the counterprotesters threw beer cans at them. One woman walked behind the march shouting "Trump 2020" at the top of her lungs; the students responded by chanting "Black Lives Matter" but seemed to have avoided direct confrontation. Several people whose intentions were unclear stood on the same side of the street as the marchers, watching in silence or recording it. One silent man stood nearby with a sign that read, "Native Lives Matter," a statement he seemed to have intended as a rebuke of the march. The marchers did not challenge him or seem concerned with his message, a message that would not have looked entirely out of place within the march, where a number of students wearing Native Strong T-shirts held signs reading "Native Lives for Black Lives." After all, the same Minneapolis police force that killed George Floyd is also known for its historic and ongoing violence against Native Americans.[10]

University, town, and tribal officials were quick to distance themselves from the counterprotesters and reiterate how eager they were to welcome the students back to Pembroke in August. Local religious and community leaders, all Lumbee, called for a unity demonstration to bring town and campus together. Presenting a new and widely mocked twist on the classic "outside agitators" trope, the chancellor's statement sought to assure everyone that the counterprotesters were not residents of Pembroke, a dodge that may have technically described the mailing addresses of the people brandishing weapons but was not at all in keeping with the social media chatter that preceded the march. Members of the faculty senate attempted to craft a statement of their own that would somehow, impossibly, unite all the things they needed to recognize—the pain and fear the chancellor's tepid response had stoked among our black students in particular, the native students who were horrified at the response to the march but also frustrated and alienated by many of their classmates' ignorance of Native American histories and cultures, the university's historic founding as a native-serving institution and current racially diverse status.[11]

There is much shared history between the black and Lumbee residents of Robeson County. Both groups faced violence and exploitation at the hands of the Confederacy, as well as generations of exclusion, disfranchisement, and oppression at the hands of the state and its leaders—and both groups found ways to assert their dignity in spite of that oppression. Community historians are quick to remind us that Henry Berry Lowry's group was triracial, much like Robeson

County, and that its members fought against the first iteration of the Ku Klux Klan. Lumbee men of a certain age are eager to regale visitors with stories of how they drove the more modern KKK out of the county in 1958; everyone, it seems, was present at Hayes Pond in Maxton to suppress an intended Klan rally and make national headlines.[12] So how did a few dozen Lumbee men and women end up on the same side of the street as the Klan, at least metaphorically speaking, when Black Lives Matter came to town?

Part of the answer lies in contemporary and recent partisan politics. The region's economy—so long dependent on tobacco, cotton, and textile manufacturing—was hit hard by economic policies of the 1990s that residents of Robeson County (rightly or wrongly) associate with the Democratic Party, while the Baptist associations that form a key component of local Lumbee identity have for the most part aligned with Republicans on cultural issues. These factors have aligned to put the county pretty reliably in the Republican camp, and it seems that a good portion of Lumbee voters are willing to overlook David Duke's endorsement of Donald Trump as long as he is also endorsed by the leaders of Moral Majority. They also share with Trump's white rural supporters a sense of profound alienation and exclusion from not just national prosperity but also the nation's attention. Trump's decision in late October to support the Lumbee Recognition Act was not so much an attempt to gain Lumbee votes as it was a way to thank them for their ongoing support of him and his allies in Congress.

Recognizing this exclusion brings us back to history. For much of their recent history, going back to the nineteenth century, Lumbee people lived in a state that frequently denied their identity as Native Americans. They live in a country that constantly changes the conditions under which it will grant them full recognition as a native nation. By sometimes lumping Native Americans in with African Americans in how laws are enforced, the states of North Carolina and South Carolina have made it far too easy for observers—including other Native Americans—to deny Lumbee people's identity. Meanwhile, academic Civil War historians have all but erased Lumbees and most other native peoples from the story of the South after the 1830s. For far too long, scholars have talked about the Confederacy, the Civil War and its aftermath, and the South as a whole in purely black and white terms. We are therefore complicit in the kind of cultural and psychological violence that accompanied impressment for the Wilmington fortifications in the days of the Confederacy.

One attempt to rectify that exclusion was also underway in the summer of 2020. A new exhibit for the visitors' center at the Fort Fisher State Historic Site, spearheaded by the staff of UNCP's Museum of the Southeast Native American, has been in the works for the past two years. The new exhibit seeks to inform visitors of the history and Civil War experiences of Lumbee people in particular—both those who were forced to build the Wilmington fortifications and those who served in either the Confederate or Union armies. It foregrounds the oral histories and community stories that earlier generations of scholars overlooked or discounted as they privileged written documentation. Ultimately, leaders of the NC Office of Archives and History hope to build a new visitors' center at Fort Fisher, one that weaves into every aspect of the interpretation the stories of the black and Native American men forced to labor on those fortifications. Telling more accurate and comprehensive stories about our shared past—while challenging and at times a bit scary—will hopefully help resolve some of the tensions on display in Pembroke, and throughout the nation, during the summer of 2020.[13]

Notes

1. Based on descriptions in Dennis Hart Mahan's 1846 *Treatise on Field Fortifications*, used by military engineers during the Civil War, and Engineer Department correspondence, discussed in Jaime Amanda Martinez, *Confederate Slave Impressment in the Upper South* (Chapel Hill: University of North Carolina Press, 2013), 47–48; Correspondence between Engineer and Commissary Departments discussed in Martinez, *Confederate Slave Impressment*, 52–54; also William McKee Evans, *To Die Game: The Story of the Lowry Band, Indian Guerillas of Reconstruction* (Baton Rouge: Louisiana State University Press, 1971; edition consulted: Syracuse University Press, 1995), 33–35.

2. Interview with Rev. Ishrael Massie in *Weevils in the Wheat: Interviews with Virginia Ex-Slaves*, ed. Charles L. Perdue et al. (Charlottesville: University Press of Virginia, 1976), 210–11; Letters from Gatlin's office, discussed in Martinez, *Confederate Slave Impressment*, 107.

3. *Public Laws of the State of North Carolina, 1862–1863*, 24–25.

4. Adolph Dial interviews with Clifton Oxendine and Charlie Oxendine, University of Florida Oral History Project, July 1969 (transcripts in possession of the Museum of the Southeast American Indian, UNC Pembroke); Evans, *To Die Game*, 35–37.

5. Laurence M. Hauptman, *Between Two Fires: American Indians in the Civil War* (New York: Free Press, 1995); Bradley Clampitt, ed., *The Civil War and Reconstruction in Indian Territory* (Lincoln: University of Nebraska Press, 2015); Ari Kelman, *A Misplaced Massacre: Struggling Over the Memory of Sand Creek* (Cambridge: Harvard University Press, 2013); Megan Kate Nelson, *The Three-Cornered War: The Union, the Confederacy, and Native Peoples in the Fight for the West* (New York: Scribner, 2020); Mary Jane Ward, *When the Wolf Came: The Civil War and the Indian Territory* (Fayetteville: University of Arkansas Press, 2013).

6. Evans, *To Die Game*, 3–18, 35–46.

7. Malinda Maynor Lowery, *Lumbee Indians in the Jim Crow South* (Chapel Hill: University of North Carolina Press, 2010), 19–119; Malinda Maynor Lowery, *The Lum-

bee Indians: An American Struggle (Chapel Hill: University of North Carolina Press, 2018), 94–127.

8. Mission Statement of the University of North Carolina at Pembroke, https://www.uncp.edu/about/mission-statement.

9. David Nelson Leek, "Hate Has No Home Here" Facebook photo album, June 26, 2020; Krista Davis Facebook photo album, June 27, 2020; Wanya Ward Facebook photo album, June 27, 2020.

10. Facebook posts by David Kalonji Walton (Department of History, now at Western Carolina University) and Lawrence T. Locklear (Office of Diversity and Inclusion), and video shared on Facebook Live by Abdul Ghaffar, June 26, 2020; Tonya Brown, "Robeson County Town Grieved by Mistreatment of People during Peaceful Protests," ABC 15 News, June 27, 2020, wpde.com; Jessica Markey Locklear, "Through Protest and Resistance, Lumbees Seek to Reconcile Past with Present," *The Conversation*, July 14, 2020, theconversation.com (accessed July 15, 2020); Malinda Maynor Lowery (Director, Center for the Study of the American South), "Behavior of Lumbees at Friday Protest Disappoints," *The Robesonian*, June 29, 2020, robesonian.com/opinion (accessed July 3, 2020).

11. Chancellor Robin Gary Cummings, "Message on Friday's March," June 27, 2020, https://www.uncp.edu/news/message-chancellor-cummings-fridays-march; Chancellor Robin Gary Cummings, "Follow-Up Message on June 26 March," July 3, 2020, https://www.uncp.edu/news/message-chancellor-cummings-and-follow-june-26-march; Town of Pembroke, "Statement Concerning June 26 Protest," June 27, 2020, https://www.pembrokenc.com/ (accessed July 3, 2020); Chairman Harvey Godwin, Statement of June 27, 2020, Shared via Facebook, https://www.facebook.com/lumbeetribenc (accessed July 3, 2020); UNCP Faculty Senate, "Resolution in Response to the Events of 26 June 2020," July 7, 2020, https://www.uncp.edu/sites/default/files/2020-07/Resolution%20in%20Support%20of%20Students_final.pdf.

12. "Raid by North Carolina Indians Balks Klan Rally," *The New York Times*, January 19, 1958; "The Natives Are Restless," *Time*, January 27, 1958; Dean Chavers, "Battle of Hayes Pond: The Day Lumbees Ran the Klan Out of North Carolina," *Indian Country Today*, January 18, 2017, indiancountrytoday.com/archive (accessed July 3, 2020).

13. Nancy Strickland Fields, Exhibit Matrix for Fort Fisher, September 2020, draft shared with author via e-mail.

3

Witnessing Ned Scott's Coffin

Spectacular Police Violence in the Age of Emancipation

John Bardes

In June 1865, two months after the Union Army liberated Richmond, hundreds of Virginians attended a funerary procession for Ned Scott, a recently emancipated man. Scott's funeral was orchestrated by federal military policemen, called provost marshals, from New York. After cutting a window into Scott's coffin lid so that spectators could view the freedman's face, the marshals escorted the coffin down Main Street, to the step of a marching band. White Richmonders "laughed" while "the colored population looked with horror and amazement." It was an exhibition unlike anything "witnessed in Richmond before," one spectator acknowledged, as the man in the coffin was still very much alive.[1]

Why did provost marshals, tasked with re-establishing order in the occupied city, host a funeral for a living man? This essay considers how police in the aftermath of emancipation deployed performative violence toward the re-establishment of rigid racial hierarchy. Prevalent representations of police violence as spontaneous, irrational, and aberrative—isolated outbursts of excessive force, performed by "a few bad apples" and driven by chaotic rage—obscure how vital these violent acts are to the maintenance and production of social relations and cultural values. Certain acts of police violence must be reconceptualized as *performative*: meaning, intent on establishing spectacle for the purpose of conveying messages to audiences.[2] It is through these acts of performative violence that states affirm power relationships, racialize bodies, and attach ideas of rights and biological differences to certain bodies (while withholding those ideas from other bodies).[3] If we seek to understand and combat racialized police violence in contemporary society—why, for example, a law-enforcement officer might kneel on a compliant detainee's neck in a city street for eight minutes and forty-six seconds—we must appreciate the ways that violent spectacles not only *reflect* imbalances of power but also *create* racial meanings.

Three days before his living funeral, Ned and his wife, Virginia Scott, had walked hand-in-hand down the same street: a gesture of love and companionship, all the more meaningful because the couple had just been freed. Two paroled Confederate veterans, vowing to never "get out of the way for damned n-----s," collided into the Scotts, groped Virginia Scott's breasts, and flung her into the gutter. Scott chased the men away, but three off-duty provost marshals, outraged by reports that white men had been "insulted by a damned n-----," ran to the scene and began beating Scott. Scott drew a pocketknife, cutting two officers.[4]

As punishment, the provost marshals choreographed Scott's living funeral. First Scott was bound and rolled through the mud in Main Street's gutter. Black passersby were seized and ordered to whip him. Next Scott was untied and marched down Main Street while wearing a placard reading "I stabbed two of the provost guard." After whitening Scott's face with flour so that he would resemble a corpse, and rubbing his body with cornmeal to attract flies, the provost marshals nailed Scott inside a pine coffin "with all the gravity which would accompany the preliminaries for burying a man alive." After parading the coffin throughout Richmond, the provost marshals propped the box in front of their headquarters. A Black Baptist preacher was summoned to deliver Scott's eulogy before massive crowds. "Hundreds of persons . . . enjoyed the spectacle hugely," the Richmond *Times* reported: "We never saw a more ludicrous or amusing scene."[5]

Simply by strolling down Main Street, the Scotts laid claim to rights previously denied: to leisure, to public dignity, to the bonds between husband and wife. Confronted by these implicit affirmations of Black social life, policemen re-affirmed Black social death by conjuring the rituals and processes surrounding death and burial. It would have been far easier to simply kill or wound Scott. Yet by parodying funerary ritual—transforming liturgy into burlesque—police ridiculed the very *idea* of Scott's personhood. By transgressing that sacred boundary between the living and the dead, police asserted that Scott's status as a living being was insignificant, marginal, unworthy of full recognition. To white audiences, this carnival of Black suffering served two purposes. First, it restored interregional white solidarity, which the Civil War had devastated, by vividly demonstrating federal commitment to white control over public space. Second, by creating a spectacle of Black Otherness—in other words, a spectacle that served to identify Blacks as separate and alien from the societal norm—the performance legitimated the re-establishment of Black disenfranchisement.[6] Meanwhile, to Black audiences, the performance was intended to terrorize. The conscription of Blacks as performers—the pedestrians forced to whip Scott, the preacher ordered to deliver Scott's eulogy—served to underscore Black powerlessness by making Blacks props within their own humiliation.

The regulation of Black bodies in urban public space is rooted in the very origins of American policing. The first modern police forces in the United States emerged in southern port cities during the early antebellum period and in response to revolutionary events within the French Caribbean island of Saint-Domingue (Haiti). Between 1791 and 1804, the enslaved of Saint-Domingue overthrew their masters, expelled all whites from the island, and declared the colony's independence as a sovereign state—events that terrorized American slaveholders, who feared that the island's sailors and refugees would disseminate their Black radicalism in the South. Indeed, events in Saint-Domingue helped inspire slave uprisings throughout the Americas, including within the US South.[7] In 1793, slaveholders of Charleston were terrorized by rumors that agents from Saint-Domingue had begun to "agitate the slaves in the United States and make them slit the throats of their masters."[8] In Richmond in 1800, a planned uprising, led by an enslaved blacksmith named Gabriel Prosser, was thwarted at the eleventh hour.[9] In New Orleans in 1804, authorities perceived that enslaved people had begun to "wander about" spreading "disorders," while Louisiana's governor described "a general Spirit of Insubordination" growing among the enslaved: "The impression is general among the Inhabitants of the City, that they are in eminent Danger."[10] "Our combustion must be near at hand," Thomas Jefferson predicted; "only a single spark is wanting."[11]

In response, the South's major port cities transformed pre-existing forces of night watchmen, civilian patrols, and state militias into the nation's first professionalized, full-time, publicly funded, and salaried municipal police forces: Richmond in 1801, New Orleans in 1805, Charleston and Savannah in 1806. London, Boston, and New York would not follow suit for another generation.[12]

Urban enslaved people had enjoyed a high degree of mobility and autonomy, compared with their rural counterparts. To counterbalance this relative freedom, early police were tasked with regulating Black access to urban public space by examining slave passes, disrupting "illicit" slave gatherings, enforcing slave curfews, and detaining fugitive slaves and free travelers of color. Antebellum visitors to southern port cities were routinely awestruck by the degree of militarization. "In the appearance of an armed police, Charleston and New Orleans do not resemble the free cities of America," one traveler noted, "but the great number of the Black population, and the way in which they are treated by the whites, render this precaution, I have no doubt, indispensably necessary."[13] A visitor described Charleston as "alive with patrolling parties" and compared the city to "a great military garrison."[14] Frederick Law Olmsted likened Richmond to "a prison or fortress," Charleston to a city "in a state of siege."[15]

During the Civil War, tens of thousands of self-emancipated Blacks fled plantations for freedom, safety, and family re-unification within federally occupied cities. This unanticipated mass migration terrified and enraged southern whites and many federal authorities, who perceived that the urban congregation of so many liberated Blacks would produce crime, disorder, and mayhem. In response, Union Army generals tasked police and provost marshals with arresting Black migrants who failed to immediately find a white employer, forcibly returning them to plantations as contracted wage laborers. Mass arrests resulted. "The military and police authorities will not allow us to walk the streets by day or night, in the regular pursuit of our business or on our way to church," Richmonders wrote in June 1865: "[their] business is the hunting of the colored people."[16] "Children going to School With there arms full of Book have Been arrested and Put up in Pens Like Sheep," reported Anthony Motley, a barber in Memphis.[17] White residents praised the reclamation of public space. While watching the

Figure 1. "Revival of the Old Slave Laws of Louisiana," 1863. Originally printed in *Frank Leslie's Illustrated Newspaper*. This image shows police arresting freeborn people of color on the false pretext that they might be "vagrant" fugitive slaves. (Library of Congress: Illustration in *Frank Leslie's Illustrated Newspaper*, March 7, 1863, p. 381.)

Figure 2. "The Provost Guard in New Orleans Taking Up Vagrant Negroes," 1863. From the same issue of *Frank Leslie's Illustrated Newspaper*. (The Miriam and Ira D. Wallach Division of Art, Prints and Photographs: Picture Collection, The New York Public Library. "The Provost Guard in New Orleans Taking Up Vagrant Negroes," New York Public Library Digital Collections. Accessed February 8, 2023. https://digitalcollections.nypl.org/items/510d47e0-fb01-a3d9-e040-e00a18064a99.)

deportation of "ten wagon loads of freedmen," one planter in Montgomery wrote that "It would please us to see a hundred or two hundred loads going off daily till our city was found almost rid of the surplus negro population. Let the good work go on."[18]

Critically, policemen at this moment not only *reflected* and *reinforced* but assumed an active role in *reshaping* social relations and racial meanings. Prior to the Civil War, southern police had typically upheld legal and social distinctions between enslaved people and those free people of color who were deemed "respectable"—those who owned property, who obeyed prescribed behavioral guidelines, and whose community status was acknowledged by their white neighbors. With emancipation, police intentionally suppressed these distinctions, systematically seizing well-to-do business owners of color and their families on the pretext that they were homeless and unemployed freedpeople. Albert Brooks, a prosperous Richmond business owner and community leader of "good character and voracity," described how an "old policeman, who had known all about me and my business for many years," arrested him on the pretense that he was a transient freedman. "I have lived here 40 years," Brooks protested, "and was never before arrested"; now, police "stop [me] on nearly every corner of the street and make it nearly impossible for me to carry on my business."[19]

Similar stories of targeted police harassment, through which police and provost marshals suppressed pre-existing class and caste privileges, emerged from cities throughout the South. "I was well known by the police to be a respectable man," Edwin Davenport, a boardinghouse keeper, wrote, "they disregarded my papers, and I was obliged to submit to arrest."[20] "The oldest Citizens of Collor in this City are hunted down like Brutes," Anthony Motley wrote from Memphis, "taken to a Corall Like Beasts to be hired or Sold to the highest Bidder."[21] "We are hunted up in the streets, in the market house, and other places whilst engaged in our daily vocations, and marched off [to] the Penitentiary, whence we are placed with [former slaves]," protested Baton Rouge residents. "We were born free, have lived free, and wish to be treated as freemen."[22] In New Orleans, 486 freeborn property holders—nearly one-fifth of that city's free nonwhite men—signed a petition protesting the "illegal arrest and confinement" of freeborn persons of color on the "frivolous, vexatious and unjust pretext" that they were transient plantation workers.[23]

Through this harassment, police helped redraw the color line. By seizing business owners as transients, police suppressed nonwhite persons' class protections and the pre-existing meanings tied to the "free person of color" category. They helped fabricate the new racial order of Jim Crow, within which all persons of any African ancestry—regardless of reputation, prosperity, or prior legal condition—lacked social standing among whites.

In the spring and summer of 1866, conflicts over urban public space exploded into police massacres. In Memphis in May, after Black residents' refusal to disperse a block party led to a skirmish with police, Memphis policemen led riotous mobs in a three-day rampage through Black neighborhoods, killing roughly four dozen Blacks and indiscriminately burning Black homes, churches, and schools.[24] In New Orleans that July, Black residents organized a parade in celebration of a state constitutional convention that had convened for the purpose of extending voting rights to Black men. Policemen opened indiscriminate fire on the parade and raided the convention hall, killing between 40 and 50 Blacks

Figure 3. Emancipation Day Parade, Richmond, Virginia, 1905. An uplifting celebration of Black Richmonders claiming access to urban public space. (Library of Congress: Detroit Publishing Co., publisher.)

and wounding nearly 200.²⁵ These consecutive massacres horrified the nation, leading directly to passage of the nation's first federal civil rights laws and to the Fourteenth Amendment—illustrating that violent spectacles, and the meanings intended by their choreographers, can be repurposed.

Performances have no intrinsic meaning; the messages are particular to specific contexts and societies.²⁶ The meanings broadcast by the Richmond provost marshals in 1865 are not the same as those sought by Chicago police as they attached electrodes to the genitals of Black and Latino detainees between 1972 and 1991, by New York City police as they sodomized Abner Louima with a broomstick in 1997, or by military police as they constructed human pyramids of naked Iraqi prisoners at Abu Ghraib in 2003. Yet never was the goal simply to inflict pain; in each instance, police sought to affirm power relations, reify racial Otherness, and normalize nonwhite suffering.

This is why the videos of Officer Derek Chauvin murdering George Floyd so captivated the world's attention: Whether we realized it consciously or not, we recognized that we had not witnessed an arrest so much as a performance of domination. Floyd's torture was *intended* for public consumption: Chauvin's statue-like position atop Floyd's neck, minutes after Floyd had gone limp, served no purpose but the performative. Officer Chauvin wanted to establish—to Minneapolis residents, to the other officers present, to George Floyd, to himself—that he exercised total power over the Black body, that his Black neighbor was as far beneath him socially as the dirt against which Floyd's face was immobilized. The witnesses-turned-participants—the officers whose faces appear contorted with moral confusion and complacency, the passersby shouting, "*Let him breathe!*"—forced us to examine whether we too are spectators and actors within this drama, watching and tolerating and participating in the relentless reproduction of Black subjugation and white power.

Floyd's murder—coupled with the police shootings in 2020 of Breonna Taylor, Rayshard Brooks, Jacob Blake, Jonathan Price, Walter Wallace Jr., and so many others—inspired global demonstrations against anti-Black state violence. Facing protests over their excessive violence, police departments responded with dramatic displays of excessive violence. We watched phalanxes of officers in full riot gear march in syncopation down American main streets, draped in clouds of tear gas and stepping to the drum of batons against riot shields. We watched police target protesters, reporters, and bystanders with rubber bullets, paint balls, batons, and pepper spray. Throughout, police knew that they were being filmed: Either they didn't care, or they intended for their violent theatrics to be seen. They seemed engaged in their own brand of street performance, much like the protesters with whom they clashed: affirming their might, the power of the state, and the immobility of the status quo through violent theatrics disguised as state-sanctioned crowd control.

It is altogether fitting that the world has witnessed Officer Chauvin's performance. We cannot help but be transfixed. As consumers of spectacle, we must gird ourselves against exacerbating the dehumanization and racial Othering that such scenes have been choreographed to perpetuate. We must reject the dangerous allure of the visually dramatic and compelling. We must repurpose these powerful images as calls to action and educative insights into the role that violence plays in the perpetuation of race, without over-circulating them in ways that numb us to pain, dull our empathy, or normalize Black suffering.

Notes

1. Richmond, VA. *Times*, June 8, 1865; Richmond, VA. *Whig*, reprinted in Louisville, KY. *Daily Journal*, June 23, 1865; New York, NY *Tribune*, June 17, 1865.

2. Yvonne Manzi, "Performative Violence: Conceptual and Strategic Implications," *E-International Relations*, February 28, 2014, www.e-ir.info/2014/02/28/performative-violence-conceptual-and-strategic-implications/.

3. David Garland, *Punishment and Modern Society: A Study in Social Theory* (Chicago: University of Chicago Press, 1993), 249–76; Saidiya V. Hartman, *Scenes of Subjection: Terror, Slavery, and Self-Making in Nineteenth-Century America* (New York: Oxford University Press, 1997).

4. Statement of Jinny Scott, wife of Ed Scott, June 8, 1865, and Statement of Richard Adams, former slave of Wm. Barret, June 8, 1865, both in Statements Relating to the Abuses of Freedmen in Richmond, June 1865, Records of the Assistant Commissioner for the State of Virginia, Bureau of Refugees, Freedmen, and Abandoned Lands, 1865–1869, Record Group 105: Records of the Bureau of Refugees, Freedmen, and Abandoned Lands (microfilm edition, National Archives and Records Administration, Washington, D.C.), M-1048, Reel 59 (hereinafter cited as Statements Relating to Abuses).

5. Richmond, VA. *Times*, June 8, 1865.

6. Grace Elizabeth Hale, *Making Whiteness: The Culture of Segregation in the South, 1890–1940* (New York: Vintage Books, 1998), 205.

7. Julius Sherrard Scott, *The Common Wind: Afro-American Currents in the Age of the Haitian Revolution* (New York: Verso, 2018); David Geggus, ed., *The Impact of the Haitian Revolution in the Atlantic World* (Columbia: University of South Carolina Press, 2001).

8. Robert Alderson, "Charleston's Rumored Slave Revolt of 1783," in *The Impact of the Haitian Revolution in the Atlantic World*, 93–111 (quotation on 98).

9. Douglas R. Egerton, *Gabriel's Rebellion: The Virginia Slave Conspiracies of 1800 and 1802* (Chapel Hill: University of North Carolina Press, 1993).

10. Meeting of June 30, 1804, Official Proceedings (translations), Bk. 1, Vol. 1, Conseil de Ville Records, City Archives, New Orleans Public Library; William C.C. Claiborne to Thomas Jefferson, September 18, 1804, *The Territorial Papers of the United States*, 26 vols. (Washington: Government Printing Office, 1940), 9:298.

11. Thomas Jefferson to St. George Tucker, August 28, 1797, *The Writings of Thomas Jefferson*, ed. Paul Leichester Ford, 10 vols. (New York: G. P. Putnam's Sons, 1892–99), 7:167–68.

12. *A compilation of the laws of the state of Georgia . . . with a copious Index to the Whole*, ed. Augustin Smith Clayton (Augusta: Adams and Duyckinck, 1812), 312–13; Austin D. Washington, "Efforts to Prevent Negro Revolts in Early Savannah," *Savannah State College Bulletin* 21 (December 1967): 39–42; *Digest of the Ordinances of the City Council of Charleston . . . which relate to the city of Charleston* (Charleston: Archibald E. Miller, 1818), 104–16; *A Collection of all such Acts of the General Assembly of Virginia . . . with a complete Index to the Whole*, 2 vols. (Richmond: Samuel Pleasants Junior, 1808), 2:174–75; Dennis Charles Rousey, *Policing the Southern City: New Orleans, 1805–1889* (Baton Rouge: Louisiana State University Press, 1996).

13. James Stuart, *Three Years in North America*, 2 vols. (Edinburgh: Robert Cadell, 1833), 2:236.

14. Louis Tasistro, *Random Shots and Southern Breezes . . . with SemiSerious Observations on Men and Manners*, 2 vols. (New York, 1842), 2:135.

15. Frederick Law Olmsted, *A Journey in the Seaboard Slave States; With Remarks on Their Economy* (New York: Dix and Edwards, 1856), 20, 404.

16. Fields Cook et al. to Andrew Johnson, June 10, 1865, in New York, NY *Tribune*, June 17, 1865; "An Appeal from the Negroes of Richmond for Protection," in Petersburg, VA. *Daily News*, June 15, 1865, in *A Documentary History of Emancipation, 1861–1867*, Ser. 3, Vol. 1: Steven Hahn et al., eds., *Land and Labor, 1865* (Chapel Hill: University of North Carolina Press, 2008), 206–7.

17. Anthony Motley to Clinton B. Fisk, September 28, 1865, in ibid., 271–72.

18. Montgomery, Al. *Advertiser*, September 6, 1865, reprinted in New Orleans, La. *Times*, September 10, 1865.

19. Statements of Albert Brooks, June 9 and June 10, 1865, Statements Relating to Abuses.

20. Statement of Ned Davenport, June 9, 1865, Statements Relating to Abuses.

21. Motley to Fisk, September 28, 1865.

22. Joseph Lofficial et al. to Don Albert Pardee, [November] 1863, Letters Received, ser. 1920, Civil Affairs, Department of the Gulf, Record Group 393, Part 1, National Archives and Records Administration.

23. Manuel Moreau et al. to George F. Shepley, [January 1863], Folder 2, Box 7, George F. Shepley Papers, Maine Historical Society, Portland.

24. Stephen V. Ash, *A Massacre in Memphis: The Race Riot That Shook the Nation One Year after the Civil War* (New York: Hill and Wang, 2013).

25. James G. Hollandsworth Jr., *An Absolute Massacre: The New Orleans Race Riot of July 30, 1866* (Baton Rouge: Louisiana State University Press, 2001).

26. Jonathan Markovitz, *Racial Spectacles: Explorations in Media, Race, and Justice* (New York: Routledge, 2011), 5.

4

Abaline Miller and the Struggle for Justice against the Employer Police State after Slavery

William Horne

Abaline Miller escaped from the plantation where she toiled after a brutal attack by her employer on the night of December 16, 1865, almost a year after Congress passed the Thirteenth Amendment to formally end slavery in the United States and just ten days after its ratification. The formerly enslaved Miller fled her employer, John J. Pringle, in the middle of the night, much as Black southerners had escaped enslavement for generations. She later testified that the overseer, Mr. Cotton, delivered a near-fatal beating and then "drove me of[f] the place he said that he would Brake more bones than ten men could put together and all drew his gun on me to shoot me." The extralegal violence applied to Miller and countless others allowed white elites to suppress Black wages and organizing, to destroy Black schools and undermine Black education, and to eliminate Black political activity. The pattern of the dispute between Miller and her employers replicated a key aspect of slavery—one that planters developed further after emancipation—an alliance between the white owner class in Pringle and the white working class in Cotton. This alliance cemented antebellum enslaver surveillance and policing power, especially in the form of the slave patrol. After emancipation, elites repurposed this alliance in violence, investing heavily in a police state and in new forms of convict leasing, debt peonage, and wage theft to keep Black workers like Miller from *ever becoming fully free*.[1]

Black workers like Miller forced emancipation on enslavers, making its formal recognition all but inevitable by the US state. Miller exemplified this process, having negotiated a verbal contract with Pringle to continue harvesting cotton for wages during the Rebellion, in 1864 and 1865. This agreement, initiated by Miller and her comrades, grew from the contested plantation landscape of Pointe Coupee, which was subject to frequent US Army raids. Enslavers in this region often made verbal agreements with enslaved people to pay them for their work if they agreed to remain on the plantation rather than break for certain freedom behind Union lines. Black workers Luke Canning and John Johnson, for example, negotiated a contract during the war and before emancipation after their planter "called upon said freedmen and urged them [to] not desert to the plantation and go over to the Yankees, but to remain and take care of it and that all they could raise in the way of crops etc should belong to them." Although enslavers and even the US Army did everything in their power to maintain slavery, enslaved men, women, and children destroyed the institution from within.[2]

Though tension between Pringle and Miller had been building since she had demanded wages during slavery, Pringle turned to violence to resolve a new contract dispute. Like many former enslavers, Pringle tested the limits of early emancipation and refused to pay Miller and her co-workers despite having made a verbal contract. He became incensed when his Black workers "wouldn't sine the [new] contract" to work for him again after he had stolen their wages from the previous year and "drove [Miller] off after the crop was gathered." She testified that, after she refused to sign away another year of her life, Pringle "beat me over the [head] with gun and tied me all night and car[ried] me to the magistrate one cold frosty night." In this respect, Miller's assault echoed those of generations of Black Louisianans who faced mutilation and murder if they dared

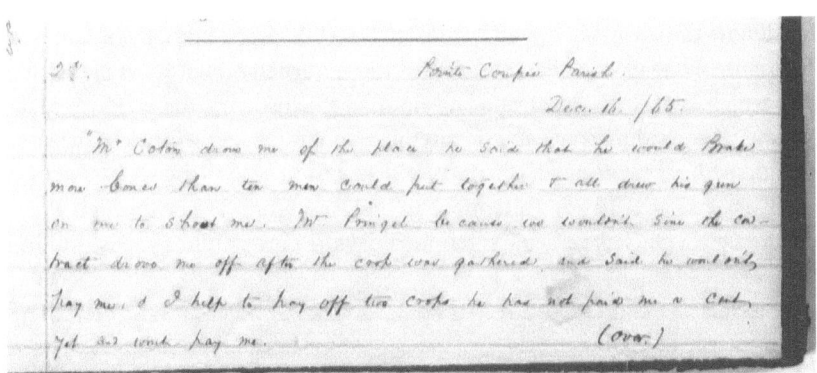

Figure 1. The opening lines from the Statement of Abaline Miller, recorded by another planter, Thomas Boyd, and sent to the local agent of the Freedmen's Bureau on Miller's behalf. Although Boyd appears to be a sympathetic character, helping Miller to file her complaint, he stole her wages for the following year, 1866. Between them, Pringle and Boyd stole three years of wages from Miller and her family. (Statement of Abaline Miller, December 16, 1865, Complaints, March 1866–August 1868, Roll 97, Records of the Field Offices for the State of Louisiana, Bureau of Refugees, Freedmen, and Abandoned Lands, 1863–1872, Record Group 105, National Archives, Washington, D.C.)

to challenge the system of racial capitalism constructed by white elites to their exclusive benefit.³

What Miller and tens of thousands of Black Louisianans experienced after slavery had almost nothing to do with freedom. Before emancipation, white enslaving elites set up a system of policing based on the surveillance and torture of Black people to enrich themselves. They found a variety of ways to profit from the lives and labor of Black Louisianans, from setting strict curfews and slave patrols to beatings, rape, and murder. Each of these were staples of white enslaver power designed to produce elite wealth in Black work and flesh. After emancipation, white elites resurrected this torture-for-profit regime, which Pringle used on Miller, through their control of policing and the courts, which remain central to white power to this day.⁴

White planters like Pringle used violence to coerce labor and to avoid paying wages because they controlled every aspect of the legal system. This had been a staple of white supremacy under slavery—white elites created a "carceral landscape" in which enslavers deputized the entire white population into a makeshift network of surveillance and policing. White elites repurposed this system after emancipation to replicate the conditions of slavery, helping planters steal Black labor, monitor Black movement, and police Black behavior. Thus, when Pringle hauled Miller to the magistrate, he brought her to a powerful ally who would not only ignore the assault charges but threaten her with imprisonment if she refused to drop the issue of unpaid wages. Authorities returned Miller to the plantation, after which she made her escape and notified the justice of the peace, William Burton, who "said he could not do anything about it." She theorized that "these men that I have mentioned," the local officials from whom she sought redress, were "bribed not to pay any attention" to her case. From slavery through emancipation, local officials and courts reinforced white power at the expense of Black residents like Miller.⁵

The cops and courts that covered up the attack on Miller and the theft of her wages gave birth to the carceral landscape that binds Black Americans to this day. Even with clear video evidence, local officials cover up and dismiss the murders of Black Americans by law enforcement and white vigilantes. Police and white vigilantes who murdered George Floyd, Trayvon Martin, Tamir Rice, Eric Garner, Ahmaud Arbery, Breonna Taylor, and countless others receive ample opportunity to cover up their crimes and, in the case of Arbery's vigilante murderers, were arrested only after damning video of the murder emerged. These cases bear the legacy of a legal system designed to treat Black bodies as objects of plunder—

one continued through *practice and precedent*—into our present-day complex of mass incarceration. This system feeds disproportionately poor and marginalized folks into an ever-expanding network of prisons, in the process employing an ever-expanding police, judicial, and prison workforce.[6]

The 2020 murders of George Floyd and Ahmaud Arbery—which helped inspire the nationwide Black Lives Matter protests later that summer—revolve around issues of race, place, and property, illuminating the policing and enforcement of racial capitalism that played a central role in the post-emancipation assault on Miller. White vigilantes shot Arbery, who was out jogging in a predominantly white Georgia suburb on February 23. His killers claimed their actions a justifiable defense of white property owners, whose belongings were presumably at risk in the presence of a Black jogger. Police likewise murdered George Floyd on May 25 in Minneapolis for allegedly trying to spend a counterfeit twenty-dollar bill. Together they show how police and armed white vigilantes have long been tasked with enforcing the racial boundaries of ownership central to American capitalism. Indeed, even the police raid and shooting of Breonna Taylor in Louisville, Kentucky, fits this mold, as the cops who raided her home wrongly believed her to be involved in an illicit drug enterprise, which, in their telling, justified her shooting. As with the 1865 attack on Miller, one way to understand the murders of Arbery, Floyd, and even Taylor, then, is as products of an alliance between the white owner class and the white working class in the police and their white vigilante auxiliaries. This alliance between elite and working-class white Americans represents a mutual investment in the patrolling of Black economic activity to (re)produce white wealth at the expense of criminalized and plundered Black communities.[7]

Abaline Miller's case, when viewed from the present, emphasizes the ways that state violence remains embedded in racial capitalism as it was in the weeks following emancipation. This is no accident. In its current form, "criminal justice" means pumping cash into police departments to prey upon Black communities made poor by decades of discriminatory education, housing, and hiring practices. It involves slathering courts, jails, and prisons with revenue to fund the imprisonment of Black Americans for being disproportionately poor and having statistically little access to representation. It means allocating resources to communities that need them the least, the very communities built upon wealth and opportunities stolen from Black, Brown, and Indigenous communities for generations. It also means—in the cases of Floyd, Arbery, and Taylor—refusing to charge or even meaningfully investigate those who kill Black Americans absent

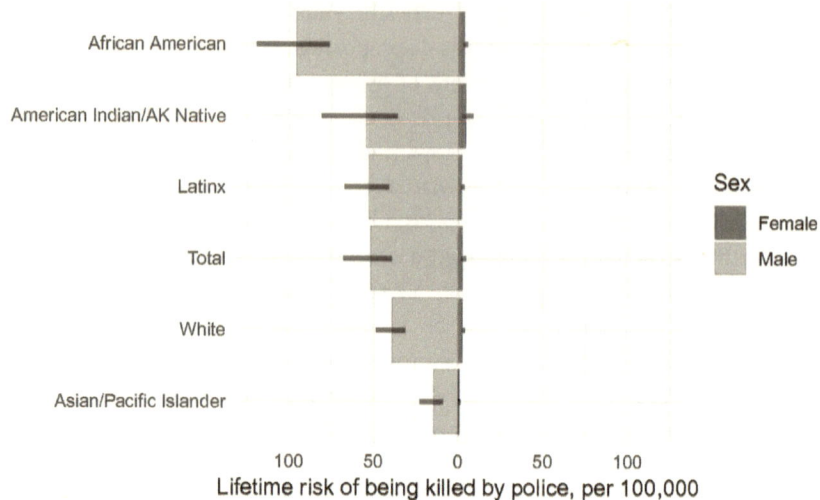

Figure 2. Today's policing—which kills Black Americans at double the rate of their white neighbors—grew from the alliance in violence that ensnared Miller, preserving the surveillance and coercion slavery to accrue new forms of plunder to the white elite. (Frank Edwards, Hedwig Lee, and Michael Esposito, "Risk of being killed by police use of force in the United States by age, race-ethnicity, and sex," *Proceedings of the National Academy of Sciences* 116, 34 [August 20, 2019]: 16793-98, https://www.pnas.org/content/116/34/16793.)

massive public outcry and protests. Whether by active participation or centripetal force, this system continues to operate, propelled by those "bribed not to pay any attention" to the plight of today's Millers.[8]

As her co-workers testified, Miller fell victim to a system that ensnared many of her neighbors and friends—a system of extortion designed by white elites like Pringle. When Miller filed a complaint with the Freedmen's Bureau agent tasked with supporting emancipation, Major Thomas Hopwood, the agent recorded several additional complaints that had somehow eluded local officials. Shepard Grant, for example, explained that he had "worked two years, and [Pringle] has not payed me any yet." Lemuel Miles testified that Pringle refused to pay for his work, adding that he "also cut 1500 lbs. of hay—he promised to pay me for it." Instead, Miles reported, he "never gave me anything for it, and when I went for the money, he drove me away." Their complaints were ignored by Burton, and even Hopwood merely dismissed them as a "misrepresentation." Miller, Miles, and Grant were left at the mercy of an employer who beat them as if they were enslaved and threatened their lives. Despite their years of labor, they were not paid by Pringle for their work from 1864 through December 1865, when they registered their complaints.[9]

Though Burton appears to have been a negligent justice of the peace regarding Pringle, his judicial neglect far exceeded Pringle's abuse of and refusal to pay his workers. In the summer of 1866, word spread that Burton had helped to cover up a murder. The first reports came in July from planters complaining that their Black workers caused a "disturbance" by protesting local officials' attempt to cover up the crime. Local authorities and Bureau officials dragged their feet, and it was only at the end of August that the Bureau agent, Major H. F. Wallace, bothered to investigate. He found that white planter Henry W. Coyle had beaten one of his Black workers and had the coroner declare "that he came to his death by disease of the heart." Frustratingly, Wallace never bothered to record the murdered man's name and, although Coyle confessed to the crime, local officials apparently took no further action. Even this small thing—the cursory investigation and admission of guilt—would never have happened absent the mass Black activism that led white planters to complain to Bureau officials. Generations of Black activists demanded protection from white elites, who were at once plunderer, judge, jury, and executioner as they plundered Black workers like Miller, Miles, and Grant of their meager wages.[10]

The Black activists whose agitation led Wallace to investigate Coyle's murder of his Black employee protested the very systems of inequality and violence that reflect the very concerns voiced by today's Black Lives Matter protesters. Today's protesters draw attention to longstanding systemic abuses by police and white vigilantes that are central to the system of racial capitalism designed to benefit and empower white elites and their auxiliaries. Just as they did after slavery, Black protestors reject the "medical incident"—the original statement of the Minneapolis Police Department on their murder of George Floyd—explanations for police violence as obvious cover-ups designed to cloak the enforcement arm of racial capitalism. BLM protesters build upon the work of the Black Louisianans who overturned slavery, protested the Coyle murder and Miller's abuse, and expressed a vision of equality that continues to inspire Black visionaries. They explain the disproportionate poverty and deprivation in Black America as rooted in America's longstanding and ongoing racist policies and practices, demanding instead a country that lives up to its ideals of democracy and equality.[11]

After emancipation, as now, Black Americans demanded fair wages for their work and basic legal protections that would allow them to live as truly free and equal members of society. Rather than accept these demands, enslavers and white supremacist successor regimes created and maintained systems of power designed to enrich themselves at the expense of everyone else. Although white Americans often complain, in response to Black Americans' protest of racial oppression, that slavery ended a long time ago, this would have been news to Abaline Miller, who suffered its effects well after its legal demise. The claim would doubtless have surprised George Floyd, Trayvon Martin, Tamir Rice, Eric Garner, Ahmaud Arbery, and Breonna Taylor, surveilled and slaughtered at the hands of the same system of oppression white elites erected generations ago as a torture-for-profit scheme. In recognizing this fundamental force in American history, we have a collective opportunity to join the freedom struggle so long suppressed by white elites and demand the just and equitable society sought by Miller as a birthright of a free society. It is long past time that we do so.

Notes

1. Statement of Abaline Miller, December 16, 1865, Complaints, March 1866–August 1868, Roll 97, Records of the Field Offices for the State of Louisiana, Bureau of Refugees, Freedmen, and Abandoned Lands, 1863–1872, Record Group 105, National Archives, Washington, D.C. (LBRFAL); Abiline Miller, 1870 Census, Ward 4, Pointe Coupee Parish, LA, dwelling 515, household 485.

2. Statement of Abaline Miller; Capt. A. H. Nickerson to Messrs Jed Smith and Edward Converse, Executors Carmena Estate, February 12, 1866, Letters Sent Vol. 1, January 1866–May 1867, Roll 64, LBRFAL. For more on the ways enslaved people destroyed the Rebellion from within, see W. E. B. Du Bois, *Black Reconstruction in America, 1860–1880* (New York: Harcourt, Brace & Co., 1935); Tera Hunter, *To 'joy My Freedom: Southern Black Women's Lives and Labors after the Civil War* (Cambridge: Harvard University Press, 1997); Thavolia Glymph, *Out of the House of Bondage: The Transformation of the Plantation Household* (New York: Cambridge University Press, 2008); Stephanie McCurry, *Confederate Reckoning: Power and Politics in the Civil War South* (Cambridge: Harvard University Press, 2012).

3. Statement of Abaline Miller. Robin Kelley gives a short articulation of racial capitalism, a term pioneered by Cedric Robinson, in "What Did Cedric Robinson Mean by Racial Capitalism?," *Boston Review*, January 12, 2017, http://bostonreview.net/race/robin-d-g-kelley-what-did-cedric-robinson-mean-racial-capitalism. For more, see Cedric Robinson, *Black Marxism: The Making of the Black Radical Tradition* (Chapel Hill: University of North Carolina Press, 2000); Destin Jenkins and Justin Leroy, *Histories of Racial Capitalism* (New York: Columbia University Press, 2021).

4. Eric Foner, *Reconstruction: America's Unfinished Revolution, 1863–1877* (New York: Harper & Row, 1988); Douglas Blackmon, *Slavery by Another Name: The Re-Enslavement of Black Americans from the Civil War to World War II* (New York: Anchor Books, 2009); Edward Baptist, *The Half Has Never Been Told: Slavery and the Making of American Capitalism* (New York: Basic Books, 2014).

5. Statement of Abaline Miller; William Burton, 1860 Census, Pointe Coupee Parish, LA, dwelling 779, household 854; J. J. Pringle, 1860 Census, Pointe Coupee Parish, LA, dwelling 781, household 856; Douglas Blackmon, *Slavery by Another Name*.

6. For more on mass incarceration and the prison industrial complex, see Angela Davis, *Are Prisons Obsolete?* (New York: Seven Stories Press, 2003); Ruth Wilson Gilmore, *The Golden Gulag: Prisons, Surplus, Crisis, and Opposition in Globalizing California* (Chapel Hill: University of North Carolina Press, 2007); Michelle Alexander, *The New Jim Crow: Mass Incarceration in the Age of Colorblindness* (New York: The New Press, 2010); Keeanga-Yamahtta Taylor, *From #Blacklivesmatter to Black Liberation* (Chicago: Haymarket, 2016).

7. "How George Floyd Died, and What Happened Next," May 25, 2021, *New York Times*, https://www.nytimes.com/article/george-floyd.html; Richard Fausset, What We Know About the Shooting Death of Ahmaud Arbery," *New York Times*, April 29, 2021, https://www.nytimes.com/article/ahmaud-arbery-shooting-georgia.html; Richard A. Oppel Jr., Derrick Bryson Taylor, and Nicholas Bogel-Burroughs, "What to Know About Breonna Taylor's Death," *New York Times*, April 26, 2021, https://www.nytimes.com/article/breonna-taylor-police.html.

8. Khalil Gibran Muhammad, *The Condemnation of Blackness: Race, Crime, and the Making of Modern Urban America* (Cambridge: Harvard University Press, 2010); Richard Rothstein, *The Color of Law: A Forgotten History of How Our Government Segregated America* (New York: Liveright Publishing, 2017); Keeanga-Yamahtta Taylor, *Race for Profit: How Banks and the Real Estate Industry Undermined Black Homeownership* (Chapel Hill: University of North Carolina Press, 2019).

9. Complaint of Shepard Grant and Abaline Miller against J. J. Pringle, March 14, 1866; Complaint of Lemuel Miles against J. J. Pringle, Undated [March or April 1866], Complaints, March 1866–August 1868, Roll 97, LBRFAL.

10. W. D. Smith, Chairman of Committee, to Maj. Wallace, July 23, 1866, Roll 97; Henry W. Coyle, 1870 Census, Pointe Coupee, LA, dwelling 557, household 525. Wallace appears to have copied the name incorrectly here as "R. W. Coyle," who appears elsewhere as "H. W. Coyle," which coincides with the census. H. F. Wallace to J. H. Malinken, August 31, 1866, Trimonthly and Special Reports, Volume 1, April 1866–May 1868, Roll 97, LBRFAL.

11. Eric Levenson, "How Minneapolis Police First Described the Murder of George Floyd, and What We Know Now," CNN, April 21, 2021, https://www.cnn.com/2021/04/21/us/minneapolis-police-george-floyd-death/index.html. Black visionaries, radicals, and reformers argued that America had yet to embrace the fullest vision of equality and freedom since the country's founding. This argument, popularized by Nikole Hannah-Jones's 1619 Project, illustrates the continuum of Black agitation for equality that Cedric Robinson termed the "Black radical tradition" and helps explain the persistence of racism as a literal investment in white power. Nikole Hannah-Jones, "Our Democracy's Founding Ideals Were False When They Were Written. Black Americans Have Fought to Make Them True," *New York Times Magazine*, August 14, 2019, https://www.nytimes.com/interactive/2019/08/14/magazine/black-history-american-democracy.html.

Resistance

5

From Eagle Buttons to Face Masks

The Dangers of Expressing Racial Equality

Emmanuel Dabney

Just after the Battle of Gettysburg, Frederick Douglass stated to a crowd in Philadelphia, "Once let the black man get upon his person the brass letters US, let him get an eagle on his button, and a musket on his shoulder, and bullets in his pocket, and there is no power on earth or under the earth which can deny that he has earned the right of citizenship in the United States."[1]

Southern states seceded between 1860 and 1861 to preserve slavery, and the Civil War began at Fort Sumter in April 1861. At that time, the Federal government, including President Abraham Lincoln, focused on putting down the rebellion and restoring the Union. On January 1, 1863, after tens of thousands of enslaved people had fled plantations, farms, and cities combined with Federal military failures, Lincoln released the Emancipation Proclamation and the war ultimately dismantled slavery in the United States.

One hundred and fifty-one years after Douglass's Philadelphia speech, police officer Darren Wilson killed Michael Brown of Ferguson, Missouri on August 9, 2014. As demonstrations occurred, protestors shouted, "Black Lives Matter" and soon #BlackLivesMatter was plastered on social media. The backlash to a majority Black protest movement that created and spread "Black Lives Matter" was prevalent from the start. Monica Anderson's and Pew Research Center's research points to 13.3 million tweets that included "#BlackLivesMatter" and the counter "#AllLivesMatter" composed between July 12, 2013 and March 31, 2016. Of that, a small minority (11%) of the posts were critical of the Black Lives Matter movement.[2] However, the commentary was disgusting. Among the most egregious was that of Laura Ingraham who in early 2014 compared cattleman Clive Bundy's militia supporters in an armed standoff with federal agents to the Civil Rights activists known as the Freedom Riders, yet called the Ferguson protesters a "lynch mob."[3] In 2015, Fox News' Katie Pavlich called Black Lives Matter "a movement that promotes the execution of police officers."[4] Despite Black Lives

Matter signs displayed in yards across America, as protests developed following George Floyd's 2020 murder, Tucker Carlson attacked celebrities, like rapper Lil Nas X, who Carlson claims helped incite "riots" or other celebrities who were "bailing out" protestors.[5]

Nevertheless, since the Ferguson protests, many people have worn Black Lives Matter pins, T-shirts, and accessories (including the accessory of 2020—face masks) to show their belief in equality. The protests and performative regalia of the Black Lives Matter movement (BLM) is a bold assertion of citizenship. Like the Civil War uniform of Black soldiers, BLM protestors' attire embraces the idea of Montague Simmons, chair of the St. Louis based Organization for Black Struggle. He explained in 2014: "The more you want to quiet us, the louder our voices will be."[6] It is important to consider how clothing and regalia worn by Black Americans demanding equality and respect was and continues to be weaponized against us.

I recognize that military uniforms and protest slogan clothing are not explicitly the same type of clothing. Uniforms are issued to soldiers whereas protest slogan clothing is made or purchased by the wearer. However, considering the volume of Black men who volunteered to enlist knowing the risks associated with being Black and in uniform, I argue that Black United States soldiers in the Civil War and contemporary Black Americans wearing BLM clothing and accessories was and is, as scholar Monica Miller wrote, a "visual presence and defiant attitude of deliberately clad black bodies."[7] Many Black Civil War veterans' comments make it clear that they believed they were fighting a righteous cause that would solidify emancipation and citizenship for Black Americans.[8] BLM protestors are not fighting to emancipate millions from legal, racialized slavery but still demand equality and fair treatment. It is the political nature of who is wearing the clothes that stitches the past and present together.

For Black Civil War soldiers (historically called United States Colored Troops or USCTs), Douglass's hopes of equality and full acceptance of Black men did not materialize. Donning the US uniform provoked verbal threats and violent, if not deadly, interactions. Their military service, however, contributed to America's second founding. In the present, Black Lives Matter clothing and accessories contribute to harassment and loss of income. In both cases, the prejudices of *some* white Americans caused or causes perceptible harm to Black Americans simply based on the fabric upon them. This essay focuses on Black people's claims to citizenship through their clothing and the policing of Black bodies.

Generally, Confederate military policies considered USCTs as slaves in insurrection and as historian David Silkenat writes massacres in 1864 battles prompted

Figure 1. Corporal Jacob Standerford (Staniford) of Co. F, 108th US Colored Troops Infantry Regiment in uniform with gun. (Library of Congress Prints and Photographs Division, Washington, D.C.)

some USCTs to fight more ferociously to prevent surrendering and questioning of their manhood.[9] However, these men's uniform-covered bodies would make them targets off the battlefield as well. Assaults on these soldiers were provoked from anger that the Federal government recruited Black men into the army. These servicemen came to understand they were not going to be celebrated by everyone.

Some white servicemen committed these deplorable acts. On September 14, 1863, Henry Hall and James Kelley of the 3rd Maryland Cavalry attacked Isaac

Freeman of the 4th US Colored Infantry. Hall broke Isaac's nose and mashed his forehead with a brick.[10] In another case, Lieutenant J. W. Glase, 104th Pennsylvania Infantry shouted to Private Nat Bruin, 33rd USCT, "If I had my will of the God damn nigger troops I would drown every one; damn you, you all will drown after the rebel war."[11]

Civilians also harassed these men. One man being protected by USCTs from potential Confederate attacks, commented days after the 1864 Battle of Fort Pillow, that Confederate general Nathan B. Forrest was justified in massacring Black soldiers. He then drew his knife upon Amos Hurd, a member of the 3rd US Colored Cavalry and "threatened to cut his throat."[12] In January 1865, some Black people gathered near Tobaccostick [now Madison], Maryland to celebrate a discharged, wounded Black soldier. A white constable in company with three other white men crashed the party. Most partygoers fled, but the white men beat the soldier.[13] In September 1865, Memphis policemen pestered Sergeant Joseph Brown of the 3rd US Colored Heavy Artillery. He wrote to the Provost Marshal that he was "sitting in my own door on Sunday night . . . about dark" talking with a friend. A policeman who lived opposite Brown said to him, "I wish I could get a chance to kill all the Damned Nigger Soldiers." When Brown said the police couldn't kill him, another policeman beat Brown to the ground, stomped on his back, ripped his shirt, and left him bruised. The white policemen then hauled him off to prison although he had not committed a crime.[14] Eight months later, Memphis was embroiled in a three-day race riot instigated by attempting to arrest a Black US soldier.[15]

Like the Civil War USCTs, Black people continue to face harassment for their clothing and had their attire affect their means to earn money. Black Lives Matter marked clothing and accessories in many ways are connected to other visual protest events like the 1917 Silent Protest Parade in Harlem, where Black men dressed in black and Black women and children dressed in white.[16] While their clothing did not display protests over racial riots and lynching, the signs of white backgrounds and black letters matched the clothing. In the modern era, Black employees and their employers have sparred over wearing Black Lives Matter attire. On July 22, 2016, Youngstown Municipal Court Judge Robert Milich noticed Andrea Burton, an attorney, wearing a nickel-sized Black Lives Matter pin in court. The judge reportedly asked her to remove it approximately five times. She refused, was held in contempt, handcuffed, and escorted away. Initially the judge sentenced her to five days in jail but stayed the order. Andrea Burton commented to the press at the time that the judge indicated "that legally I wasn't allowed to wear it and I deferred and said that I'm respecting my First Amendment right.

That I'm not neutral in injustice, and to remain neutral becomes an accomplice to oppression." She continued:

> It's an act of civil disobedience I understand that. I'm not anti-police I work with law enforcement and I hold them in the highest regard, and just to say for the record I do believe all lives matter. But at this point they don't all matter equally, and that's a problem in the justice system.[17]

Wearing the pin affected Burton's finances. From late July to early September she was not appointed to any criminal cases which had accounted "for 90 percent of her income" before the incident.[18]

Other people have experienced negative interactions at their jobs. They felt that their employer did not support racial equality. For example, in February 2017, Alton Edmond, a resident of Cocoa, Florida and an assistant public defender, wore a Black Lives Matter tie to court and to the office. He was fired afterwards. Edmond claimed that he had previously worn his tie a number of times in court without problems. Public defender Blaise Trettis admitted Edmond was fired but said "it was an accumulation of things . . . the tie had no significance in his firing." One of these alleged "things" was a Facebook post Edmond made during work hours criticizing his boss. Trettis added, "People can talk about politics, of course. But there's a big difference about talking politics and wearing politics on your tie."[19] It is clear that Edmond's accessory was policed even as he attempted to defend his clients and led to his forced departure from his work.

As COVID-19 bore down in the United States, the policing of BLM regalia increased. Costco required its employees to wear face masks. In June 2020, some workers in Louisville, Kentucky wore Black Lives Matter face masks, but a manager told them to remove them. A Black employee posted his resignation letter on Facebook calling out the disconnect between Costco CEO Craig Jelinek's public statements on the repulsiveness of racism in a city reeling from the murder of Breonna Taylor.[20] Other Black Lives Matter face mask incidents happened at a Wawa, Taco Bell, and Publix.[21] For some businesses, policing Black essential workers who use BLM regalia as an expression of citizenship continued to be important even as the pandemic raged.

Collectively these events illustrate how Black Americans have engaged in the freedom struggle. Statement regalia and clothing are part of Black America's material culture which expresses their citizenship and humanity. Those involved with the Black freedom struggle have long taken pride in their attire and endured the risks. Failing to face racism and injustice head on would cede the fight for our rights as Americans and humans and be an insult to our past, present, and future. William Henry Singleton, who served in the 35th United States Colored Infantry during the Civil War later wrote, "I wore the uniform of those men in Blue, who through four years of suffering wiped away with their blood the stain of slavery and purged the Republic of its sin."[22] Singleton would no doubt join outraged Americans today over how Black people are still treated as we express the belief that our lives are endangered and deserve to be respected. Black people are told to adhere to certain social guidelines (including dress) as a way to be respected. The reader should now see that regardless of how and what Black people say or wear, for too many Americans it is our presence that is feared. America is still on the road to true equality and freedom and for Black people, the way we clothe our bodies is part of the visual culture of our need to be appreciated and celebrated.

Notes

1. Philip Foner and Yuval Taylor, *Frederick Douglass: Selected Speeches and Writings* (Chicago: Chicago Review Press, 2000), "Address for the Promotion of Colored Enlistments, delivered at a mass meeting in Philadelphia, July 6, 1863," 536.

2. Monica Anderson, "The hashtag #BlackLivesMatter emerges: Social activism on Twitter," https://www.pewresearch.org/internet/2016/08/15/the-hashtag-blacklivesmatter-emerges-social-activism-on-twitter/ (accessed July 21, 2020).

3. Brian Powell, "'Lynch Mob' Or 'Freedom Riders': Laura Ingraham's Take On Ferguson Protests Vs. Bundy Ranch Standoff," https://www.mediamatters.org/laura-ingraham/lynch-mob-or-freedom-riders-laura-ingrahams-take-ferguson-protests-vs-bundy-ranch (accessed June 22, 2023).

4. German Lopez, "Fox News says Black Lives Matter incites violence. Critics said the same of MLK," https://www.vox.com/2015/9/1/9239643/black-lives-matter-fox-news (accessed August 2, 2022).

5. Mitchell Peters, "Lil Nas X Fires Back at Fox News' Tucker Carlson Over Inciting Riot Comments," https://www.billboard.com/music/music-news/lil-nas-x-fires-back-at-fox-news-tucker-carlson-over-inciting-riot-comments-george-floyd-protests-black-lives-matter-9397372/ (accessed August 2, 2022).

6. Carey Gilliam, "Rights struggle to continue after Missouri violence fades, organizers vow," https://wtvbam.com/news/articles/2014/aug/22/rights-struggle-to-continue-after-missouri-violence-fades-organizers-vow/460518/ (accessed July 21, 2020).

7. Monica L. Miller, *Slaves to Fashion: Black Dandyism and the Styling of Black Diasporic Identity* (Durham, N.C.: Duke University Press, 2009), 185.

8. Edwin S. Redkey, ed., *A Grand Army of Black Men: Letters from African-American Soldiers in the Civil War* (Cambridge: Cambridge University Press, 1992), 141.

9. David Silkenat, *Raising the White Flag: How Surrender Defined the American Civil War* (Chapel Hill: University of North Carolina Press, 2019), 162.

10. Isaac Freeman, Compiled Service Record, www.fold3.com; *The Baltimore Sun*, September 15, 1863. The assailants temporarily escaped but they were arrested.

11. Glase was censured and returned to duty. "General Court Martial Orders: Department of the South, 1862–1868," http://rs5.loc.gov/service/lawlib/law0001/2012/201200203998880/201200203998880.pdf?fbclid=IwAR2se_v8RnnOE7acX9uGdY28Fy4ZuNdc5WO6pSkbvW8qDW1LySuQgSfi3fA (accessed July 18, 2020). I thank Rich Condon for making me aware of this record's being digitized and for sharing the link with me.

12. *The Times-Picayune* [New Orleans], May 12, 1864. The assailant, B. W. Wooster, was hanged for this action; also see John Cimprich, *Fort Pillow, a Civil War Masssacre, and Public Memory* (Baton Rouge: Louisiana State University Press, 2005); and Brian Steel Willis, *The River Was Dyed with Blood: Nathan Bedford Forrest & Fort Pillow* (Norman: University of Oklahoma Press, 2014).

13. *The Baltimore Sun*, January 30, 1865.

14. Statement by Sgt. Joe Brown, [September 11] 1865, Affidavits & Statements, series 3545, Memphis TN Provost Marshal of Freedmen, Bureau of Refugees, Freedmen, & Abandoned Lands, Record Group 105, National Archives, available online at http://www.freedmen.umd.edu/JBrown.html (accessed July 24, 2020).

15. Stephen V. Ash, *A Massacre in Memphis: The Race Riot That Shook the Nation One Year After the Civil War* (New York: Hill and Wang, 2013).

16. Miller, 185.

17. Joseph D. Lyons, "Ohio Attorney Found 'In Contempt' for BLM Pin," https://www.bustle.com/articles/175137-who-is-andrea-burton-the-ohio-attorney-jailed-for-the-black-lives-matter-pin-she-refused (accessed July 18, 2020).

18. "Youngstown attorney settles suit over Black Lives Matter button," https://www.wfmj.com/story/32991028/youngstown-attorney-settles-suit-over-black-lives-matter-button (accessed July 18, 2020). For more on the legal precedent of clothing in the courtroom, see this article graciously provided to me by Shana Haines, https://lawprofessors.typepad.com/conlaw/2015/11/can-a-trial-judge-prohibit-defendants-and-spectators-from-wearing-black-lives-matter-shirts.html.

19. J. D. Gallop, "Brevard public defender fired, says Black Lives Matter tie raised eyebrows," https://www.floridatoday.com/story/news/2017/02/03/brevard-assistant-public-defender-fired-says-black-lives-matter-tie-raised-eyebrows/97409412/ (accessed July 20, 2020).

20. Billy Kobin and Sarah Ladd, "Louisville Costco employees say they were asked to leave over Black Lives Matter masks," https://www.courier-journal.com/story/news/local/2020/07/06/louisville-costco-black-lives-matter-masks-not-allowed-workers-say/5375680002/ (accessed July 20, 2020).

21. Matt Gray, "Wawa amends uniform policy after worker told he can't wear 'Black Lives Matter' mask," https://www.nj.com/burlington/2020/06/wawa-revisits-uniform-policy-after-worker-told-he-cant-wear-black-lives-matter-mask.html (accessed July 20, 2020); Kate Taylor and Palmer Haasch, "Taco Bell apologizes and says that it does not ban employees from wearing Black Lives Matter masks, after a worker was fired for doing so in a viral video," https://www.businessinsider.com/taco-bell-apologizes-worker

-fired-for-black-lives-matter-mask-2020-6 (accessed July 20, 2020); and Cliff Pickard, "Taco Bell apologizes after Ohio worker says he was fired for wearing Black Lives Matter mask," https://www.cleveland.com/nation/2020/06/taco-bell-apologizes-after-ohio-worker-says-he-was-fired-for-wearing-black-lives-matter-mask.html (accessed July 20, 2020); Caroline Silva, "Publix won't let employees wear Black Lives Matter face masks," https://www.orlandoweekly.com/Blogs/archives/2020/06/15/publix-wont-let-employees-wear-black-lives-matter-face-masks (accessed July 20, 2020).

22. William Henry Singleton, "Recollection of My Slavery Days," https://docsouth.unc.edu/neh/singleton/singleton.html (accessed July 20, 2020).

6

"Give Me My Rights"

Patriotism and Protest Among Black Civil War Soldiers and Black Lives Matter Activists

Jonathan Lande

John Payne resigned his teaching post in Bellefontaine, Ohio, to enlist in the Fifty-fifth Massachusetts in the spring of 1863.[1] Like many northern Black men, he joined the Army to improve Black lives, but he found himself serving the nation only to be mistreated in its military. He wished to continue soldiering yet acknowledged ongoing injustices in a letter to the A.M.E. Church newspaper, the *Christian Recorder*. "I am not willing to fight for anything less than the white man fights for," the soldier said. He continued in a tone similarly strident to Patrick Henry's famed 1775 declaration, "Give me liberty or give me death!"[2] "Give me my rights," Payne penned, "the rights this Government owes me, the same rights that the white man has." He concluded his letter, writing, "Liberty is what I am struggling for."[3] For the Ohioan, service was not merely an endeavor to preserve the Union but also a means of achieving liberty at home and in the ranks.

Like Payne, Black northern men serving in the US Army drew on a vibrant tradition of protest to combat injustice and establish equality as they fought for the Union and to end slavery. They reaped the rewards of military service, such as the chance to prove their mettle and themselves citizens. Yet they suffered numerous indignities. They refused to suffer in silence, however, issuing protests and sometimes turning to violence to fight back against racism.[4] These men did not distinguish their protests from their patriotism: They understood that protest did not in itself make one unruly or unpatriotic. Protest, even expressed violently, has been central to freedom movements in America since its founding. The Black soldiers who grappled with injustice while fighting for their country are fitting to remember following the backlash against Black Lives Matter (BLM) activists as they protest anti-Black racism in the twenty-first century. Recalling the connections made between patriotism and protest among Black soldiers allows us to transcend the distractions, including those that characterized BLM activists as un-American or lawless, so we can make sober assessments of activists' prescriptions to advance the nation beyond 2020.

In 1863, Black northern leaders articulated the stakes of the war as they recruited Black men, explaining that service would end slavery and bring about greater equality. As such, when Black northerners enlisted, they harbored distinctive understandings of the political objectives of their service. When the Army re-created racial violence, the men responded, relying on political tactics Black northerners had adapted from popular political tactics to counter their marginalized status in the polity. Black activists had written to newspapers, addressed politicians, and hosted rallies in the streets.[5] Many, including Frederick Douglass and Sojourner Truth, had embraced American nationalism, too, and spent July 4th simultaneously criticizing inadequacies and articulating a vision of the country as antislavery and antiracist.[6] Black northerners, including Black soldiers, carried these tactics into the Civil War years.

Protests against unequal treatment began soon after enlistment when Black soldiers discovered that the Federal government meant to pay them less than white soldiers. Dissent spread. Soldiers followed the Black political tradition of protest, which had been particularly potent in Massachusetts and thus, unsurprisingly, appeared early on in Massachusetts' Black regiments.[7] As early as May 1863, troops of the Fifty-fourth Massachusetts wrote letters to politicians and newspapers demanding equal pay. Sergeant Frederick Johnson reported to Governor John Andrew that the men felt "duped." Several soldiers rejected their pay until it equaled white men's. This protest was not easy, given that the refusal could be interpreted as insubordination and the men's families grew hungry, yet the men thought the injustice too important to overlook. Their protests went unheeded and frustration crept into their resolve. They nevertheless remained nonviolent. Their patience won them equal pay in June 1864.[8]

Some men opted for more violent methods and, in doing so, drew on an American tradition of adopting force as a means of combating injustices, a tradition visible most clearly during the Revolution. Americans in the mid–nineteenth century knew well the patriotism that swelled in the breasts of colonists in the 1770s—as well as the militancy that followed. In 1837, residents gathered in Massachusetts to dedicate a monument to the militiamen who confronted British soldiers in 1775. At the dedication, Ralph Waldo Emerson honored the militiamen's sacrifice, clearly drawing a connection between their bold action and American freedom. "Spirit, that made those heroes dare / To die, and leave their children free," read the sage of Concord.[9] In the 1850s, thanks to Black historian William Cooper Nell, Americans grew to appreciate the role of Crispus Attucks at the Boston Massacre, and Douglass's 1852 July 4th oration evoked the Founders' dogged pursuit of liberty.[10] Yet when resorting to political violence during the Civil War, Black soldiers were often charged as mutineers, not as militant patriots. Many officers issued formal charges of mutiny, furnishing evidence of the trials. Courts-martial transcripts reveal that Black soldiers, like white soldiers, understood mutiny as a legitimate protest against poor conditions and inferior leadership.[11] Black northerners also saw their protests as a means of eradicating racial injustices, however. Their decision to confront officers with the threat of violence was, in effect, a continuation of the strategy adopted by Black abolitionists.

By 1860, some Black northerners had turned toward the possibility of force as a means of overturning slavery and racism. Black northerners looked to military leaders, such as Toussaint Louverture, for inspiration and adopted political violence—a strategic tool to end oppression using the threat of force—when moral suasion failed to liberate or uplift Black lives.[12] Black men in the Army facing brutal, unjust punishment were following a well-trod path when they invoked in letters to newspapers the possibility of using violence.

On January 28, 1864, an anonymous soldier from the Forty-third US Colored Infantry (USCI) described the insults of ruthless officers. Most officers in Black regiments were white, and many white officers cared deeply for their men, inspiring respect by Black soldiers for their commanding officers.[13] However, some officers mistreated men, and the Forty-third USCI troop detailed the actions of such abusive officers for readers of the *Christian Recorder*. He said that the officers sometimes "strike the men with their swords, and jog and punch them in their side to show them how to drill." The protester added, "I do not think it right that soldiers should be cuffed and knocked around so by their officers, especially as we colored soldiers are." The soldier then ominously remarked, "Our officers must stop beating their men across the head and back with their swords, or I fear there will be trouble with some of us."[14] The soldier never wrote whether the cruelty ended in the Forty-third USCI, but in other regiments the abuse continued, leading to conflict between the men and their officers.

In April 1864, perceived injustices shattered the bonds forged in battle for the men and officers of the Fifty-fifth Massachusetts. The dispute over unequal pay continued to strain the relationship between the men and officers, and a defeat at the Battle of Olustee weakened morale further. During the ride back to South Carolina aboard the steamship *Sentinel*, the camaraderie finally broke down when Second Lieutenant Josiah Bean overheard the men grumbling about unsavory rations of salted horse and hardtack. He demanded that the alleged culprit, Private Sampson Goliah, step forward. Goliah said he would not do so for "any damned white officer" and threatened to hit Bean. The conflict escalated, and Captain William Nutt handcuffed Goliah. Several men, including Privates Nelson Browning and John Lewis, thought Nutt had treated Goliah unjustly and decided to liberate him. They confronted their officers. Browning said that there were "other ways of punishing a man without having him tied up," and they freed Goliah.[15] Later, officers arrested several men and tried them for mutiny. The courts-martial convicted Goliah, as well as Browning and Lewis, and imprisoned them for the remainder of their enlistment terms before dishonorably discharging them. The men of the Fifty-fifth Massachusetts protested injustice, an act condemned as mutiny in the Army yet revered in other contexts as quintessentially American.

Black Civil War troops struggled against racism, not unlike BLM activists. The BLM movement began in July 2013, when activists tweeted #BlackLivesMatter following the acquittal of George Zimmerman for the killing of Trayvon Martin, an unarmed Black teenager. Then police shot and killed Michael Brown, an unarmed Black man, in Ferguson, Missouri, and BLM activists moved from cyberspace to the public sphere to stress the value of Black lives in a nation that historically undervalued Black people.[16] BLM activists continued to struggle for change, but they intensified their demands in 2020 following the murders of George Floyd, Breonna Taylor, and Ahmaud Arbery.[17] Activists hosted more than 550 protests or vigils in 2020 to remember Floyd, Taylor, and Arbery and call for justice, better treatment by authorities, and extensive alterations to social, political, and legal structures, such as the reduction or abolition of police departments.[18] These demands echo those issued by Black soldiers. Of course, the circumstances in the 1860s differed from those in 2020. Yet the demands for racial justice course beneath both groups of protesters. However, while Black soldiers have been remembered as patriots on and off the battlefield, most notably in the film *Glory* (1989), many in America have disparaged BLM protesters as unpatriotic, reduced their activism to disorder, and disregarded their plight.

Critics frequently referred to BLM demonstrations as un-American, a criticism that NFL quarterback Colin Kaepernick faced in 2016. While he played for the San Francisco 49ers, Kaepernick dove into texts describing historic racial injustices, including Carter G. Woodson's *The Mis-Education of the Negro* (1933) and *The Autobiography of Malcolm X* (1965), and grew wearier of American racism. To demonstrate his protest, he knelt during the National Anthem.[19] When asked why, he said, "I am not going to stand up to show pride in a flag for a country that oppresses Black people and people of color."[20] Responses to his protest varied. The 49ers explained that they wished to "honor our country" with the pre-game ceremony, but the team did not require players to participate. "In respecting such American principles as . . . freedom of expression, we recognize the right of an individual to choose and participate, or not, in our celebration of the national anthem," the team said.[21] In an open letter, Army veteran and NFL long snapper Nate Boyer voiced his disagreement with Kaepernick yet noted that his protest was the quarterback's "inalienable right." "Even though my initial reaction to your protest was one of anger," Boyer added, "I'm trying to listen to what you're saying and why you're doing it."[22] Not all were so magnanimous. Critics piled on, charging Kaepernick with disloyalty. Then–presidential candidate Donald Trump said, "Maybe he should find a country that works better for him."[23] Witness to continued violence against Black lives, many Americans shifted their views, and other athletes knelt without censure. The NFL even changed its tune before the 2020 season, admitting that the organization was "wrong for not listening to NFL players earlier." As president, Trump sustained his attack, however, tweeting that the players had been "disrespecting our Country & our Flag."[24] Trump persisted in ignoring the patriotic roots of the protests and the causes generating dissatisfaction too. The president even overlooked the hypocrisy of issuing criticism of peaceful protests while encouraging violence against his opposition. At a 2015 rally, when activist Mercuito Southall Jr. declared, "Black lives matter!" Trump shouted, "Get him the hell out of here." Trump supporters then attacked Southall as security removed him. After the rally, reports emerged that Southall had been punched, kicked, and nearly choked. Trump said of Southall, "Maybe he should have been roughed up."[25] In 2020, Trump's blasé response continued, as he refused to condemn a counterprotester (and avowed Trump supporter) charged with killing Wisconsin protesters who had assembled after police shot Jacob Blake, an unarmed Black father.[26] The critics, including the president, condemned BLM activists not only as "un-American"; BLM activists faced criticism for their tactics too.

Frequently, critics have described BLM activists as a disorderly mob, a theme reminiscent of assaults on Black activism during the civil rights movement. As BLM activists prepared for a peaceful rally in Minneapolis to demand justice, for instance, Trump tweeted a phrase steeped in white-supremacist denunciations of Black activists: "Once the looting starts, the shooting starts." A Miami police chief known for bigotry first used the phrase in response to 1967 civil rights protesters. George Wallace recycled the phrase during his presidential run on a third-party ticket supporting segregation in 1968. Trump received criticism for invoking the phrase and denied knowing its history, yet he denigrated protesters again in June. To bring attention to violence against Black Americans, BLM protesters congregated near the White House. Kishon McDonald, a Navy veteran, participated and said that "we were peaceful [and] we wanted no trouble." Yet at the protest, the police advanced on the crowd, shooting protesters with rubber bullets and beating a reporter with a baton. The president, showing no remorse, labeled protesters "thugs" and "terrorists" before threatening to enforce "total domination" with military force. Several days later, he further rebuked resistance, equating activists with traitors. All the while, antagonists and Trump overlooked the calls for policy change.[27]

BLM protests, even when they turned confrontational, were the essence of patriotism, despite the condemnations. Indeed, the resolve to confront injustice shown by BLM activists mirrored that of the militia at Concord and of the colonists who refused to abide by the violation of their inalienable rights in 1776. Only the race of the protesters and the specific injustices protested against allowed critics' comments to go so uninterrogated and the plight of protesters to go unexamined. James Baldwin succinctly captured this point on the *Dick Cavett Show* in 1968. "[W]hen any white man in the world says, 'Give me liberty or give me death,'" Baldwin said, "the entire white world applauds, but if a Black man says exactly the same thing, word for word, he is judged a criminal and treated like one."[28] The author's words seem prophetic when reflecting on Trump's response to violent white supremacists demonstrating against the removal of a Confederate monument in Charlottesville, Virginia. At the rally, a white supremacist drove his sports car into a crowd of counterprotesters, killing Heather Heyer, yet the president said that there were "very fine people on both sides." Trump sympathized with the white supremacists, even as they spewed xenophobia, brandished Nazi symbols, and fought to preserve the statue of a man who had led a domestic insurgency.[29] Yet when BLM protesters spoke up at Trump's rally, assembled peacefully outside the White House, and marched against anti-Black racism in Wisconsin, the president encouraged his supporters, watched the police subjugate activists, and refused to condemn a man charged with murder. Trump used stronger language to condemn the peaceful BLM protests than the violent counterprotests of white nationalists toting AR-15s. In so doing, Trump turned a conversation about injustices into a discussion of the protesters' legitimacy.

With such rhetoric being leveled against BLM activists, it is important to recall Black soldiers' protests. Black men from across the North entered the ranks to fight and die for a Union forged in protest, and they would not abide by the injustices. They agitated, but their actions were not unpatriotic denunciations. They expressed the grandest hopes of America while serving it and confronting injustices, just as the Founders had in the 1770s and 1780s. It remains essential to remember the patriotism at the heart of Black soldiers' protests, so we can transcend the noise created by those wishing to discount activists and, as the veteran Nate Boyer said, "listen." Only then can the BLM activists' critical engagement with how to improve America be heard and carefully considered, rather than derided as lawlessness. Only then can the America Black soldiers fought for be realized.

Notes

1. John H. Payne, Compiled Service Record, Record Group 94, National Archives, Washington, D.C. (Hereafter "RG 94").

2. Patrick Henry, "Give Me Liberty or Give Me Death," The Avalon Project: Documents in Law, History, and Diplomacy, Lillian Goldman Law Library, Yale University, https://avalon.law.yale.edu/18th_century/patrick.asp.

3. Quoted in Christine Dee, ed., *Ohio's War: The Civil War in Documents* (Athens: Ohio University Press, 2014), 172.

4. For the sake of brevity, this essay addresses Black soldiers from the North only, though much that is described here also holds true for Black troops from the South. On resistance among Black southerners, see Jonathan Lande, "Trials of Freedom: African American Deserters during the U.S. Civil War," *Journal of Social History* 49, no. 3 (Spring 2016), 693–709.

5. Patrick Rael, *Black Identity and Black Protest in the Antebellum North* (Chapel Hill: University of North Carolina Press, 2002); and Manisha Sinha, *The Slave's Cause: A History of Abolition* (New Haven: Yale University Press, 2016).

6. Jonathan Lande, "'Lighting Up the Path of Liberty and Justice': Black Abolitionist Fourth of July Celebrations and the Promise of America from the Fugitive Slave Act to the Civil War," *Journal of African American History* 105, no. 3 (Summer 2020), 364–95.

7. Stephen Kantrowitz, *More Than Freedom: Fighting for Black Citizenship in a White Republic, 1829–1889* (New York: Penguin Press, 2012).

8. Donald Yacovone, "The Pay Crisis," in *Hope and Glory: Essays on the Legacy of the 54th Massachusetts Regiment*, ed. Martin H. Blatt, Thomas J. Brown, and Donald Yacovone (Amherst: University of Massachusetts Press, 2001), 38–42, quotation on 39; John David Smith, *Lincoln and the U.S. Colored Troops* (Carbondale: Southern Illinois University Press, 2013), 69–71.

9. Ralph Waldo Emerson, "The Concord Hymn," thepoetryfoundation.org, https://www.poetryfoundation.org/poems/45870/concord-hymn.

10. Mitch Kachun, *First Martyr of Liberty: Crispus Attucks in American Memory* (New York: Oxford University Press, 2017), 46–58; Lande, "Lighting Up the Path," 373–75.

11. Steven J. Ramold, *Baring the Iron Hand: Discipline in the Union Army* (DeKalb: Northern Illinois University Press, 2009), 198–208.

12. Matthew J. Clavin, *Toussaint Louverture and the American Civil War: The Promise and Peril of a Second Haitian Revolution* (Philadelphia: University of Pennsylvania Press, 2009), 78–80; Kellie Carter Jackson, *Force and Freedom: Black Abolitionists and the Politics of Violence* (Philadelphia: University of Pennsylvania Press, 2019), 7, 15–17.

13. Joseph T. Glatthaar, *Forged in Battle: The Civil War Alliance of Black Soldiers and White Officers* (Baton Rouge: Louisiana State University Press, 1990), especially chapters 7–9.

14. Quoted in Edwin S. Redkey, *A Grand Army of Black Men: Letters of African-American Soldiers in the Union Army, 1861–1865* (New York: Cambridge University Press, 1992), 262.

15. Sampson Goliah Compiled Service Record, RG 94; Josiah Bean Compiled Service Record, RG 94; Nelson Browning Compiled Service Record, RG 94; John Lewis Compiled Service Record, RG 94; Sampson Goliah Court-Martial Trial, File NN 2479; Nelson Browning Court-Martial Trial, File NN 2479; and John Lewis Court-Martial Trial, File NN 2479, Record Group 153, National Archives, Washington, D.C. For further discussion of the mutiny, see Christian G. Samito, *Becoming American Under Fire: Irish Americans, African Americans, and the Politics of Citizenship During the Civil War Era* (Ithaca, NY: Cornell University Press, 2009), 78, 90–92, 95; Glatthaar, 222–24.

16. Alvin B. Tillery, "What Kind of Movement Is Black Lives Matter? The View from Twitter," *Journal of Race, Ethnicity, and Politics* 4, no. 2 (September 2019), 297.

17. Manny Fernandez and Audra D. S. Burch, "George Floyd, from 'I Want to Touch the World' to 'I Can't Breathe,'" *New York Times*, June 29, 2020, https://www.nytimes.com/article/george-floyd-who-is.html.

18. Jiachuan Wu, Nigel Chiwaya, and Savannah Smith, "Map: Protests and Rallies for George Floyd Spread Across the Country," *NBC News*, June 1, 2020, https://www.nbcnews.com/news/us-news/map-protests-rallies-george-floyd-spread-across-country-n1220976; Michael Balsamo, "When Protesters Demand 'Defund the Police' at George Floyd Demonstrations, What Does It Mean?," *Chicago Tribune*, June 7, 2020, https://www.chicagotribune.com/nation-world/ct-nw-cb-george-floyd-protesters-defund-police-20200607-kiupi5allvgehinzidz3jund5e-story.html; Sam Levin, "What Does 'Defund the Police' Mean?: The Rallying Cry Sweeping the US—Explained," *The Guardian*, June 8, 2020, https://www.theguardian.com/us-news/2020/jun/05/defunding-the-police-us-what-does-it-mean.

19. Ameer Hasan Loggins, "The True Colin Kaepernick . . . from Someone Who Has Been There and Calls Him a Friend," *The Athletic*, August 26, 2017, https://theathletic.com/89431/2017/08/26/guest-column-the-true-colin-kaepernick-from-someone-who-has-been-there-and-calls-him-a-friend/.

20. Steve Wyche, "Colin Kaepernick Explains Why He Sat During the National Anthem," NFL.com, August 27, 2016, https://www.nfl.com/news/colin-kaepernick-explains-why-he-sat-during-national-anthem-0ap3000000691077.

21. John Branch, "The Awakening of Colin Kaepernick," *New York Times*, September 7, 2017, https://www.nytimes.com/2017/09/07/sports/colin-kaepernick-nfl-protests.html.

22. Nate Boyer, "An Open Letter to Colin Kaepernick, from a Green Beret–Turned–Long snapper," *Army Times*, August 30, 2016, https://www.armytimes.com/opinion/2016/08/30/an-open-letter-to-colin-kaepernick-from-a-green-beret-turned-long-snapper/.

23. John Branch, "The Awakening of Colin Kaepernick," *New York Times*, September 17, 2017, accessed September 23, 2020.

24. Brakkton Booker, "Trump Questions NFL Commissioner's Reversal on Protests During Anthem," *NPR News*, June 8, 2020, https://www.npr.org/sections/live-updates-protests-for-racial-justice/2020/06/08/871899132/trump-questions-nfl-commissioner-on-anthem-debate.

25. Jenna Johnson and Mary Jordan, "Trump on Rally Protester: 'Maybe He Should Have Been Roughed Up,'" *Washington Post*, November 22, 2015, https://www.washingtonpost.com/news/post-politics/wp/2015/11/22/black-activist-punched-at-donald-trump-rally-in-birmingham/.

26. Matthew Choi, "Trump Defends Gunman Charged with Murdering 2 in Kenosha," *Politico,* August 31, 2020, https://www.politico.com/news/2020/08/31/trump-defends-kenosha-gunman-406377.

27. Barbara Sprunt, "The History Behind 'When the Looting Starts, the Shooting Starts,'" *NPR News*, May 29, 2020, https://www.npr.org/2020/05/29/864818368/the-history-behind-when-the-looting-starts-the-shooting-starts; Angela Dewan and Jennifer Hansler, "Is the US Still the World's Moral Leader? Not After What Trump Just Did This Week," *CNN*, June 6, 2020, https://www.cnn.com/2020/06/06/politics/us-protests-george-floyd-world-moral-leader-intl/index.html; Catie Edmondson, "Trump's Response to Protests Draws Bipartisan Rebuke in Congress," *New York Times,* June 2, 2020, https://www.nytimes.com/2020/06/02/us/politics/trump-congress-protesters-tear-gas.html; Barbara Sprunt, "'Scared, Confused and Angry': Protester Testifies About Lafayette Park Removal," *NPR News*, June 29, 2020; https://www.keranews.org/2020-06-29/scared-confused-and-angry-protester-testifies-about-lafayette-park-removal.

28. *I Am Not Your Negro*, directed by Raoul Peck (2016; New York: Velvet Films), 1:06.

29. Rosie Gray, "Trump Defends White-Nationalist Protesters," *The Atlantic*, August 15, 2017, https://www.theatlantic.com/politics/archive/2017/08/trump-defends-white-nationalist-protesters-some-very-fine-people-on-both-sides/537012/.

7

A Lens Through Which We Can View Society

Sports and Race in America

Daryl A. Carter

America has many pastimes. One of our most important pastimes is sports. There are several major sports historically in the United States: baseball, football, basketball, golf, hockey, and, more recently, soccer. Other sports, such as swimming, track and field, and cross-country, have also been a part of the American sports landscape. Sports are important to understanding American society. Sports are often the windows through which we can both view and understand the society around us.

Athletic competition tells us about ourselves, our hopes, our dreams, and our fears. It peels back the veneer of the gentility of our work and social lives and reveals what animates us.[1] Over the course of three weeks, Americans seemingly live and die with every made field goal, slam dunk, and foul. The productivity of the American workforce declines somewhat as Americans play hooky in order to watch games and, when possible, travel to see their favorite teams play.[2] We live vicariously through those young athletes. When I was in graduate school at the University of Memphis in 2007 and 2008, I watched as Memphis slowed to a crawl as the Memphis Tigers went deep into the NCAA tournament in 2007 and played for the national championship in 2008.

Yet sports also reveal our politics, prejudices, and baser instincts. Storytelling, sportsmanship, and passionate displays of emotion are central to our sports adventurism. They reveal societal norms, personal political affiliations, and individual belief systems. As a result, race is at the center of so many of our national conversations about sports. Segregation. Immigration. Integration. Is O. J. Simpson innocent or guilty of murdering his ex-wife Nicole Brown Simpson and her friend Ron Goldman in June 1994? Should LeBron James stop advocating for Black Americans and "just dribble"? Why in the hell is Colin Kaepernick kneeling during the national anthem? These questions have animated our national discourse.

Sports and Black activism have also been tricky because most Black athletes have historically been very careful when it came to activism. Renford Reese has noted that "Until the late 1960s, many black athletes had been effectively socialized to be nonpolitical."[3] This began to change in 1968. A year of tremendous upheaval in the United States included Tommie Smith and John Carlos raising their gloved fists in Black Power salute at the Olympic games in Mexico City. Over the next fifty years Black athletes grew bolder as their fame and income and wealth grew to astronomical heights.

Many Americans believe that political issues have no place in sports. ESPN journalist Howard Bryant notes, "*Political*, fans think, describes an individual act of dissidence, not a collective one perpetrated against the public by the state, the mainstream media or your local sports team."[4] This mistaken belief is all around us. Sports, therefore, is a window through which we can understand the world around us. Nowhere has this been more evident than in baseball.

Baseball dates back to the first half of the nineteenth century. In major cities such as New York, Philadelphia, and Washington, baseball took root. From its early days, many of its earliest advocates and promoters sought to make the game national in both appeal and influence. Henry Chadwick, who claimed to have fathered the sport, spoke after the Civil War of a "national game."[5] Ryan A. Swanson, who has examined race and baseball's origins, expertly notes, "The fanatical desire by white baseball leaders to foster a 'national game' was the preeminent force behind baseball's segregation. Northern baseball leaders worked tirelessly to spread baseball's popularity south of the Mason-Dixon line."[6] Few records from before the Civil War survive to recount Black Americans and baseball. Slavery in the South and poverty's generally being the economic condition of the vast majority of Black Americans usually meant that white Americans were playing the sport. In spite of this, Black Americans too would take a strong interest in the game. At least by 1867, the historian Benjamin G. Rader notes, all-Black baseball teams were playing baseball or "black ball."[7] Yet the National Association of Base Ball Players (NABBP) argued ferociously against integration in the 1860s. Black ball clubs and players were not to be accepted.[8]

By 1884, Blacks were prohibited from playing on professional teams with white players. As in much of the rest of the South, however, there were growing desires to control Blacks. This meant "the racist backlash felt by the black players . . . had everything to do with the national mood regarding racial relations."[9] Baseball followed the country, from Progressivism to the New Negro to World War II, as America developed new ideas about citizenship yet kept Black Americans in second-class status.

Nearly two full years after the end of World War II, the color line was finally broken. Brooklyn Dodgers executive Branch Rickey signed Jackie Robinson to play for the team in 1947. It was a watershed moment, one that heralded the integration of Major League Baseball as the civil rights movement was beginning to heat up and President Harry S. Truman was just a little more than a year away from integrating the US Armed Forces. Today we celebrate Jackie Robinson and his contributions to the game. But at the time it was a controversial decision. Robinson suffered horrendous abuse from fans, teammates, opposing players, and others. A giant crack had emerged in professional sports, a crack that over the next thirty years would lead to full integration of America's professional and collegiate sports.

For me, the summer of 2020 did not occur in a vacuum. What triggered the explosive responses from so many Americans were the graphic and disturbing images of a murderer in a policeman's uniform gleefully kneeing on the neck of a Black man in handcuffs. The video was recorded by a then-seventeen-year-old girl, Darnella Frazier. For many white Americans who watched the video, it was brutal and undeniable that Derek Chauvin had murdered an unarmed man who was begging for his life. Black Americans were outraged and livid, but not surprised. Just as when the video of the Rodney King beating was released in 1991, Black Americans were all too aware of the potential for lethal force being used against them by police officers. On the night of March 2–3, 1991, George Holliday recorded Los Angeles Police officers severely beating King following a high-speed chase. The video was broadcast countless times on television, and Americans watched police officers beat a Black man within an inch of his life. A lot of white Americans were caught by surprise, forced to confront with their own eyes what Black Americans had been pointing out for decades.[10]

The protests of 2020 were the result of the nearly fifteen searing years of backlash and economic developments. President George W. Bush had made repeated attempts at growing the Republican Party by trying to appeal to Black and Brown voters. As I noted several years ago, "During his [Bush's] administration he would make inroads with some African Americans. But he would also anger many others as he appeared to be tone deaf to events such as Hurricane Katrina."[11] But President Bush was also being squeezed by his right flank. The modern right wing and conservatism were animated by race. It was central to their political core. Joseph Lowndes has accurately pointed out that "[r]acial identifications have become linked to political grievances and aspirations when political actors . . . successfully developed credible language through which to make these links. In the case of modern conservatism, race has been both an open and coded signifier for popular mobilizations against redistribution, regulation, labor protections, and myriad other aspects of neo-liberal opposition to 'big government.'"[12]

These were Americans increasingly angry over demographic change. Since the 1960s the country had become much more diverse. The 2000s underscored what many white Americans believed was a real and existential threat to their well-being—namely, diversity. Fewer white Americans were having children. In 1960, white Americans made up 88.3 percent of the population. In contrast, white Americans made up 72.4 percent of the population in 2010. Ten years later that number dropped to 61.6 percent. The social dynamics were changing as well.[13]

There was no greater evidence of this than the election of Barack Obama. Born in Hawaii in 1961 to an interracial couple, Obama seemingly came out of nowhere. He was biracial. He'd graduated from Columbia University and Harvard Law School. He was a law professor. His wife had gone to Princeton University and Harvard Law School. Compared with the average American, he was wealthy. The future president benefited from the end of Jim Crow, integrated education, and affirmative-action policies.

Some claimed that America became post-racial because of Barack Obama. The truth was far different and sad. As David Maraniss and others have noted, Barack Obama was a direct beneficiary of the civil rights movement and its successes.[14] Yet those successes were tempered by the fact that race is so deeply intertwined in our national history and cultural DNA that we are never far removed from the pernicious effects of race, nor are we isolated from the charlatans, opportunists, racists, and politicians willing to beat the nativist and white supremacist drums of raw fury for electoral advantage. Ta-Nehisi Coates presciently notes, "The election of an African American to our highest political office was alleged to demonstrate a triumph of integration. But when President Obama addressed the tragedy of Trayvon Martin, he demonstrated integration's great limitation—that acceptance depends not just on being twice as good but on being half as black. And even then, full acceptance is still withheld."[15] While President Obama struggled politically as various politicians fanned the flames of racial resentment, the rest of Black America was catching hell.

The election of President Obama threw gasoline on a fire that had been growing since the civil rights movement. It was and is personal for me. My parents were Baby Boomers. They experienced the 1950s and 1960s in real time. My father was a first-generation college graduate from Georgia. My mother was in the same boat. They were an interracial couple married in 1975 in Sacramento, California. At the time, Ronald Reagan was wrapping up two terms as California's governor. During his years in Sacramento, Reagan embraced the rhetoric and politics of the Southern Strategy, which he used to great effect during his insurgent campaign against President Gerald Ford in 1976 and, successfully, against

President Jimmy Carter in 1980. I was born in Sacramento in 1979. The state was at the forefront of many of these hot-button issues: race, identity, immigration, sexuality, nativism, etc.

As the 1990s dawned, Major League Baseball seemed to shed more and more Black players. Some of this was the result of the growing popularity of American football and basketball. No one could reasonably deny the appeal of Magic Johnson, Michael Jordan, Lawrence Taylor, or Jerry Rice. But a cultural shift was taking place. This affected baseball as fewer Blacks played the sport and MLB teams replaced their Black players with immigrant talent of other races. While the increase in immigrants into baseball was long overdue, it raised concerns about Blacks' being excluded once again.[16] In 2020, as protests were gripping the country, *Sports Illustrated* ran a feature story that highlighted why Blacks were leaving the sport.[17] Open racism and exclusionary tactics played a big part in driving Blacks away. The conservative nature of baseball, with its traditions and unwritten rules, has proven an insurmountable hurdle for too many young athletes.

The year 2020 was an awakening for the country. While many Americans preferred sports to be an entertaining form of escapism, athletes took it upon themselves to fight back against injustice, to highlight abuse of power, and to demand meaningful reform. This was often in spite of the wishes of many owners, front-office personnel, and others who wanted to focus on the games at hand. Jerry Brewer of the *Washington Post* noted in August 2020, "Sports escapism has been suspended. There is a chance the ol' reliable expectation of games as breezy diversions may never return."[18] Escape was no longer feasible. We saw this on the campus of East Tennessee State University in the spring of 2021.

East Tennessee State University men's basketball players began to kneel during the playing of the national anthem during the 2020–2021 season. The controversy over kneeling spread from Colin Kaepernick to the Appalachian Highlands of northeastern Tennessee. The *New York Times* noted in the summer of 2020 that the kneeling issue was unavoidable now.[19] In February 2021, local news outlets wrote stories about the team, and the public became aware of the story. Outrage followed as local politicians, wannabes, those with a political agenda, and others through crocodile tears bemoaned the state of America. Some whined about how disrespectful it was to veterans and current servicepersons. The team was blasted in the public. The head coach was no longer head coach after a few weeks. A local automobile dealership owner petulantly demanded back the free cars he had been providing to coaches. People threatened to not attend the university or come for events. Others said they would not give money anymore. Tennessee legislators quickly threatened public institutions across the state. It was a debacle, one rooted not in the play of the team on the court, nor in the performance of the head coach. This brouhaha was rooted in the outrage many felt at young Black athletes engaging in peaceful protests against racism, police brutality, and injustice.[20]

Nearly a year and a half later the campus is still dealing with the fallout from the peaceful, constitutionally protected free speech exhibited by ETSU's student athletes. Members of the community remain angry, both those protecting the rights of the students as well as those uncomfortable with what those peaceful protests represented. In West Virginia, at the same time as the ETSU kerfuffle, the men's basketball team at Bluefield College was targeted for retribution for kneeling during the national anthem.[21] Conversations and debates about kneeling were taking place in every state, university and college, and athletic department. White student athletes were increasingly supportive on a scale that had not been seen before. White alumni, donors, and stakeholders were increasingly uncomfortable and making disturbing suggestions that students, faculty, coaches, and administrators should be held to account because an individual and/or group decided to engage in constitutionally protected free speech.

The establishment of baseball as America's national pastime and its meaning to Americans reflect the growth of America. All of the good, bad, and ugly that has defined our national existence is reflected in sports. The horrors of the Civil War. The sickening re-establishment of white supremacy in the American South. The political and policy desires of elected officials, bureaucrats, and others to expand freedom for many yet impede justice for Black people is seen in the ridiculous fact that professional and collegiate sports largely denied justice and hid opportunity until late in the twentieth century. Justice remains incomplete in America. At least half of the country dislikes even discussing these issues. The fact that one of the two major political parties has embraced a neo-Confederate stance is reflective of this reality. In spite of this reality, it is heartwarming to see millions of Americans reject the bigotry of the past and embrace a brighter future for all Americans. The 2020 and 2022 elections, despite the blemishes, demonstrate the progress the country has made in these spaces. Further, while the fever of discrimination, extremism, hatred, and xenophobia has not gone away, recent developments make one believe that there is light at the end of the tunnel.

Notes

1. Every year, for example, tens of millions of people watch the NCAA's March Madness basketball tournament. For three weeks, tens of millions of Americans live and die with every made basket, missed shot, foul call, and slam dunk.

2. Jessica Dickler, "March Madness takes a toll on productivity," *CNBC*, March 7, 2018, https://www.cnbc.com/2018/03/06/march-madness-takes-a-toll-on-productivity.html, accessed July 11, 2022.

3. Renford Reese, "The Socio-Political Context of the Integration of Sport in America," *Journal of African American Men* 3, no. 4 (Spring 1998), 16.

4. Howard Bryant, *The Heritage: Black Athletes, a Divided America, and the Politics of Patriotism* (Boston: Beacon Press, 2018), 4.

5. Ryan A. Swanson, *When Baseball Was White: Reconstruction, Reconciliation, and Dreams of a National Pastime* (Lincoln: University of Nebraska Press, 2014), viii.

6. Swanson, *When Baseball Was White*, viii.

7. Benjamin G. Rader, *Baseball: A History of America's Game, Second Edition* (Chicago: University of Illinois Press, 2002), 10–11.

8. Rader, *Baseball*, 28.

9. Mark Ribowsky, *A Complete History of The Negro Leagues: 1884 to 1955* (New York: Kensington Publishing Corp., 2002), 30.

10. Tensions in Los Angeles boiled over when the officers involved in the beating—Sgt. Stacey Koon, Laurence Powell, Timothy Wind, Ted Briseno, and Roland Solano—were acquitted by an all-white Simi Valley jury in April 1992. The murder of Latasha Harlins on March 16, 1991, by Soon J. Du, a liquor store owner, also fueled the anger of the Black community. After Du was convicted of manslaughter, Judge Joyce Karlin sentenced Du to probation. The two incidents were the catalysts for the explosion of violence and property destruction in Los Angeles in April and May 1992.

11. Daryl A. Carter, "The Birth of a New Political Era," in *The George W. Bush Presidency: Domestic and Economic Policy*, Volume 2, ed. Meena Bose and Richard Himelfarb (New York: Nova Publishers, 2016), 137.

12. Joseph E. Lowndes, *From the New Deal to the New Right: Race and the Southern Origins of Modern Conservatism* (New Haven: Yale University Press, 2008), 7.

13. Table 56—Race of the Population, by Regions, Divisions, and States: 1960, Supplementary Reports, 1960 Census of Population, September 7, 1961, https://www2.census.gov/library/publications/decennial/1960/pc-s1-supplementary-reports/pc-s1-10.pdf, accessed July 13, 2022; Nicholas Jones, Rachel Marks, Roberto Ramirez, Merarys Rios-Vargas, "2020 Census Illuminates Racial and Ethnic Composition of the Country," US Census Bureau, https://www.census.gov/library/stories/2021/08/improved-race-ethnicity-measures-reveal-united-states-population-much-more-multiracial.html, accessed July 13, 2022.

14. David Maraniss, *Barack Obama: The Story* (New York: Simon & Schuster, 2013).

15. Ta-Nehisi Coates, *We Were Eight Years in Power: An American Tragedy* (New York: One World, 2017), 124.

16. "¡Pleibol! In the Barrios and the Big Leagues," National Museum of American History, Behring Center, Smithsonian, https://americanhistory.si.edu/pleibol, accessed December 21, 2022.

17. Stephanie Apstein, "Why Baseball Is Losing Black America," *Sports Illustrated*, July 17, 2020, https://www.si.com/mlb/2020/07/17/preston-wilson-baseball-black-lives-matter, accessed July 18, 2022.

18. Jerry Brewer, "Sports used to be an escape from the world. Now they're a window into it," *The Washington Post*, August 5, 2020, https://www.washingtonpost.com/sports/2020/08/05/sports-used-be-an-escape-world-now-theyre-window-into-it/, accessed July 18, 2022.

19. John Branch, "The Anthem Debate Is Back. But Now It's Standing That's Polarizing," *The New York Times*, July 4, 2020, https://www.nytimes.com/2020/07/04/sports/football/anthem-kneeling-sports.html, accessed December 21, 2022.

20. Michael A. Fletcher, "After kneeling and coach's departure, a tough reckoning on race at East Tennessee State," ESPN, May 27, 2021, https://www.espn.com/mens-college-basketball/story/_/id/31510891/after-kneeling-coach-departure-tough-reckoning-race-east-tennessee-state, accessed July 18, 2022.

21. Greta Anderson, "College Stands on Principle, Students Kneel for Theirs: After the Bluefield College men's basketball team was punished for kneeling during the national anthem, fellow students and alumni are rallying to support them," *Inside Higher Ed*, February 25, 2021, https://www.insidehighered.com/news/2021/02/25/debate-about-kneeling-during-anthem-continues-bluefield-college, accessed July 18, 2022.

8

Slave Agency, the Emancipation Monument, and History's Reckoning

Karen Cook Bell

The narrative of President Abraham Lincoln as the "Great Emancipator" has undergone scrutiny in the midst of the Black Lives Matter protests that enveloped the nation after the death of George Floyd, who died after police officer Derek Chauvin placed his knee on Floyd's neck for nearly nine minutes. A national reckoning of slavery has taken place that has led to reassessments of Confederate and other monuments as well as American leaders with ties to slavery. The Lincoln Emancipation Memorial in Washington and the Emancipation Monument in Boston, which portrays a kneeling slave at the feet of Abraham Lincoln, became the target of protesters who viewed the memorials as racist subservience and historically inaccurate in light of recent scholarship on self-emancipation and what many regard as Lincoln's racist views of African Americans. Frederick Douglass, who met with Lincoln several times during the Civil War and who gave the address at the unveiling ceremony of the Emancipation Memorial, underscored Lincoln's ambivalence toward issuing the Emancipation Proclamation and his racial animus toward Black people. Speaking to a crowd of 25,000 mostly African Americans who gathered to commemorate the eleventh anniversary of President Lincoln's assassination on April 14, 1876, Douglass stated of Lincoln, "He was preeminently the white man's president, entirely devoted to the welfare of white men. He was ready and willing at any time during the first years of his administration to deny, postpone, and sacrifice the rights of humanity in the colored people to promote the welfare of the white people of this country." Douglass asserted the immutable fact that President Lincoln was forced by military necessity to establish the groundwork for the destruction of slavery by issuing the Emancipation Proclamation on January 1, 1863. Historians now recognize that enslaved men and women created the impetus for emancipation by running away to the lines of the Union Army and consequently were the "great emancipators."

Throughout much of the twentieth century, historians framed the Civil War as a political- and military-driven historical process that largely involved and affected men. Within the academy, social and cultural historians have now shifted the focus of the Civil War away from military battles to what the war meant for soldiers, white women, and enslaved men and women. The Civil War has constituted an important pillar of dialogue and debate over the meaning of freedom, free labor, and citizenship. In his seminal study *Black Reconstruction in America*, W. E. B. Du Bois argued that "the Civil War meant emancipation and the black worker won the war by a general strike which transferred his labor to the Northern invader in whose army lines workers began to be organized as a new labor force."[1] DuBois's emphasis on the "agency" of slaves set the terms of the debate in modern scholarship, which continues to emphasize the agency of enslaved men and women. Du Bois also ushered in a period of new scholarship by social historians during the 1970s that wrote against the silences and omissions of the US historical profession.

Emphasizing the agency of soldiers and civilians has led to diverse perspectives over the process of wartime emancipation and its impact on the agency of former slaves. Self-emancipation and Black agency are critical to the study of African American and Black diaspora studies. For too long, Black people have been portrayed as passive victims of slavery who lacked any agency of their own and who were thus acted upon by others. Emancipation had been achieved in many parts of the Confederate South prior to the passage (and later ratification) of the Thirteenth Amendment on January 31, 1865, by Congress. Self-emancipation forced the national government to legitimize a reality that already existed in Union-controlled areas, despite the language of the Emancipation Proclamation, which ostensibly excluded those regions under Union control; African Americans were proclaiming themselves free.

Self-emancipation refers to the idea that enslaved people escaped *en masse* and took the lead in forcing the president and Congress to act on emancipation. The esteemed historian John Hope Franklin brought the idea of self-emancipation to the forefront in his scholarship, which critically examined the ways in which enslaved men and women emancipated themselves during the chaos of the Civil War by running away to the lines of the Union Army. Nancy Bercaw's *Gendered Freedoms* and Sharon Ann Holt's *Making Freedom Pay* have complicated the narrative of self-emancipation by demonstrating how the struggles within plantation households among Black and white women defined the dimensions and directions of freedom.[2] Recently, David Williams in *I Freed Myself* has argued that by the late 1850s, there were 50,000 escapes annually, temporary and permanent, and that the resulting freedom was neither an isolated event nor an endpoint in itself.[3] Freedom was not a linear process. Runaway slaves lived a precarious life punctuated by the threat of being brought back to bondage by the enactment of the more stringent Fugitive Slave Act of 1850. Williams demonstrates that Blacks in the South contributed mightily to the war as well. They helped refugees, Black and white, escape to Federal lines. They served as spies, guides, and informants to Union forces.[4] Slave resistance took many forms during the war. Southern Blacks staged work slowdowns, refused instruction, resisted punishment, demanded pay for their work, gathered freely, traveled at will, and took freedom for themselves long before the Union Army arrived.

Emancipation in the United States stretched over a century from the Revolutionary War to the end of the Civil War.[5] This period was punctuated by intermediate struggles for freedom before the Civil War and more struggles to define and claim the freedom promised after the official end of slavery. African Americans used the chaos of the American Revolution, the War of 1812, and the Civil War to forge alternative and expanded paths to self-liberation. Black women figured prominently in this "long emancipation" as they developed resistance strategies to challenge enslavement. Enslaved women malingered, feigned illness, destroyed property, committed infanticide and suicide, and escaped slavery to undermine the system.[6] Given that the woods, swamps, and slave cabins were spaces where the enslaved could exercise more autonomy than the fields and other open spaces on the plantation, bonded men had more autonomy than bonded women because the latter were more confined to the plantation.[7] Although men made up the majority of runaways and truants, women were also truants and truancy facilitators, providing food and information, which served to make these two forms of resistance individual and collective at the same time.[8]

The Civil War disrupted the spatial arrangements of slavery; Blacks and whites, men and women, were all figuratively and literally "out of place," enabling and increasing Black resistance to white domination.[9] Scholars have frequently drawn on Federal documents to show that slaves escaped during the American Civil War. These documents also describe women's and children's orientation toward Federal lines. In late May 1861, Union Major General Benjamin F. Butler, based in Fortress Monroe, southeastern Virginia, informed US General-in-Chief Winfield Scott: "Up to this time I have had come within my lines men and women with their children—entire families—each family belonging to the same owner."[10] Octave Johnson, who freed himself and became a Corporal in Company C, Fifteenth Regiment of Corps d'Afrique, testified that there were thirty runaways in his Louisiana parish encampment in 1861 "of whom ten were women."[11] "Many come in," wrote Brigadier General Thomas W. Sherman from Hilton Head, South Carolina, at the close of 1861, "but where we get one good, able-bodied man, we have five or six women and children."[12] The actions of men, women, and children to achieve freedom through self-emancipation illustrates their agency in the midst of challenging circumstances and environments.

More than 150 years after the end of the Civil War, the controversy surrounding Lincoln's legacy as the "Great Emancipator" and the Emancipation Monument has erupted as protesters demanded the removal of the monument, as an act of restorative justice. Police built barriers around the monument to protect it after some protesters threatened to tear it down. Washington, D.C., Mayor Muriel E. Bowser announced that the city should debate the removal of the statue, and "not have a mob decide they want to pull it down."[13] The kneeling slave, whose visage was based on that of Archer Alexander, a formerly enslaved man, depicted in the Emancipation Monument was most likely inspired by an old abolitionist image used to fight for freedom for enslaved Black people. The white sculptor, Thomas Ball, was likely influenced by the abolitionist poster with the words "Am I Not a Man and Brother," which depicts a kneeling slave. At the time of the monument's commissioning, Harriet Hosmer, who was considered one of the first female professional sculptors, designed an alternative sculpture that would have depicted several figures, including a Black Union soldier. However, her design was too expensive and perhaps too revolutionary.[14]

Douglass used his speech at the April 14, 1876, unveiling of the Emancipation Monument "to clean up and clarify exactly what Lincoln's contributions were with respect to black people."[15] According to Douglass, for Black people, "Lincoln was neither our man nor our model."[16] In his speech, Douglass told the crowd that Lincoln "was important in the struggle and we honor that." But Douglass wanted Lincoln to emerge from the myth. In August 1862, Lincoln told a group of Black leaders during a visit to the White House that they were to blame for the Civil War. He stated, "But for your presence amongst us, there would be no war."[17] Lincoln was not an abolitionist. By stating that Lincoln freed the slaves, we dismiss the agency of slaves and the sacrifices of US Colored Troops and those who served in the Navy and fought and died for freedom.

It was a poor, recently freed enslaved woman, Charlotte Scott, who, distraught over Lincoln's assassination in 1865, declared, "Colored people had lost their best friend on earth. . . . I will give five dollars of my wages towards erecting a monument to his memory."[18]

Scott's request and contribution to the Western Sanitary Society, a charity run by white abolitionists for freedmen and Union veterans, grew as Black Union veterans and freedmen exclusively gave thousands more dollars to the project. Donations poured in with "$4,200 from colored troops at Vicksburg; $3,200 from another colored regiment; $500 from a battery unit; and more, until over $16,000 was amassed." Congress appropriated the remainder of the funds to finish the project.[19]

During the early years of the Civil War, Douglass expressed his exasperation with Lincoln's unwillingness to take decisive action on emancipation. He criticized Lincoln as not moving fast enough to free thousands of enslaved Black people, stating:

> When he tarried long in the mountain; when he strangely told us that we were the cause of the war; when he still more strangely told us that we were to leave the land in which we were born; when he refused to employ our arms in defense of the Union; when, after accepting our services as colored soldiers, he refused to retaliate our murder and torture as colored prisoners; when he told us he would save the Union if he could with slavery; when he revoked the Proclamation of Emancipation of General Fremont; when he refused to remove the popular commander of the Army of the Potomac, in the days of its inaction and defeat, who was more zealous in his efforts to protect slavery than to suppress rebellion; when we saw all this, and more, we were at times grieved, stunned, and greatly bewildered; but our hearts believed while they ached and bled.[20]

Douglass also said that Lincoln's slow pace was frustrating and bewildering. In short, Douglass said, Lincoln tried the patience of abolitionists who wanted a speedy end to slavery. Militant abolitionists, like Douglass, not only demanded an immediate end to slavery but also advocated for racial equality and justice for Black Americans, ideas that Lincoln rejected.

The Emancipation Monument fed a narrative that white men like Lincoln led emancipation, rather than show how the struggle for freedom was driven by the millions of African Americans who fought for their liberation from the institution of slavery. Lincoln was slow to embrace the ideas of emancipation and abolition, and as noted by Douglass in his dedication address that day, "the Union was more to him than our freedom or our future." It was African Americans who fought for their abolition, with the often-reluctant support of the Federal government.[21]

Today, we are having a national reckoning with slavery and our nation's history. As Confederate monuments are removed throughout the South, as statues of Christopher Columbus are taken down by activists who rightly point out the problem of commemorating a man who began the colonization of the Americas, we also need to look at other memorials and monuments that dot the commemorative landscape across the United States, including those that were placed with the best of intentions. Newly freed slaves funded the Emancipation Monument, but they had no voice in the process of creating it, and their voices and work are lost in the story the memorial now conveys.[22] The deaths of George Floyd, Rayshard Brooks, Breonna Taylor, and Ahmaud Arbery have removed the veil over self-congratulatory Civil War–era myths in America. Floyd, Brooks, and Taylor were unarmed and killed by negligent police action. Ahmaud Arbery was pursued by three white residents and shot to death by one of them, Travis McMichael, as he jogged in his community. Each of these deaths speaks to the absence of racial equality in the United States and the continuing legacy of slavery.

Because monuments embody what we deem important enough to place in public spaces, they must change as society changes. In the past, changing monuments led to the tearing down of a King George III statue in New York City in 1776. More recently, the debate over changing monuments has been focused on the long-awaited removal of former US Vice President John C. Calhoun's statue in Charleston, South Carolina, and the news that the American Museum of Natural History in New York City is getting rid of the often-denounced statue of former US President Theodore Roosevelt outside its entrance.[23] In his address at the dedication of the Emancipation Monument, Frederick Douglass said that in commemorating Lincoln, African Americans were "doing highest honor to ourselves and those who come after us."[24] To fulfill this effort, we should create something that commemorates not just Lincoln but also those who funded the memorial in the first place and whose efforts were at the heart of emancipation.

Notes

1. W. E. B. Du Bois, *Black Reconstruction in America, 1860–1880* (New York: Harcourt Brace, 1935), 55.

2. Nancy Bercaw, *Gendered Freedoms: Race, Rights, and the Politics of Household in the Delta, 1861–1875* (Gainesville: University Press of Florida, 2003); Sharon Ann Holt, *Making Freedom Pay: North Carolina Freedpeople Working for Themselves, 1865–1900* (Athens: University of Georgia Press, 2001).

3. David Williams, *I Freed Myself: African American Self-Emancipation in the Civil War Era* (New York: Cambridge University Press, 2014), 17; see also the recent work of Ann Murrell Taylor, *Embattled Freedom: Journeys through the Civil War's Slave Refugee Camps* (Chapel Hill: University of North Carolina Press, 2018); Thavolia Glymph, *The Women's Fight: The Civil War Battles for Home, Freedom, and Nation* (Chapel Hill: University of North Carolina Press, 2019); and Joseph P. Reidy, *Illusions of Emancipation: The Pursuit of Freedom and Equality in the Twilight of Slavery* (Chapel Hill: University of North Carolina Press, 2019).

4. Williams, *I Freed Myself*, 17.

5. Ira Berlin, *The Long Emancipation: The Demise of Slavery in the United States* (Cambridge: Harvard University Press, 2015).

6. Gerald Horne, *The Counter-Revolution of 1776: Slave Resistance and the Origins of the United States of America* (New York: New York University Press, 2014), 234–49; Cheryl Janifer LaRoche, "Coerced but Not Subdued: The Gendered Resistance of Women Escaping," in Mary E. Frederickson and Delores M. Walters, eds., *Gendered Resistance: Women, Slavery, and the Legacy of Margaret Garner* (Urbana: University of Illinois Press, 2013), 49–70; Richard Bell, "Slave Suicide, Abolition, and the Problem of Resistance," *Slavery and Abolition* 34, no. 4 (2012): 1–25.

7. Stephanie M. H. Camp, *Closer to Freedom: Enslaved Women and Everyday Resistance in the Plantation South* (Chapel Hill: University of North Carolina Press, 2004), 59.

8. Ibid., 35–59.

9. Ibid., 12–33.

10. Benj. F. Butler to Lt. Gen. Scott, May 27, 1861, in Ira Berlin, Barbara Fields, Steven F. Miller, Joseph P. Reidy, and Leslie S. Rowland, eds., *Free at Last: A Documentary History of Slavery, Freedom, and the Civil War* (New York: The New Press, 1992), 9; Robert Engs, *Freedom's First Generation: Black Hampton, Virginia, 1861–1890* (Philadelphia; University of Pennsylvania Press, 1979), 14–15.

11. Deposition of Octave Johnson, Feb. ?, 1864, in Berlin, *Free at Last*, 51–52.

12. William A. Dobak, *Freedom by the Sword: The U.S. Colored Troops 1862–1867* (Washington: Center of Military History, 2011), 29.

13. DeNeen L. Brown, "Frederick Douglass delivered a Lincoln reality check at Emancipation Memorial Unveiling," *The Washington Post*, June 27, 2020, https://wapo.st/3vJcHYr.

14. Ibid.

15. Ibid.

16. "An 1876 speech given by Frederick Douglass at the unveiling of the Freedmen's Monument in Lincoln Park, Washington, D.C.," https://dp.la/primary-source-sets/frederick-douglass-and-abraham-lincoln/sources/104.

17. Ibid.

18. Sean Kennedy, "Lincoln Park's memorial to the Great Emancipator should stand," *The Washington Post*, June 25, 2020, https://wapo.st/3RQG6aI.

19. Ibid.

20. "An 1876 speech given by Frederick Douglass at the unveiling of the Freedmen's Monument in Lincoln Park, Washington, D.C.," https://dp.la/primary-source-sets/frederick-douglass-and-abraham-lincoln/sources/104.

21. Ibid.; Rebekah Bryer, "Yes, D.C.'s Emancipation Memorial advances white supremacy," *The Washington Post*, June 25, 2020, https://wapo.st/48BibTY.

22. Rebekah Bryer, "Yes, D.C.'s Emancipation Memorial advances white supremacy," *The Washington Post*, June 25, 2020.

23. Ibid.

24. "An 1876 speech given by Frederick Douglass at the unveiling of the Freedmen's Monument in Lincoln Park, Washington, D.C.," https://dp.la/primary-source-sets/frederick-douglass-and-abraham-lincoln/sources/104.

9

Fighting for Black Humanity

Political Action of Post-Emancipation Black Christians

Nicole Myers Turner

The murder of George Floyd under the knee of a Minneapolis police officer on Memorial Day weekend 2020 touched off a summer of global protests that centered on issues of police brutality and amplified calls for police reform. These protests took off in the midst of a global pandemic that disproportionately affected and killed Black and Brown people and that had heightened awareness about the ills of the moment, and also the unresolved legacies of the Reconstruction era. The inequitable treatment and outcomes, the depraved indifference to Black life instantiated in laws and practices, hearkens back to the limitations of Reconstruction's early policies and practices in contraband camps and points toward the strategies that free and freedpeople deployed to challenge the underlying anti-Black logic that supported slavery and needed to be undone in order to make meaningful freedom. They also deployed political strategies of participation to achieve their goals. The work of post-emancipation Black Christian associations suggests that we need the marriage of policy change and reform of ideas about the recognition and acknowledgment of Black humanity in order to finally realize the promises of Reconstruction.

Disparate Outcomes and COVID-19

Like much of the country, I was transfixed by the coverage of COVID-19 cases in New York City from March through the climax in April and on to the subsiding reports in May of 2020. I paid keen attention to New York Governor Andrew Cuomo's daily briefings, in which he reported the exponentially increasing number of people infected, the rapidly declining capacity of the city to care for the sick, the struggle to supply the city's first responders with personal protective equipment (PPE), and the state's initiatives to educate the public about how to fight the spread of the virus. As a native New Yorker with family and friends still living there, I felt particularly connected to the unfolding public health emergency. What started as an epic public health crisis already hitting close to home in a matter of weeks became dramatically more personal.

When it became clear that COVID-19 was not only easily spread and very deadly but also that it was killing Black and Brown people at a much higher rate than others because in part of the prevalence of comorbidities like diabetes, high blood pressure, and heart disease in these populations, my anxiety ratcheted up several notches. The escalating demands on the medical system and the rationing of scarce medical resources suddenly made it difficult to focus on much else. I quickly found myself researching triage procedures, realizing that if doctors considered comorbidities in determining whom to ventilate, or to whom to administer different treatments, then by default Black folks would be shunted to the bottom of the treatment list. I learned that triage guidelines were rooted in battlefield scenarios. Their evaluation criteria prioritized those who were most likely to recover to be returned to the battlefield and neglected those who were most underserved or who had children and other dependents, or any number of other criteria that might have been more apt for this particular public health crisis.[1] If the triage guidelines with underlying military rationales continued to be applied, then having a comorbidity linked to poor outcomes might affect negatively the tough decisions medical providers were having to make moment by moment. The situation called for new criteria that would remove the bias from the system and give Black and Brown people a better chance at fighting the disease. But I was struck by the way one description of triage guidelines made no explicit mention of race, but by allocating provider resources to patients likely to have good outcomes, almost assured negative outcomes for patients with comorbidities—disproportionately Black and Brown persons. The high death rates during those early days of the pandemic because of the overwhelmed system and the decision-making practices that our first responders had to engage still haunt me today.

Disparate Outcomes and Police Violence

As Memorial Day 2020 approached and the numbers of cases began to wane, we looked forward to the relief of summer sun and more time outdoors after several months cooped up inside sheltering in place. But that exhalation of tension—in the Northeast at least—caught abruptly in our collective throats as reports of the death of George Floyd under the knee of a police officer in Minneapolis flooded the news. Those reports precipitated a summer of protests in streets across the nation, calling attention to the structures of racial inequality that link the twin global medical and social pandemics of COVID-19 and police violence.

Though Black Studies scholars put out the call to collect data about COVID-19 that included race, even now, months later, that information is still unevenly reported. Similarly, statistical data about the prevalence of police violence is incomplete because police departments are not required to report these cases publicly or to any centralized body where the true scale and scope of the issue could be ascertained.[2]

But perhaps it is just as well that we do not have complete numbers: The qualitative distinctions between the treatment of Black and Brown people accused of crimes compared with that of white people are stark and telling. Take, for instance, the treatment of Dylann Roof, who, in Charleston, South Carolina, in 2015, massacred nine Black people in a church Bible study and fled. When he was arrested on suspicion of mass murder, police took him to Burger King to get something to eat before he was taken to the police station because he said he was hungry. Compare that with the treatment of George Floyd, who died while in police custody, arrested on suspicion of using a counterfeit $20 bill. A police officer knelt on his neck, suffocating him, for eight minutes and forty-six seconds despite his repeatedly crying out, "I can't breathe."

Two people, each alleged to have committed crimes, each declaring a fundamental human need (sustenance and oxygen, respectively), met two very different fates. One was white, the other Black; one accused of multiple murders, the other accused of a minor theft of property. In these cases, we can see how race mitigates punishment and the very disparate outcomes for these two individuals' lives and their communities.

The crushing weight of these twindemics of COVID-19 and police violence against Black persons, along with the lack of legal or procedural protections to address the inequalities and the maturing Black Lives Matter and Prison Abolition movements, prompted thousands to rush out into the streets in a physical vote of solidarity and resistance to draw attention to these blatant inequities. Declaring that Black Lives Matter, activists called for the redistribution of public fund budgeting priorities and the abolition of prisons.

Though the current moment can easily be compared to the civil rights movement for political rights because of the mass-protest strategies being deployed, today's protests differ significantly in terms of the geographic scope, duration, and racial composition of the protesters. Perhaps a more apt comparison or at least a more informative comparison might be to the era of Reconstruction and the immediate post-emancipation period. The health disparities and police violence may be understood as the lingering effects of the incomplete overhaul of the United States' national policies and procedures and the underlying ideologies of white supremacy and anti-Blackness. The lack of a clear plan to aid the freedpeople demonstrates the problem, while the responses of freed Black church people to the circumstances illuminates a part of the solution—political solutions—and how those political solutions can address ideologies.

What can we learn from the historic moment of emancipation, a period of political and social tumult and upheaval? What did free and freed Black people do back then in their religious and political activism to confront and overcome the racial disparities of the time?

Emancipation as the Moment of Disproportionate Impact

By turning to that moment of upheaval, we see that the shared context of the post-emancipation period and the current pandemic of racial inequality becomes clear. In looking back at the moment of emancipation today, we might focus more on the hope and gloss over the uncertainties that abounded on April 9, 1865, when Confederate General Robert E. Lee surrendered to Union General Ulysses S. Grant at Appomattox Court House in Virginia. There was not yet a plan as to what do with these freed people, and as the plans unfolded, the priorities focused more on capital—the needs of the government, of planters—than on the needs of the formerly enslaved people. This was a moment of upheaval because relations and structures of the slave society and of the nation had been ruptured and now needed to be restored, repaired, or re-organized. The designation of self-emancipated people as *contraband of war* was a far cry from *citizen*, and the 1863 Emancipation Proclamation freed enslaved people only in places in rebellion against the Union, leaving people enslaved in Maryland, Delaware, and Kentucky. The Union had to be rebuilt and slavery destroyed, but there was not a clear vision of what new labor and social relations would be put in place for the 4 million newly emancipated people.

The lack of a national plan led to false starts, like General William T. Sherman's Preserve and Field Order No. 15, which provided forty acres and a mule to freedpeople to live and work so that they would have a place to go instead of following Sherman's army through the South. It was a military necessity to figure out what to do with the self-emancipating folks that prompted Sherman to develop this land-based solution. But this speedy decision, marred by limited vision, allowed that policy to be replaced, snatching away land and with it the fruits of the labor of these freedpeople when it became clear that redistributing property was not part of the national plan for Reconstruction. The retraction of this policy threw freedpeople into a state of upheaval, setting the stage for them to be disproportionately poor and landless.

The lack of a clear national plan is what created the upheaval. Given the absence of an assertive plan to end slavery and address the needs of emancipated people, the Federal government's lack of vision caused disorder. Enslaved people saw in the war the opportunity to strike for freedom. They ran to Federal camps, establishing what came to be called contraband camps and forced the dissolution of slavery where Lincoln's Emancipation Proclamation went only part of the way. Once they had fled, the dissolution of the system could not be stopped. As an enslaved woman said, upon establishing her intent to leave and follow her freedom, "answering bells is played out."[3] But without a national/Federal plan, adequate protections and resources could not be marshaled for the care and protection of these refugees. The lack of a national plan meant that these marginalized people with freedom in their grasp lacked the fundamental needs of human life. As a result, they suffered death and disease in these contraband camps. The historian Jim Downs wrote that they became "sick from freedom."

No, enslaved people's lives were not better under slavery. These freedpeople were the ancestors of civil rights activists like the late John Lewis, who marched for freedom, voting rights, and justice in the 1960s—a century later—*while being waterhosed and beat over the head*. These freedpeople of the post-emancipation era were the comrades and descendants of those self-emancipating people who, preferring isolation, distance, lack of food and employment in Canada, in swamps, and in other distant locations, risked life, limb, and even the most basic comforts to be free. No, slavery was not better than freedom. Nevertheless, freedom was incomplete.

Certainly, we can applaud Black resilience and creativity in this context. But not without first marking the roots of systemic racism that persisted in the government's failure to think about the humanity of the enslaved. A nation not ready to live out the full meaning of its creed had to be goaded along in this process by Black people and their allies who shaped the Reconstruction of the government at the Federal and state levels. Black people engaged in the political system as a means of declaring their humanity and to make the system and its instruments honor their humanity.

Filling in the Breach: Process, Intention, and Content

It was the US Constitution that needed to be revised in order to make a more complete freedom. The national plan and compact needed to be revised, and freedpeople knew that. So, if they had any hope, it was in the foundational principles and practices of the democratic republic created in the Constitution. Before they could participate in state constitutional conventions, they demonstrated this hope through their church conventions and political participation practices.

In these conventions, freed Black Christians created their own constitutions—foundational governing documents—that reflected their covenants and their beliefs. These constitutions outlined who the leaders were, what the mission and vision of the organizations were, and how they would be organized. In the Baptist Church, the associations were established by Black people who separated from white Baptist associations with similar constitutions, so the constitutions these Black Baptists created were not completely original documents.

These freed and free Black people were able to produce and reproduce these documents of social and political cohesion. They demonstrated this by their capacity for political participation, which also underscores how already at emancipation there were Black religious people ready and able to participate in the body politic. Surely, many more people fostered their skills of organizing and public speaking and leadership as independent Black churches proliferated on the post-emancipation landscape, but those skills had been established in the context of an already extant political skill and engagement that pre-dated emancipation. It was the scope and operation of that political skill which changed after emancipation with the changed status from freedpeople to citizens. Eventually, these churches and associations influenced the politics of the time by shaping political claims-making. These early constitutions and the organizational practices themselves were all evidence of Black political capacity. Organizers of the associations understood the need for this when they explained in their convention minutes that they were in còmpetition with other organizations but were the ones most capable of aiding the freedpeople.

These freed Black Christians envisioned the Constitution and their practices of governance as the tools of participation in the body politic. Their mastery of the forms and procedures were their badges of inclusion. They demonstrated this by their democratic fitness, their readiness to participate in the body politic. Through their actions they claimed their humanity, dignity, and capacity.

These skills and practices were on display in the realm of state politics, too. Freedmen played an important role in transforming the government documents. This was most evident at the state level, where hundreds of Black men served as delegates to the state constitutional conventions in 1868 and 1869, where they worked on amending the constitutions to end slavery and secure education and other rights for Black people. More than 25 percent of the delegates to the state conventions were Black, and in Virginia an extraordinary 90 percent of Black people who registered also voted in the constitutional convention elections.[4]

At the state and local levels of government, Black men seized the opportunities to vote. When the Federal government required that elections be held for delegates to the state constitutional convention to revise the Constitution to abolish slavery and allow Black men the franchise, Black men debated the issues of the day, addressing issues like integrated public schools, interracial marriage, and even the language of race itself. By their participation they showed their commitment to removing slavery and caste from the formal structure of government.[5] At the 1867 Virginia Constitutional Convention, one Black delegate, Thomas Bayne, argued that it was his obligation to ensure that race not be used in the document at all as a way to preserve rights for all human beings.[6] Bayne was hopeful that this would be for the greater good, even though the evidence of how politicians read the absence of the words *slaves* and *slavery* proved otherwise.

It was in such instances of constitutional politics at the state level that freedpeople had the most influence. The results of the lack of plans in the post-emancipation period stemmed from a failure to view Black humanity and persisted in the upheavals in the contraband camps. But Black people tried to set that right through their participation in the process and through upholding the principles and values of America's founding documents.

Conclusion

What lessons, principles, or insights might we derive from the Black political struggle in which religious folks engaged during the post-emancipation era? To create a livable world out of the ashes of slavery, free and freedpeople recognized the inequities and sought to address them, especially by engaging in political processes. They determined that the United States had failed to live up to the true meaning of its creed, and yet they nonetheless tried to redeem the nation's founding texts, using them to deconstruct and counter the denials of Black humanity and human dignity, actions reflected in the documentary record of their associations, conventions, and writings.

The conditions under which freedpeople labored to make freedom more complete were inflected by slavery's dehumanizing force and the racism that supports the continuing inequality. Still, free and freed Black people found in the process of writing and revising constitutions and democratic practices possibilities for living into the creed that all persons are created equal with inalienable rights to life, liberty, and the pursuit of happiness. Though they labored to make the process more comprehensive and the language in the founding documents more inclusive—accomplishments, no doubt—the work was incomplete. We know now from the Jim Crow era that even founding documents that did not explicitly call for racial inequality produced that outcome. In the new nation, slavery persisted through counting enslaved people for representation purposes but not allowing them to vote. In the Jim Crow era, voting rights were limited on the basis of lineage, literacy, and legacy.

This political reality has contemporary analogs. The triage guidelines for COVID-19 patients do not have to be explicit about placing Black people at the bottom of the list of priorities for that to occur. Police departments do not have to mandate different procedures for Black and white people for that to happen. The persistence of these differential outcomes suggests that it is not just political participation or political instruments that affect the outcomes—though they are surely important. It is the underlying denial of and equivocation about Black humanity that allows the ideology of slavery to persist without the words being uttered.

It is, therefore, the fundamental principles, founding assumptions, worldview, and ideology that must be excavated. We cannot end our analysis with the words on the page but instead must dig into our cultural milieu and the meanings we convey by the collections of words and practices we enact, and we must call out where the processes discriminate against Black people. We are at a moment in which we can see even more clearly the need to protect and follow the procedures, and, if we are to have wholly different outcomes—not disparate outcomes but different outcomes—then we must confront and declare definitively and more decisively the inherent value of all humanity. We must declare that Black Lives Matter.

Notes

1. Ken Kipnis, "Triage and Ethics," *AMA Journal of Ethics* 4, no. 1 (January 1, 2002), https://doi.org/10.1001/virtualmentor.2002.4.1.puhl1-0201.

2. Mapping Police Violence, "2015 Police Violence Report," accessed September 24, 2020, https://mappingpoliceviolence.org/2015; College of Liberal Arts. "Projects // Purdue College of Liberal Arts." https://cla.purdue.edu/academic/sis/p/african-american/covid-black/projects.html.

3. Tera W. Hunter, *To 'joy My Freedom: Southern Black Women's Lives and Labors After the Civil War* (Cambridge and London: Harvard University Press, 1997).

4. Steven Hahn, *A Nation Under Our Feet: Black Political Struggles in the Rural South from Slavery to the Great Migration* (Cambridge and London: The Belknap Press of Harvard University Press, 2003), 205.

5. Hahn, *A Nation Under Our Feet*, 205.

6. W. E. B. Du Bois, *Black Reconstruction in America, 1860–1880* (New York: The Free Press, 1935, 1962), 541–42; W. H. Samuel, "The debates and proceedings of the Constitutional Convention of the State of Virginia, Assembled at the city of Richmond, Tuesday, December 3, 1867; being a full and complete report of the debates and proceedings of the convention, together with the Reconstruction Acts of Congress and those supplementary thereto, the order of the Commander of the First Military District assembling the convention, and the new constitution" (Richmond, Virginia, 1868).

10

Jim Crow Then, Jim Crow Now

Police Violence, Tort Law, and Black Resistance in the Twentieth and Twenty-First Centuries

Myisha S. Eatmon

On March 10, 1912, Lawson Burford Jr. made his way home to a basement apartment that he rented from his employer, W. R. Cole, in Nashville, Tennessee. Burford was likely tired after a long day of chauffeuring Cole around Nashville. Relaxing in the safety of his home, where he could escape the dangers of Jim Crow and white prejudice, was a reasonable desire after an honest day's work. But the advent of Jim Crow in the aftermath of the Civil War and white prejudice—then and now—did not always afford Black people such luxuries.

Cole, Burford's employer and landlord, and the other property owners in the neighborhood had recently hired Captain Z. T. Terry, a white police officer, to patrol their property at night after a series of break-ins. "Private policemen, like Terry, were employed and paid by the citizens whose property they were detailed to protect and were subject to the orders of those employing them." White property owners hired Terry to protect white property, but from whom: criminals, Black people, tenants?

The night before the fatal shooting, Terry saw Burford on the property and allegedly suspected him of trespassing. On March 10, Terry approached Burford. Likely uneasy about the situation, as a Black man living under Jim Crow, Burford told Terry that he lived there and that he was the property owner's tenant and driver. Terry, unwilling to accept that Burford lived on the property and likely assuming Black criminality, ordered Burford to prove his residency by opening the door to his apartment. According to witness testimony, he also told Burford that he would shoot Burford if he did not open his apartment. When Burford refused to open his home to the officer—because why should he have to open his home to a police officer without a warrant?—Terry fired two or three shots, leaving Burford to die on the steps outside his apartment.

Lawson Burford Jr.'s bereaved father sued Officer Terry and the property owners who hired him in civil court for wrongful death. Terry had taken Burford Jr.'s life for no reason. He had not committed a crime, and he was trying to enter his own home. At the trial, an all-white jury awarded Lawson Burford Sr. $3,500 (about $107,000 in 2023 USD) in damages, despite the off-duty policeman's claims "that he had exercised his right to self-defense" in the killing.[1] Though it may seem commonsensical to sue for wrongful death, Burford Sr.'s challenge to his son's murder was revolutionary and a form of resistance. The move to use litigation to counter police violence and killings by police was a part of Black legal culture during Jim Crow.[2] Black Americans used and have continued to use private law, not criminal law, to challenge and seek recourse for police violence, including murders by police, for more than a century. This chapter covers cases from 1912 into the twenty-first century, though Black Americans' use of civil courts—specifically of tort law—to combat police violence extends back even further.

More than one hundred years after Lawson Burford Jr.'s murder, images of similar murders flash across our screens almost daily. Police officers continue to arbitrarily murder Black American citizens, those they swore to serve and protect. Black citizens are not safe even in their homes, as Burford Jr. and Breonna Taylor's cases show us. Like Burford Jr., Breonna Taylor was murdered in her home by police in 2020. Like Burford Jr., Taylor had not committed a crime, but officers barged into her home in the middle of the night and executed her as she slept. The prosecutor did not charge the officers for her murder.[3] Like those of us who are still fighting for justice for Black Americans executed by police officers in the twenty-first century, Black Americans living under Jim Crow used tort law to gain recourse for white-on-Black and police violence.

Tort doctrine is an area of miscellaneous private wrongs that matured during the late nineteenth century.[4] Remedies for such wrongs are sought in civil courts, rather than criminal courts, though some torts could be classified as criminal and civil wrongs. As is the case with many instances of physical violence, prosecutors could have easily charged violent white vigilantes and police officers for the assaults, batteries, murders, and property destruction that Black people suffered at whites' hands. Prosecutors refused to challenge white supremacy, and they likely did not see white vigilante and police violence as violating public peace.

Police officers swear an oath to the Constitution, to protect American citizens, and to protect public peace. Despite their duty to protect citizens and public order, individual police officers have violated individuals' rights to their persons. When white police officers abused Black people, even in the Jim Crow South, Black victims had the option to sue. To counter the threat of lawsuits, "some

States . . . enact[ed] laws and [included] provisions in municipal charters exempting either the municipality or the officer, or both, from liability."[5] Despite qualified immunity, Black plaintiffs still named municipalities in their claims and brought damage suits against officers as private citizens.

In the face of an ambivalent criminal justice system and qualified immunity, many Black Americans filed civil lawsuits for civil assault, battery, wrongful death, and negligence for the violence they suffered at the hands of white police and sheriffs during Jim Crow. Some, like Lawson Burford Sr., even won damages. By using race-neutral tort law principles, Black victims were able to convince white jurors to side with Black people who had experienced violence at white people's hands.[6] Though it may not seem revolutionary, it was. For Black Americans confronting Jim Crow, such suits were one of the few remedies available.

When Black plaintiffs sued police officers and their employers for situations involving individual white people's violent attacks and state violence, they asserted their "fundamental rights of personhood" in civil courts.[7] According to the historian Barbara Welke, "personhood . . . rests most fundamentally on legal recognition and protection of *self*-ownership, that is, of a right to one's person, one's body."[8] Black Americans used the principle of self-ownership, a "right to be free from physical abuse or coercion without due process of law," to make claims in a judicial system that white people never meant to protect Black people. White people have always used the US judicial system to uphold white supremacy, but Black plaintiffs found a way to make the system work for them: torts. When Black plaintiffs sued municipalities, surety companies, and individual whites for incidents that involved white violence, they asserted their legal personhood and their right to be free from physical abuse without due process of the law. Though they did not frame their arguments in terms of legal personhood, their suits demonstrated an understanding of self-ownership and a right to live free of extrajudicial violence from the state and individual whites.

Policing—formal and informal—was a tool of white supremacy. Jim Crow was about social control over Black life, and its purpose was to "reaffirm and remind the Black population of their lesser status or 'place' in larger society."[9] If Jim Crow was about social control, then state violence and social control would play a central part in reinforcing the racial caste system. C. Vann Woodward famously wrote that "the Jim Crow laws put the authority of the state or city in the voice of the street car conductor, the railway brakeman, the bus driver," and "the hoodlum of the public parks and playgrounds."[10] Jim Crow endowed ordinary whites with the power to police Black life within local communities. Formal police officers, on the other hand, "represented the South's repressive civil order and the ideology of white supremacy overall."[11] White supremacy permeated a system that was said to protect the public peace but did not protect Black Americans' most basic rights or afford Black people human decency or the rights of personhood. Despite the authority vested in police officers and their profession's legal immunity as arms of the state, not all Black Americans submitted to white police officers' abuse without protest. In the case of the plaintiffs mentioned here, that challenge arose through tort lawsuits.

Black people, like Burford Jr., who were attacked by police officers, had to argue that they were not a threat and that they had not committed a crime merely by going home. Since police officers were arms of state, county, and municipal governments, they were able to invoke their legal authority to cloak, explain, or excuse their targeting and mistreatment of Black people. For this reason, Black people argued or attempted to prove that they were not a threat to public peace when they were stopped, arrested, harassed, or assaulted by police officers. When up against white police officers, Black Americans were guilty until proven innocent.[12] Despite a long history of more stringent policing of Black people that extended back to the antebellum period with slave patrols and Black codes, Black Americans living under Jim Crow could and did argue that the Founders included the police powers in the Constitution to protect citizens, including Black Americans. That duty was supposed to supersede white people's prejudices.[13] Like abolitionists during the antebellum period, Black Americans living under Jim Crow had to invoke not only citizenship rights but also their rights of personhood—specifically the "right to live free from physical abuse or coercion without due process of the law"—to challenge police officers' mistreatment.[14]

Four hundred years after the first people of African descent arrived in North America, Black Americans still must prove their humanity, worth, and value as people and members of the United States' body politic. The Black Lives Matter movement and Black Twitter organizing hold new meaning when considered within a longer historical context of violations of Black Americans' rights of personhood, Black civil litigation, policing, and Black legal culture. Twenty-first-century Black activists' use of civil litigation as a weapon against a racist criminal justice system has its roots in the nineteenth century. Even with its limitations, this form of resistance was revolutionary. Black Americans worked around criminal courts and convinced the same white juries that would have sentenced a Black man to hang for a crime he did not commit to award them thousands of dollars in monetary damages. This tactic continues to represent Black Americans' faith in the promise of systems that have historically oppressed them (us).

The families of Black Americans killed by police officers in the twenty-first century have often filed wrongful death or civil rights suits in response to their loved ones' murders. Bereaved families and friends have sued local municipalities like New York; the city of Ferguson, Missouri; North Charleston, South Carolina; Waller County, Texas; and countless others. They have also sued white police officers and city council members after officers have literally gotten away with murder.[15] For those left to mourn Black men and women murdered by police, civil lawsuits seem to offer promise for a semblance of justice. Black Americans continue to challenge white vigilante and state-sanctioned police violence, working around an anti-Black criminal justice system and relying instead on civil law. Black Americans and activists continue to push America to live up to its promise and the ideals enshrined in its founding documents.

Jim Crow left yet another stain on American history. Despite how white Americans have tried to oppress their Black neighbors, Black Americans continue to find ways to resist. In the same way that white supremacy and racism manifest themselves differently in different historical periods, so too do our methods of resistance. Before Oscar Grant, Eric Garner, Michael Brown, Walter Scott, Freddie Gray, Laquan McDonald, Tamir Rice, Philando Castile, Terence Crutcher, Antwon Rose II, O'Shae Terry, John Crawford, Sandra Bland, Breonna Taylor, George Floyd, Jacob Blake, and the countless other unarmed Black people who were killed by twenty-first-century police officers, there was Lawson Burford Jr. and others like him. Since our arrival, Black Americans have suffered physical violence and death at the hands of white supremacists. Still, for more than a hundred years, Black Americans have used civil law to resist. As we, Black Americans, continue to fight our oppression, it is essential to remember that our methods and our legal culture were born in slavery and matured under Jim Crow. And like a phoenix, our methods and our resistance have been reborn in the twenty-first century.

Notes

1. *Terry et al. v. Burford*, 131 Tenn. 451 (1914).
2. Myisha S. Eatmon, "Public Wrongs, Private Rights: African Americans, Private Law, and White Violence during Jim Crow," Ph.D. diss., Northwestern University, 2020. ProQuest Dissertation and Theses Global.
3. The Kentucky attorney general did not give grand jurors the option of bringing murder charges against the police involved, though the jurors were given the option to charge officers for property damage. Taylor's life was less important than someone's material possessions.

4. Hilliard Francis, *Law of Torts or Private Wrongs* (Boston: Little, Brown, 1859), 49 (Chapter 1, Section 1), https://heinonline.org/HOL/P?h=hein.beal/tortpw0001&i=49.

5. Henry S. Fraser, *Civilian Defense Manual on Legal Aspects of Civilian Protection* (Washington: US Government Printing Office, 1943), 66.

6. Historians have given little attention to Black people's use of tort law to gain recourse for violence and insults under Jim Crow. Barbara Welke and Kate Masur have investigated Black Americans' use of tort law to combat discrimination during Reconstruction and the post-Reconstruction period. Masur, *An Example for All the Land: Emancipation and the Struggle Over Equality in Washington, D.C.* (Chapel Hill: University of North Carolina Press, 2010), 111; Masur, "Patronage and Protest in Kate Brown's Washington," *Journal of American History* 99, no. 4 (2013): 1047–71; Barbara Young Welke, *Recasting American Liberty: Gender, Race, Law, and the Railroad Revolution, 1865–1920* (New York: Cambridge University Press, 2001), 359.

7. Barbara Young Welke, *Law and the Borders of Belonging in the Long Nineteenth Century United States* (New York: Cambridge University Press, 2010), 7.

8. Welke, *Law and the Borders of Belonging*, 3. Original emphasis.

9. Sandra Bass, "Policing Space, Policing Race: Social Control Imperatives and Police Discretionary Decision," *Social Justice* 28, no. 1 (Spring 2001): 161.

10. C. Vann Woodward, *The Strange Career of Jim Crow* (New York: Oxford University Press, 1994), 107–8.

11. Bass, "Policing Space, Policing Race," 161.

12. Laura F. Edwards was the first historian to make this point. Here, I am extending it to the Jim Crow period. Laura F. Edwards, *The People and Their Peace: Legal Culture and the Transformation of Inequality in the Post-Revolutionary South* (Chapel Hill: University of North Carolina Press, 2009). And see Kate Masur, "The People's Welfare, Police Powers, and the Rights of Free People of African Descent," *American Journal of Legal History* 57, no. 2 (June 2017): 242.

13. Edwards, *The People and Their Peace*; Masur, "The People's Welfare, Police Powers, and the Rights of Free People of African Descent," 240; Bass, "Policing Space, Policing Race," 156.

14. Welke, *Law and the Borders of Belonging*, 3.

15. J. David Goodman, "Eric Garner Case Is Settled by New York City for $5.9 Million," *The New York Times*, July 13, 2015; "Michael Brown's Family Received $1.5 Million Settlement with Ferguson," NBC News, June 23, 2017, https://www.nbcnews.com/storyline/michael-brown-shooting/michael-brown-s-family-received-1-5-million-settlement-ferguson-n775936 (accessed June 8, 2020); Greg Botelho and Sonia Moghe, "North Charleston reaches $6.5 million settlement with family of Walter Scott," CNN, October 9, 2015, https://www.cnn.com/2015/10/08/us/walter-scott-north-charleston-settlement/index.html (accessed June 8, 2020); Monica Davey, "Chicago Pays $5 Million Over Killing of Teenager," *The New York Times*, April 16, 2015; Lauren Hodges, "Cleveland to Pay $6 Million to Settle Tamir Rice Lawsuit," NPR, April 25, 2016, https://www.npr.org/sections/thetwo-way/2016/04/25/475583746/cleveland-to-pay-6-million-to-settle-tamir-rice-lawsuit (accessed June 8, 2020); Alanne Orjoux, "Philando Castile's family reaches $3 million settlement with city of St. Anthony," CNN, June 26, 2017,

https://www.cnn.com/2017/06/26/us/philando-castile-family-settlement/index.html (accessed June 8, 2020); Joshua Barajas, "Family of Terence Crutcher files civil lawsuit, seeking Tulsa police reform," PBS, June 16, 2017; https://www.pbs.org/newshour/nation/family-terence-crutcher-files-civil-lawsuit-seeking-tulsa-police-reform (accessed June 8, 2020); "Family of O'Shae Terry files $1M lawsuit against Arlington, fired officer for his death," Fox 4 News (Arlington, Texas), September 4, 2019, https://www.fox4news.com/news/family-of-oshae-terry-files-1m-lawsuit-against-arlington-fired-officer-for-his-death (accessed June 8, 2020); Ismail Turay Jr., "Beavercreek, Crawford family settle lawsuit for Walmart shooting death," *Dayton Daily News* (Dayton, Ohio), May 13, 2020; Carma Hassan, Holly Yan, and Max Blau, "Sandra Bland's family settles for $1.9M in wrongful death suit," CNN, September 15, 2016; https://www.cnn.com/2016/09/15/us/sandra-bland-wrongful-death-settlement/index.html (accessed June 8, 2020).

11

"How wonderful a country"

Black Lives Matter and the Long History of Aboriginal Resistance

Samuel Watts

As upsetting and terrible that the murder that took place—and it is shocking, that also just made me cringe—I just think to myself how wonderful a country is Australia.... [T]here's no need to import things happening in other countries here to Australia.... Australia is not the United States.

—Prime Minister SCOTT MORRISON on the death of George Floyd[1]

David Dungay Jr., a Dunghutti Aboriginal man, died with a knee in his back, screaming for help, in Sydney's Long Bay Prison hospital on December 29, 2015. Dungay repeatedly yelled, "I can't breathe" as he lay flat, forcibly restrained and sedated, before going into cardiac arrest.[2] Like Eric Garner, Javier Ambler, Derrick Scott, George Floyd, and so many others, Dungay uttered the same harrowing cry for help, "I can't breathe." "If you're talking, you're breathing," the guards told him, just as guards and police had told Robert Richardson in Ohio and Willie Ray Banks in Texas as they lay dying.[3] CCTV footage from a Western Australia police station on August 4, 2014, shows an extremely distressed twenty-two-year-old Yamatji Aboriginal woman (Ms. Dhu*) crying out in pain and being repeatedly mocked by police officers. Ms. Dhu was arrested for unpaid fines. Her previously broken ribs had become infected. Police officers and doctors alike ignored her pain, and she died in her cell of advanced septicemia.[4] Five days after Ms. Dhu died in police custody in Western Australia, Michael Brown was shot dead by police in Missouri. Their deaths were caused by the same toxic combination of white supremacy and unchecked police authority, albeit on two different continents. Four hundred and eighty-nine Aboriginal and

---

* Following Aboriginal naming protocols, this article does not use Ms. Dhu's full name.

Torres Strait Islander people have died in custody since 1991 (when a royal commission first released a report on this issue), and to this date no convictions of any police or prison authorities have been recorded.[5] In Australia, police violence against Indigenous people has been a central element of colonization since the beginning of white settlement. Rather than a dark stain on Australia's history, it represents the thread that has held together the narrative of settlement and nationhood.

It is also part of a transnational history of racial violence that connects to both Indigenous dispossession in North America and American slavery. The formation of police forces in nineteenth-century Australia and the United States were linked not only by the development of the modern nation-state but also by the violent dispossession of people of color. Antebellum slavery and Australian colonization were both maintained through the constant surveillance by and interventions of police forces. It was in the late antebellum and early Civil War era—when police surveillance and enforcement of slavery were at their peak in the United States—that a majority of Australia's current police forces were formed. For many Australians, including the tens of thousands of protesters who took to the streets and marched in support of Black Lives Matter in June 2020, the murder of George Floyd by a Minneapolis police officer represented a legacy of violent white supremacy that is as much Australian as it is American.[6]

Historians have lagged behind Indigenous activists who have long noted the comparison between Black struggles and resistance in both countries and who are now leading a national debate on structural racism in Australia.[7] In the week prior to the BLM protests in Australia in June 2020, Prime Minister Scott Morrison dismissed the protests, claiming that Australia had been "a pretty brutal place, but there was no slavery" after having previously said that "we shouldn't be importing the things that are happening overseas to Australia."[8] While Morrison has since apologized for these comments, they reflect a set of false assumptions that many, if not most, white Australians share about their history and cultural identity. Despite these assumptions, slave labor was not only prevalent in Australia's tropical North for much of the nineteenth century but was also common on pastoral stations in central and northern Australia well into the mid–twentieth century.[9]

The history of slavery in Australia is directly linked to the American Civil War. As a result of the blockade of Confederate ports, global demand for cotton grew and prices rose dramatically, motivating Robert Towns (early Queensland settler colonist and founder of Townsville) to cash in on this opportunity in 1863 by kidnapping, transporting, and coercing South Sea Islanders to work on his

Queensland plantations.[10] The end of the Civil War also led to a global emigration of ex-Confederates, including to Australia, where many ex-slaveholders applied their expertise to Australian plantations and the kidnapping and coercion of South Sea Islanders.[11] While the nature of the Civil War changed in 1863, as a result of President Abraham Lincoln's Emancipation Proclamation and the participation of Black soldiers in the US military, it was in this historical moment that slavery in Australia entered a new and prolonged phase, with more than 62,000 South Sea Islander people brought to Australia between 1863 and 1904.[12] When Prime Minister Morrison dismissed the applicability of BLM in Australia, he demonstrated a blindness not only to the truly global nature of white supremacy but also to basic Australian history. A shared history of white supremacy exists in both countries' histories of slavery and in their historical foundation and development as settler colonies dependent on Indigenous dispossession. Yet this shared history of slavery, genocide, and dispossession only partly explains why the Black Lives Matter movement has resonated so deeply with both Indigenous and non-Indigenous Australians.

The Black Lives Matter movement in Australia has engaged with and built upon a longstanding tradition of Indigenous protest and resistance, and that has been key to its impact on Australian politics and society. This is seen most clearly in the success and activism of the Warriors of the Aboriginal Resistance (WAR). WAR burst onto the national political consciousness in 2020 when it organized a peaceful protest in Melbourne in solidarity with BLM and to protest deaths in police custody.[13] Yet the group had formed in 2014, and developed an activist network alongside the initial growth of BLM in the United States.[14] While being clearly influenced by BLM activists in the United States and protesting in solidarity with this movement, WAR has positioned itself as carrying on a legacy of resistance that dates back to 1788 and the first settlement of white colonists.

As in the United States, white settlement and incursions onto Aboriginal and Torres Strait Islander lands were met with Indigenous resistance from the very beginning, and, as in the United States, Indigenous resistance was often met with overwhelming and brutal force.[15] As WAR's founding manifesto states: "The colonization of our lands and lives began with English invasion in 1788, an unprovoked and undeclared war, one nation against another nation. This war never ended."[16] WAR was founded on a philosophy of Aboriginal nationalism that specifically rejects Australian citizenship. Its principal aims include decolonization through the restoration of tribal sovereignty and Aboriginal legal, political, and economic self-determination.[17] WAR not only draws on a legacy of resistance specific to Aboriginal and Torres Strait Islander people and their fight against colonial exploitation, but it also engages with ideas of self-determination and nationalism that are rooted in global Black struggles.

WAR and other activist groups in Australia's growing BLM movement are continuing the work of previous generations of Indigenous activists who advocated for greater Indigenous independence and freedom. By identifying themselves as Warriors of the Aboriginal Resistance, these advocates connect themselves with the legacy of Indigenous resistance leaders who fought British colonists in the 1780s and 1790s. WAR's advocacy, however, draws more directly on twentieth-century Indigenous activists like William Cooper, Pearl Gibbs, Jack Patten, and others. These activists were all crucial in organizing Aboriginal activist networks and protests during the 1930s, arguing principally for civil and citizenship rights for Aboriginal people. Like WAR, this group of activists highlighted the illegality of first settlement and its traumatic consequences for Indigenous Australians by staging a Day of Mourning Protest in 1938 on the 150th anniversary of the First Fleet's landing—a protest tradition still observed on that date in every major city since then.[18] Like WAR, these activists used examples of international racial oppression to highlight racial injustice in Australia. In 1938, William Cooper organized a protest at the German Consulate immediately following Kristallnacht, an organized night of brutal anti-Jewish violence and destruction across Germany. As Gary Foley has highlighted, Cooper purposely drew attention to the similarities between the white government's treatment of Aboriginal Australians and the Nazis' treatment of Jews.[19]

From the 1960s onward, Indigenous activists have drawn more directly from the United States. Civil rights protests in Australia came to a head during the 1960s. Inspired by activism in the United States, Charles Perkins, Ann Curthoys, and more than thirty other university students from Sydney organized a "Freedom Ride" into rural New South Wales to protest racial discrimination.[20] These activists used the language of the US civil rights movement to highlight the similarities between American and Australian white supremacy, including Australia's own system of racial segregation—the history of which still receives little public acknowledgment—and similarities between Black political consciousness and activism in each country.[21] Similarly, during the 1970s Aboriginal activists, including Gary Foley, led Australia's own Black Power movement, linking Aboriginal struggles for self-determination with Black American, Native American, and anti-colonial struggles throughout the world.[22] Given this long history of Aboriginal activism and resistance, which has often taken inspiration from both Black American and global Black struggles, it should be no surprise that a new generation of activists was ready to respond to the Black Lives Matter movement when it first emerged in 2013.

To focus solely on high-profile activist networks, however, ignores the breadth and depth of resistance that helped propel BLM protests in Australia and the United States. Resistance to oppression exists in many different forms and can sometimes be hard to identify. From the early twentieth century until the 1970s, the Australian government forcibly removed countless Indigenous children and placed them either into domestic labor, foster families, or state or church institutions. These children, known as the Stolen Generations, were violently separated from their culture, communities, and families with devastating consequences. Despite a national apology from the then–prime minister, Kevin Rudd, in 2008, the case for reparations remains an ongoing fight. The intergenerational trauma caused by this practice is impossible to separate from contemporary Indigenous issues. For the Stolen Generations and their descendants, survival is in itself an act of resistance.

Similarly, the most powerful acts of defiance and resistance have often come from the families of victims of police violence and from the families of Aboriginal people who have died in custody. It was the relentless advocacy of Mavis Pat, the mother of murdered teenager John Pat (who was beaten to death by Western Australia police officers), that sparked the Royal Commission into Aboriginal Deaths in Custody in 1988. It was the children of Tanya Day, an Aboriginal woman who died of traumatic injuries while in police custody, who successfully pushed for the state's coroner to consider systemic racism as a contributing cause of death—an important step in forcing the state and the judiciary to confront white supremacy.

Much like the families of George Floyd and Eric Garner, these families have all played an important part in sharing their grief and anger with the media and the public and highlighting the damage and loss caused by racism and police brutality. While organizations like WAR have proven to be extremely effective in organizing major protests and focusing public and political attention on the issue of white supremacy, it has been the voices of bereaved Aboriginal families that have had the most impact. Responding to Scott Morrison's dismissive comments quoted earlier in this essay, David Dungay Jr.'s sister, Christine, told the prime minister on national television, "You sat there, you made a comment that you did not want USA issues brought to Australia. Come on, brother, they have been here. It is here. It has always been here." She lamented that "you do not ever, ever hold them accountable. And that's why we stand here today. Me and my mother, still fighting, five years later. And believe me, all the families, we are still suffering." Finally, she warned the prime minister and the world, "And I'm telling you, until we get justice, brother, you are not going to get any peace. Because we are going to keep fighting."[23]

Notes

1. Prime Minister of Australia, *Transcript of Interview with Ben Fordham, 2GB*, 2 June 2020. Retrieved from https://issuu.com/brisbaneblacks/docs/war_manifesto_d91595ceee8754. Accessed August 27, 2020.

2. Coroner's Court of New South Wales (2019), *Inquest into the Death of David Dungay*. 2015/381722. Retrieved from https://issuu.com/brisbaneblacks/docs/war_manifesto_d91595ceee8754. Accessed August 27, 2020.

3. Mike Baker, Jennifer Valentino-DeVries, Manny Fernandez, and Michael LaForgia, "Three Words. 70 Cases. The Tragic History of 'I Can't Breathe.'" *The New York Times*, 29 June 2020. Retrieved from https://issuu.com/brisbaneblacks/docs/war_manifesto_d91595ceee8754. Accessed August 27, 2020.

4. Coroner's Court of Western Australia, *Inquest into the Death of Julieka Ivanna Dhu* (2016), 11020–14. Retrieved from https://issuu.com/brisbaneblacks/docs/war_manifesto_d91595ceee8754. Accessed August 27, 2020.

5. Laura Doherty, *Deaths in Custody in Australia 2020–21*. Statistical Report No. 37. Canberra: Australian Institute of Criminology, 2021. Retrieved from https://doi.org/10.52922/sr78436; Alison Whittaker, "Despite 432 Indigenous deaths in custody since 1991, no one has ever been convicted. Racist silence and complicity are to blame," *The Conversation*, 3 June 2020. Retrieved from https://theconversation.com/despite-432-indigenous-deaths-in-custody-since-1991-no-one-has-ever-been-convicted-racist-silence-and-complicity-are-to-blame-139873. Accessed August 27, 2020.

6. "Australia protests: thousands take part in Black Lives Matter and pro-refugee events amid Covid-19 warnings," *The Guardian*, 13 June 2020. Retrieved from https://www.theguardian.com/world/2020/jun/13/australia-protests-thousands-take-part-in-black-lives-matter-and-pro-refugee-events-amid-health-warnings. Accessed August 27, 2020.

7. Aboriginal activist and academic Gary Foley highlights this point in his Ph.D. thesis. Gary Foley, "An Autobiographical Narrative of the Black Power Movement and the 1972 Aboriginal Embassy." History Ph.D. thesis. The University of Melbourne.

8. Prime Minister of Australia, *Transcript of Interview with Ben Fordham, 2GB*, 11 June 2020. Retrieved from https://www.pm.gov.au/media/interview-ben-fordham-2gb-4. Accessed August 27, 2020.

9. See Tracey Banivanua-Mar, *Violence and Colonial Dialogue: The Australian–Pacific Indentured Labor Trade* (Honolulu: University of Hawai'i Press, 2007); Stephen Gray, "The Elephant in the Drawing Room: Slavery and the Stolen Wages Debate," *Australian Indigenous Law Review* 11: 1 (2007): 30–54.

10. Tracey Banivanua-Mar, *Decolonisation and the Pacific: Indigenous Globalisation and the Ends of Empire* (Cambridge: Cambridge University Press, 2016), 35.

11. Gerald Horne's *White Pacific* provides an excellent overview of this fascinating transnational history. See Gerald Horne, *The White Pacific: U.S. Imperialism and Black Slavery in the South Seas After the Civil War* (Honolulu: University of Hawai'i Press, 2007).

12. Horne, *The White Pacific*, 2.

13. Tarneen Onus-Williams, Crystal McKinnon, and Meriki Onus, "Why we organized Melbourne's Black Lives Matter rally," *The Saturday Paper*, June 13, 2020. Issue 305.

14. Warriors of the Aboriginal Resistance, "Warriors of the Aboriginal Resistance Manifesto." November 2014. Retrieved from https://issuu.com/brisbaneblacks/docs/war_manifesto_d91595ceee8754. Accessed August 27, 2020.

15. See digital mapping project, *Colonial Frontier Massacres in Australia, 1788–1930*. Retrieved from https://c21ch.newcastle.edu.au/colonialmassacres/. Accessed August 27, 2020.

16. Warriors of the Aboriginal Resistance, "Warriors of the Aboriginal Resistance Manifesto." November 2014. Retrieved from https://issuu.com/brisbaneblacks/docs/war_manifesto_d91595ceee8754. Accessed August 27, 2020.

17. WAR, "Manifesto." November 2014. Retrieved from https://issuu.com/brisbaneblacks/docs/war_manifesto_d91595ceee8754. Accessed August 27, 2020.

18. "Day of Mourning 1938," *The Dictionary of Sydney* (2008). Retrieved from https://dictionaryofsydney.org/entry/day_of_mourning_1938. Accessed August 27, 2020.

19. Gary Foley, "Australia and the Holocaust: A Koori Perspective," *The power of whiteness and other essays*, Aboriginal studies occasional paper (1). Centre for Indigenous Education, The University of Melbourne (1999): 74–87.

20. See Ann Curthoys, *Freedom Ride: A Freedom Rider Remembers* (Sydney: Allen & Unwin, 2002).

21. Russell McGregor, *Indifferent Inclusion: Aboriginal People and the Australian Nation* (Canberra: Aboriginal Studies Press, 2011), 100 and 147.

22. Sian Vate, "Black Power in White Australia: An Interview with Gary Foley," *Jacobin*, 24 January 2020. Retrieved from https://issuu.com/brisbaneblacks/docs/war_manifesto_d91595ceee8754. Accessed August 27, 2020.

23. Natalie Wolfe, "David Dungay's family issue warning to Scott Morrison: 'You won't get peace,'" *News.com.au*. Retrieved from https://issuu.com/brisbaneblacks/docs/war_manifesto_d91595ceee8754. Accessed August 27, 2020.

Memory

12

Carpetbagging the Colfax Riot Marker

LeeAnna Keith

I missed the summer of 2020.

I know you are thinking that everyone did that, that all of us missed everything in 2020 once the coronavirus came to call. For me, though, the missing-out started earlier, began in fact at 3:40 P.M. on November 25, 2019, when the tires of a cement mixer tapped gently on the side of my bicycle two times, slamming me to the ground on Fifth Avenue at 59th Street and breaking my left leg below the knee. Breaking my leg caused me to re-evaluate my habits and even my values, especially as demonstrations for causes I had long embraced began to proliferate after the deaths of George Floyd and Breonna Taylor. I was no John Lewis or Fannie Lou Hamer, I discovered, willing to face down bodily harm for my beliefs. Watching scenes of police cruisers driving into crowds six months after my accident, I wondered if I would ever take part in political demonstrations again.

The protests addressed Civil War history, my research interest, targeting Confederate monuments in public spaces including in my hometown, Huntsville, Alabama. So many disunionist and white supremacist displays were shouted at, spray-painted, and removed by negotiation that 2020 gained distinction as the most active year in the history of commemorating the Civil War! Housebound in my recovery, I pondered how I could be a part of this solution. As it happened, my telephone started to ring with inquiries about the Colfax Massacre, the subject of my first book, published in 2008. In the end I had a chance to add my voice—and even to bring my high school students into a micro-scale social justice campaign.

The Colfax Massacre is the subject of what one expert has called the worst Confederate marker in the United States. Strictly speaking, the event took place eight years after the collapse of the Confederacy, in 1873, when white supremacist militiamen overran a Black town, destroyed a courthouse, and killed or executed an estimated 150 victims in post-election political violence. The spirit of the Lost Cause permeated the attack on Colfax, however, in which white Confederate veterans and their younger relatives took part in the camaraderie of men in arms.

The perennial commemoration of the original event in the town of Colfax starting soon after 1873 channeled the same passions and employed the same civic-minded white racists that constructed monuments to Civil War soldiers and generals across the South. Choosing the reconstructed Grant Parish courthouse as the site of their observances, white citizens placed placards on lynching trees, publicized a flaming fountain on the site of the mass grave of 69 victims in *Ripley's Believe It or Not*, and finally persuaded the state to erect an historical marker upon the gravesite, its text spare and threatening in iron letters.

"Colfax Riot," it reads: "On this site occurred the Colfax Riot in which three white men and 150 negroes were slain. This event on April 13, 1873 marked the end of carpetbag misrule in the South."

The strange career and antecedents of the Colfax Riot marker have resonated with my own. Having turned up in the Historical Markers Database amid my early searches, it inspired me to become an author who could do justice to its tale at a time when I had not yet started to study the Civil War. Its story churned up unfamiliar elements of my own experience as a white woman from an old Huntsville, Alabama, family. A large percentage of the Black families residing on the massacre site in 1873 had traveled there involuntarily from my hometown, I discovered. They were penned awaiting transport on a plantation later sold to build mill homes, including my grandmother's house, where my father lives today. By chance, my sister came to own the site of the townhouse of Meredith Calhoun, the impresario who brought 1,000 captives from Huntsville to his wilderness estates around the area that later became the town of Colfax.

Louisiana people would see me as an outsider, imagining me as a latter-day carpetbagger—like the "Yankees" and regional migrants who had stirred up trouble in the name of Black equality and the Republican Party in the times of the Civil War and Reconstruction. In fact, despite my New York City address, the subject of the Colfax Massacre found me close to home, and during my tense research and publicity visits to the region I stayed with my aunt and first cousins in nearby Shreveport.

Back in the early 2000s I had been shocked to find the text of the Colfax Riot marker on the Internet, and I never fully believed that it was still standing until I saw it with my own eyes. I had arrived in Colfax in the company of my father, who came armed in light of the town's reputation as a white supremacy stronghold. In fact, while we photographed the marker and a nearby obelisk that mourns the white men who died "fighting for white supremacy," a friendly man approached us, offered documents, and let us know that he was in the Ku Klux Klan.

My book *The Colfax Massacre* took part in a siege of outsider inquiries about Colfax. While white citizens of the town may have seen me as a carpetbagger, African Americans might reasonably inquire about my credentials to tell a story with so much historical and emotional weight. I felt the glare of my whiteness and that of my counterpart, Charles Lane, another 2008 author whose own book *The Day Freedom Died* won critical praise. It was our privilege to have a platform from which to give the Colfax Massacre its full accounting, and to follow in the footsteps of a Black novelist with ties to the area, Lalita Tademy, whose books *Cane River* and *Red River* were national bestsellers, and an intrepid band of Black journalists serving life sentences at Louisiana's state prison, who published the first historical account of the massacre in its journal *The Angolite*. Over the years I have heard news of and participated in television shows, theatrical productions, academic symposia, and documentary films about the events. I made calls and wrote letters to local newspapers and elected officials, mostly looking foolish, and in 2015, President Barack Obama's National Parks Service initiated plans for a proper commemoration at the site of the massacre. As of summer 2020, even as famous names retold the story of the Colfax Massacre in *New York Times* editorials, none of this attention had resulted in a new public discourse in Colfax and its vicinity. The marker planted in the mass grave remained the only local commemoration of events.

What I could not do, I resolved to teach. Students—responding to the brief account of the Colfax Massacre in Eric Foner's *Reconstruction* in some of the earliest classes I taught—had originally inspired my interest in the story by their horrified questioning. Ever since the original publication, moreover, I had found ways to share my expertise about the subject with them, sharing documents and making use of passages and auxiliary writings. Now in the summer of 2020, I prepared a research project centered on the Colfax Riot marker and similar public commemorations that were still standing. I was lucky to be offering a remote summer course for high school students interested in historical research. Taking inspiration from the impasse of the Colfax Riot marker, we would seek out other markers that offered racist or outdated interpretations of the past and propose alternatives.

Collegiate School in New York City, where I have taught since 2005, has felt the sting of historic cultural shifts, having interrogated its all-male traditions, questioned the appropriateness of the Dutchman mascot embodied by a cartoon Peter Stuyvesant, and weathered the uncomfortable departure of Black faculty and administrators in the same school year marked by the outbreak of the COVID-19 pandemic. A degree of our enjoyment of the history of the school—dating back to 1628 and interrupted only by the Revolutionary War—has been diminished. The summer course was for stalwarts, however, determined to feather their caps with prizes for research papers, essays, and podcasts. Some embraced the markers project, forming a loose coalition of related independent researchers.

Students used the Internet and worked to identify the best search terms to identify outdated language: *negro*, as found in the Colfax Riot marker; *colored*, *Confederate*, *slave*, and the names of specific events. A surprisingly large number of pro-Confederate markers and monuments were found by searching for Nathan Bedford Forrest. One student chose a Georgia marker erroneously celebrating the made-up Br'er Rabbit stories as an African tradition as the point of departure for his research into Walt Disney Corporation's racist film *Song of the South*. Another asked why no monument marked the site of a riot that challenged the authority of Black US troops in Charleston in 1865. A small group pursued the story of the Colfax Riot marker and other commemorations in Louisiana, exploring records that had been digitized or published in the years since *The Colfax Massacre*. What my students discovered helped me better understand the reasons for the persistence of the Colfax Riot marker through decades of social change.

First there was a tree on the courthouse grounds, the scene of some especially heinous cruelty, blessedly unspecified in surviving records. After photographing and tending the tree into the twentieth century, local whites obtained a special placard from a national organization, its text lost to time, and when it finally fell, a scrapbook organizer wrote in a tribute that the old pecan had been sacred. The recognition of the tree and other remembrances had helped to "write in blood upon the pages of history," as an 1881 newspaper editorial described it, "the oft taught lesson that the Anglo Saxon will not be the slave of an inferior race."

Students linked events in Colfax to a national surge of pro-Confederate sentiment. World War I and the fiftieth anniversary of the Civil War occasioned an outpouring of public remembering, as hundreds of thousands of southern men enlisted in the armed forces for the first time since the Civil War, and membership in heritage organizations such as the United Daughters of the Confederacy and Sons of Confederate Veterans peaked. In Colfax, a reunion on the site of the massacre brought together nearly all the surviving white veterans of the courthouse fight for a tearful and solemn ceremony. By 1921, the eleven-foot obelisk, now relocated to the cemetery, was positioned by the courthouse entrance. "In Loving Remembrance," it read in granite, "Erected to the Memory of the Heroes . . . Who fell in the Colfax Riot fighting for White Supremacy."

Students identified new records while I worked to help them contextualize them. In the 1930s, as New Deal politics and changes in the Democratic Party rocked the South, whites in the vicinity of Colfax saw fit to remind their neighbors of the dangers of Black voting and political alliances. "[W]ithin the memory of men now living," warned the *Bunkie Eagle*, "other white men sought the organization of Negroes for political purposes. . . . Better stop it now for the benefit of all concerned." The town high school circulated a student paper called "The Colfax Riot," its pages filled with smiling whites. A WPA researcher going through the courthouse files identified a trove of written remembrances of the terrible event, recorded by white participants and their families and lovingly preserved by a largely female cadre of local historians. The story of the massacre was one that whites in the vicinity of Colfax liked to tell again and again, we observed.

The national trend favored fewer new Confederate monuments between the 1920s and the mid-century civil rights movement. But the Colfax remembrances surged forward in 1950 with the placement of the historical marker. Roadside markers grew up alongside the highway network and worked in harmony with civic boosters and tourism interests. In the case of Colfax, the marker also responded to new anxieties about race relations that arose during World War II and its aftermath.

Northern Louisiana played host to major military mobilizations in the 1940s, bringing thousands of African Americans into the region, many of whom hailed from areas where Jim Crow practices and deferential manners remained unknown. The demands of wartime production in the West and in northern states lured Black workers away with high wages, and local employers recoiled from seeing their labor force "on the train and gone" and sending money home so relatives could follow. A number of prominent incidents brought whites in the vicinity of Colfax and Alexandria, home to military bases, to the streets for racially motivated violence. Both during the war and afterward, Black men in uniform were lynched by mobs and shot by police. The placement of the new marker allowed white citizens an opportunity to reiterate the message of the white supremacy obelisk, described as "the means of a more complete understanding between the races."

In the years after 1950, public commemorations of the "riot" and its white heroes faded from view. The town and its vicinity did not experience demonstrations or boycotts during the civil rights movement—despite the discovery in 1957 that hundreds of ballot applications from Black citizens of Grant Parish had been improperly discarded. An uneasy peace prevailed, as the expansion of

Black voting under Federal supervision after 1964 created opportunities to elect Black mayors, police jurors, and state legislators. None addressed the problem of the Colfax Riot marker, though the current African American mayor, Ossie Clark, has expressed the wish "to come together and have a conversation," to address the subject in the local schools and to correct the language of the marker to acknowledge that the event was a massacre and not a riot. "[J]ust because there is an absence of protest doesn't mean that everything is perfect," noted another African American leader, Avery Hamilton, who was descended from one of the first Black men to die in 1873.

My young New Yorkers found it easy to believe that white supremacist violence persists in the rural South. The Klan remains entrenched in Colfax, though the evidence of its presence is ghostly. Aside from my personal encounter with the smiling man whose "friend" was in the KKK in 2005, its invisible empire has come into view only in events surrounding the Jena Six anti-racist protests in 2007, which unfolded in the immediate vicinity of Colfax and Alexandria. During demonstrations against the display of nooses on a high school campus, a pair of teens dragged a noose from a pickup truck and were arrested. The younger of the two, the same age as my students, wore a Ku Klux Klan tattoo and lived in Colfax, population 1,659, of whom fewer than 550 are white.

Though roughly one hundred Confederate and racist monuments were removed before the end of 2020, the Colfax Riot marker and the majority of the offensive monuments in the United States remain in place. State lawmakers have responded to public protests with legislation to protect the status quo, and white supremacy extremists have manifested their willingness to kill and injure in the name of historic preservation at Charlottesville and in other confrontations. Although the marker was finally removed in May 2021, the history of commemorations on the site of the Colfax Massacre suggests that the price of its removal might easily become a matter of life and death for local people.

My students and I, in consideration of these obstacles, made no formal bid to revise or remove the Colfax Riot marker. What we learned about Colfax, public memory, and the racial justice reckoning of our awful times lives only in our understanding.

13

"Moving History"

The Life and Afterlife of Louisville's Confederate Monument

Anne E. Marshall

Louisville, Kentucky's Confederate monument first caught my scholarly interest nearly twenty-five years ago because of its context. As I researched my dissertation on Kentucky's post–Civil War Confederate identity, I paid special attention to the monument as a paeon to the rebel cause in what was, during the Civil War, a decidedly Union city. The monument's story has become even more complicated, as has my own view of it in the years since I first investigated the circumstances surrounding its construction. In the past twenty years, Kentuckians have historically contextualized, removed, relocated, and re-contextualized the monument. In the short essay that follows, I explore the shifting contexts of the monument, and what it might (and might not) mean in light of renewed public consciousness of the connection between Confederate symbols and racial injustice.[1]

The monument, featuring an eight-foot-tall bronze infantryman atop a 62-foot-tall pedestal, flanked by another pair of bronze soldiers at its base, was completed and unveiled in 1895. It was the product of several years of hard fundraising by the Kentucky Women's Monument Association, a group that would later become the Albert Sidney Johnston chapter of the United Daughters of the Confederacy. While it was one of many such monuments that went up throughout the South in the same period, it was different because it stood as a towering symbol of the Confederate sympathy in a city and a state that had remained in the Union. Indeed, during the Civil War, Louisville served as a Federal supply base as well as a center of Union Army recruitment. However, as I wrote in my 2010 book, *Creating a Confederate Kentucky*, it seemed that white Kentuckians were bent on celebrating a cause they had not actually lost.[2]

The Louisville monument was not an aberration in Kentucky. Dozens of Confederate monuments appeared in town squares and on courthouse lawns between 1880 and 1925. As I argued in my book, however, the proliferation of statues is

Figure 1. Confederate Monument, Louisville, Kentucky, circa 1906. (Library of Congress Prints and Photographs Division, Washington, D.C.)

more reasonable than it might first seem. Kentucky was a former slave state, and most white Kentuckians signed on to the Union cause in order to preserve the peculiar institution, rather than destroy it. After the war they committed to maintaining white political, economic, and social supremacy through Jim Crow laws and lynching just as white citizens of former Confederate states did. Like the hundreds of other Confederate monuments erected during the late nineteenth and early twentieth centuries across the South, Louisville's imposing contribution to secessionist statuary was about more than honoring brave soldiers. As historians have pointed out in a growing scholarship about Civil War memory in the past twenty-five years, these statues were part of a much larger effort to both enshrine a Lost Cause memory of the Civil War and to shape a present in which African Americans remained legally, economically, and socially subservient.[3]

Louisville's Confederate memorialists built their monument on what was then the periphery of Louisville, but the booming city quickly grew around it. By the late twentieth century, the monument sat amidst the University of Louisville's Belknap campus, where it stood as an unwelcoming presence to a diverse student body. Lost Cause symbolism extended beyond the monument itself, as the corner on which it stood became known as "Confederate Place," and a nearby student dorm was dubbed "Confederate Apartments." Students protested the monument and these place names from time to time, and by the beginning of the new millennium, both university and city officials acknowledged that the statue did not reflect their modern values of inclusivity. In 2002, the university embarked on a project to remodel the area around the monument and to turn it into a space they called "Freedom Park."[4]

The initial plan was ambitious. It called for a Civil War memorial that would honor all fallen soldiers, an area designated to honor "global struggles for freedom," and space for other unspecified historical markers and exhibits, both permanent and temporary. As J. Blaine Hudson, chair of U of L's Pan-African Studies department, and a longtime champion of the new space, stated, "We want Freedom Park to represent as accurately and as completely as possible the late-antebellum and Civil War experience of Louisville and Kentucky—all the different players in that drama." University vice president Larry Owsley explained, "When people look back at it 100 years from now, we hope they have something that will help interpret the Civil War. As it is now, we just have a Confederate monument without context."[5]

Owsley's use of the word *context* was key. The city and university hoped to carry out what public historians referred to as "contextualizing" the Confederate monument. *Contextualization* refers to both explaining and offsetting the origins and intent behind the construction of public historical displays. In the case of Confederate monuments, this means explaining how the same white southerners who built these monuments were concurrently implementing policies of racial discrimination, disenfranchisement, and segregation. Sometimes this is done by adding additional text on or around monuments that explains the full intent of the monument to present-day onlookers who might otherwise simply take monuments at face value and see them only as genuine tributes to lost soldiers and brave veterans. Other times, as in the case of Freedom Park, promoters install additional monuments representing and paying homage to people or groups who were silenced or marginalized by those represented by the original monument, with the idea that doing so destabilizes and undercuts the power of the monument in the present.

Contextualization was, until not long ago, seen by many professional historians as a sort of *de facto* best practice when it came to public history. It had the benefit of seeming to represent multiple historical voices and to portray the past as one of conflict, rather than consensus, amongst groups. It also precluded the actual removal of troublesome monuments. While most academic and public historians bore absolutely no reverence toward these monuments, many saw them as valuable historical resources. The prominent historian Gary Gallagher expressed this opinion, writing that he sees "memorial landscapes as similar in nature and value to graphic and literary sources—all compose part of the historical record and should be interpreted as such." Gallagher was in favor of adding text to existing monuments and creating new ones. "But eliminating monuments is tantamount to destroying records or images," he warned, "potentially inhibiting a real understanding of our past, warts and all, and obscuring important themes, movements, and eras."[6]

While researching and writing my book in the early 2000s, I felt much the same way. I studied and visited dozens of the monuments about which I wrote in an effort to understand, first-hand, their physical presence as well as to gain a sense of the enormous scope of their interpretational influence. As much as I disagreed with their message, I felt about them as I would feel about any historical document. I did not want these relics of the past destroyed; rather, I wanted them to testify to the power of the white supremacists who erected them and, by extension, bear witness to the strength and tenacity of the African Americans who struggled mightily against them in the intervening years.

So it was with keen interest and appreciation that I read about the completion of Freedom Park in 2011. The finished park included ten obelisks (some of which flanked the Confederate monument) inscribed with information about the city's history from settlement to the present day. The text on each obelisk highlighted the role that Native Americans and African Americans (both enslaved and free) played in the city's history, growth, and development. The park also featured nine glass panels, each of which depicted the achievements of twentieth-century civil rights leaders in Louisville. To many of the park's advocates (myself included) the finished product was a model of historical contextualization. While the old monument remained in place, the exhibits surrounding it reoriented the narrative in an effort to rebalance the power equation.[7]

Many Louisville residents did not feel the same, however. Even before Freedom Park's completion, Black residents of Louisville cast doubt on the notion that a broadened, inclusive portrayal of history could mitigate the symbolism of the Confederate monument. During Freedom Park's design and development stage, members of Louisville's African American community voiced their opinion that the statue should be removed. Park opponents included civil rights leader Reverend Louis Coleman and Mattie Jones, head of Louisville's Justice Resource Center, who decried the new installation as a "compromise," asking why any of the descendants of the Black figures to be honored in the park would want tributes to their relatives placed near a symbol of oppression. In short, implied Freedom Park critics, no amount of counternarrative could counteract the offensiveness of the original statue.[8]

In the intervening years, more and more people seemed to agree with the park's detractors, especially in light of the increasingly visible veneration of Confederate symbols by avowed white supremacists. In 2015, photos of Dylann Roof, who massacred nine African American churchgoers at Charleston's Emanuel AME Church, showed him posing next to multiple Confederate flags. These images reinforced the connection between Confederate history and present-day white supremacy and racial injustice. Dr. Ricky Jones, who succeeded Blaine Hudson as the head of U of L's Pan-African Studies program, used this moment to demand the monument's removal. "For twenty years we have been plagued by confusion, compromises, excuses and half measures," he wrote in a *Courier-Journal* editorial. "It's time for the statue to go." Eschewing a drawn-out debate over what to do with the monument, Jones blasted: "If 21st century Confederates want it, sell it to them and put it on one of their lawns . . . move it wherever you want. Frankly, there would probably be very little protest if you strapped a C4 or TNT to it and blew the damn thing up in the middle of the night. We just want it gone."[9]

Under pressure, Mayor Greg Fischer and University President James Ramsey announced days later that they intended to remove the monument. The Kentucky Division of the Sons of Confederate Veterans quickly responded with a restraining order. Local attorney Everett Corley, who represented the SCV, described the removal as "the 2016 version of a book burning." Corley also charged that the city was deceptive in its claims to move the monument and actually intended to "destroy it and throw it away." This was not true, however, and even before the judge in the case lifted the restraining order later in May, the city began looking for a place to re-home the monument.[10]

Louisville's Commission on Public Art entertained numerous ideas for potential destinations before accepting the offer from officials from the town of Brandenburg, Kentucky, to re-home the monument in their town. Located forty-four miles west of Louisville along the Ohio River, Brandenburg already boasted a riverfront park where the locals hosted a biennial reenactment of Kentucky cavalryman John Hunt Morgan's cross-river invasions of Indiana. Town officials felt that they had a fitting spot for the Confederate monument and that its presence in their town would help boost local tourism. It seemed that Ricky Jones's words about selling the monument to "twenty-first-century Confederates" were prophetic, except that the city didn't sell the monument, but instead gave it away. The city and the university, together, spent $400,000 to move the statue to its new home.[11]

Despite the expense, Louisville officials seemed pleased with the solution. It allowed them to rid their city of the statue's troublesome presence with an apparently clear conscience. As Mayor Fischer told the PBS *NewsHour*, "Some people said 'Mayor, you're the Taliban, you're destroying history.' I said, 'No, I'm not. We're not destroying history, we're just moving it.'" "You're moving history?" asked incredulous correspondent Jeffrey Brown. Fischer replied, "History is dynamic. It can always be interpreted in different ways." What he and other city and university officials seemed to be implying was that Brandenburg, a town whose population was only 3 percent African American, was a likelier home for the monument and that it was fine to leave it to locals there to contextualize it as they wished. As the chairman of the University of Louisville Foundation, Brucie Moore, said, "We are glad to find this process moving to completion in a way that respects the campus community's wishes while preserving the historic value of the monument." Residents of Brandenburg seemed, for the most part, to welcome the second-hand statue. Months after the announced move, Mayor Ronnie Joyner claimed he had received only a handful of calls opposing it, including one from a white woman asking whether he had consulted with the town's African American community. He dismissed the question, saying, "We don't have an African American community as such. By that I mean we don't have just a place where Blacks all live."[12]

Brandenburg officials planted their new monument near two other more modest riverfront markers that recognized the town's role in the Underground Railroad and the region's early Native settlers. They held a dedication ceremony on Memorial Day, 2017, complete with Confederate color guard. An estimated 400 to 500 people attended, along with a very small group of protesters. On the occasion, Mayor Joyner told a reporter, "I never looked at this statue as a Black versus white thing or that it had a link to slavery or anything like that . . . it is actually a monument to Confederates who fought in the Civil War." Denuded of its Freedom Park context, Louisville's monument had gone back to being revered by many as a symbol of the Lost Cause, just as it was at its unveiling in 1895.[13]

By the time Louisville officials relocated their monument, my views on contextualization had changed, in large part because I saw how it had failed in that city. I had realized, as I wrote in a 2017 op-ed advocating the removal of two Confederate statues in Lexington, Kentucky, that "in a present in which racial injustice pervades the everyday life of so many, it turns out that no amount of historical context is particularly helpful." Along with many former advocates of the process, I realized that as long as there were white supremacists who actively rallied around these symbols of the Lost Cause (as they did at the Unite the Right rally in Charlottesville, Virginia, in 2017) to promote their current agenda, it was impossible to offset or counterbalance that meaning. "Contextualization in public spaces doesn't work," I wrote, "because monuments speak not only to who had power in the past, but who has it in the present." In the wake of the violent killings of Ahmaud Arbery, George Floyd, and Breonna Taylor, more academic and public historians seemed to come around to this position. The National Trust for Historic Preservation, which had continued to advocate for contextualizing Confederate monuments in the wake of Charlottesville, shifted positions in June 2020, calling for their removal. In a statement, the NTHP proclaimed, "we believe that their removal may be necessary to achieve the greater good of ensuring justice and equality."[14]

And yet, the fate of the Louisville monument should also give pause to historians like me who have lost faith in the process of contextualism. In its new home in Brandenburg, it has become the object of white adulation not unlike that which it received in 1895, and that is troubling. Without the accompanying exhibits of Freedom Park, the history it tells once again allows visitors to honor the Lost Cause without confronting the racial oppression on which white southerners founded the Confederacy. It also casts doubt on the process of removal and relocation. In hastening to hand the monument off, as if it were a hot potato, as quickly as possible to anyone who would take it, Louisville city and university officials revealed their poor understanding of just why Confederate monuments are problematic. In an effort to remove it from their own midst and make it another community's opportunity (or, alternately, another community's problem), they abandoned all duty to interpret the statue responsibly. All of these issues seem to indicate that though the practice may not work perfectly, contextualization may be a more responsible approach to dealing with monuments than simply relinquishing them to other groups who will interpret them in a manner that directly contradicts the spirit in which they were removed in the first place.

Louisville's experience also raises the question of whether alterations in the historical landscape will lead to real policy change that will lead to a better quality of life for African Americans. Events in the city cast this question in bold relief in 2020. In March of that year, police invaded Breonna Taylor's Louisville apartment during a botched drug raid, shooting her dead in her bed. In the aftermath of the shooting, angry but nonviolent protesters filled the city's streets night after night, demanding systemic change in policing and other areas of public policy. In response, police confronted them with batons and tear gas. During protests in June, National Guard members enlisted by Mayor Fischer fired upon and killed a local restaurant owner. Meanwhile, on June 12, 2020, forty-four miles down the Ohio River in Brandenburg, it was a very different scene as hundreds of people formed a human chain around their new Confederate monument to protect it from such protesters. Wielding guns, they responded to the cries of "Black Lives Matter" with vociferous assertions that "all lives matter," along with other, obscenity-laden replies.[15]

All of this made clear that removing the Confederate statue from Louisville has not resulted in better health or housing, or fairer law-enforcement measures for the city's African American citizens. It did not prevent Kentucky's African American attorney general (who earned both his undergraduate and law degrees from the University of Louisville, where he must have passed by the monument regularly) from effectively shielding the officers involved from direct legal charges in Taylor's death and refusing to release the grand jury testimony to the public. In the end, statues and monuments are inanimate memorials and representations of the values and meanings we see in them. They are both meaningful and meaningless at the same time. Just as the removal of monuments does not erase the past, neither does it disassemble the unjust systems that they represent. It is incumbent upon communities that choose to remove monuments to think about how they will be interpreted in their new settings, but, more importantly, to use their riddance as a starting point for conversations and actions that lead to real change. It is also imperative for historians to remind communities that "moving history" is often easier than dismantling mechanisms of white power in the present.[16]

Notes

1. For more on the monument's construction, see Joy M. Giguerre, "The (Im)Movable Monument: Identity, Space, and the Louisville Confederate Monument," *Public Historian* 41, no. 4 (November 2019): 63–69.

2. Anne E. Marshall, *Creating a Confederate Kentucky: The Lost Cause and Civil War Memory in a Border State* (Chapel Hill: University of North Carolina Press, 2010).

3. Ibid.
4. *Louisville Courier-Journal*, November 18, 1989, and December 9, 2002.
5. *Louisville Courier-Journal*, December 9, 2002.
6. See, for example, David B. Allison, ed., *Controversial Monuments and Memorials: A Guide for Community Leaders* (New York: Rowman & Littlefield, 2018); for examples of contextualization purpose and protocol, see the Atlanta History Center's process: https://www.atlantahistorycenter.com/assets/images/Pages-from-AHC_History_Matters_Fall_2019_Web.pdf, accessed August 12, 2020; Gary Gallagher, "In the Thickets of History and Memory: Using Charlottesville's Memorial Landscape," in Gary W. Gallagher and J. Matthew Gallman, eds., *Civil War Places: Seeing the Conflict through the Eyes of Its Leading Historians* (Chapel Hill: University of North Carolina Press, 2019), 117.
7. *Louisville Courier-Journal*, January 19, 2011, https://louisville.edu/freedompark, accessed July 29, 2020.
8. *Louisville Courier-Journal*, February 22, 2005, and March 7, 2005.
9. *Louisville Courier-Journal*, April 20, 2016.
10. *Louisville Courier-Journal*, April 30, 2016; May 3, 2016; and May 26, 2016.
11. *Louisville Courier-Journal*, November 16, 2016, and November 17, 2016.
12. PBS *NewsHour*, September 14, 2017, https://www.youtube.com/watch?time_continue=31&v=JpsKCULkwwI&feature=emb_logo (accessed July 29, 2020); Philip M. Bailey, "Monument Will Cost $400,000 to Move," *Louisville Courier-Journal*, November 17, 2016.
13. Joseph Gerth, "Brandenburg Celebrates Monument to Slavery," *Louisville Courier-Journal,* May 29, 2017; Jonah Engel Bromwich, "Confederate Monument Shunned by One Kentucky City, Is Welcomed in Another," *New York Times,* May 30, 2017.
14. Anne E. Marshall, "Historian on Ky. Confederacy: Time to Remove the Statues," *Lexington Herald-Leader*, August 16, 2017; Makeda Easter, "Why the National Trust for preservation changed its stance," https://www.latimes.com/entertainment-arts/story/2020-06-20/confederate-monuments-national-trust-historic-preservation (accessed October 10, 2020); "National Trust for Historic Preservation Statement on Confederate Monuments," https://savingplaces.org/press-center/media-resources/national-trust-statement-on-confederate-memorials#.X4IPPC2zonU, accessed October 10, 2020.
15. Bailey Loosemore, "Breonna Taylor Protests in Louisville: What Activists Want—and What they've Accomplished," https://www.usatoday.com/story/news/nation/2020/10/02/breonna-taylor-what-you-need-know-louisville-protests/5879867002/, accessed (October 10, 2020); Richard Opel Jr.,Derreck Bryson Taylor, Nicholas Bogel-Borroughs, "What to Know about Breonna Taylor's Death," https://www.nytimes.com/article/breonna-taylor-police.html (accessed October 10, 2020); Victoria Albert, "Kentucky Attorney General Files Motion to Keep Grand Juror from Speaking Publicly About Proceedings," https://www.cbsnews.com/news/breonna-taylor-grand-juror-daniel-cameron-motion-silent/, (accessed October 10, 2020); New York Times, July 16, 2020; Eddy Rodriquez, "Armed Civilians in Kentucky Guard Confederate Statue Against Black Lives Matter Protesters," https://www.newsweek.com/armed-civilians-kentucky-guard-confederate-statue-against-black-lives-matters-protesters-1510664, (accessed August 14, 2020).
16. Azi Paybarah, "Louisville May Be Latest City to Declare Racism a Public Health Crisis," https://www.nytimes.com/2020/07/30/us/louisville-racism-crisis.html, (accessed October 10, 2020).

14

Goodbye, Calhoun. What's Next?

The Future of Charleston's Commemorative Landscape

Adam H. Domby

The statue of John C. Calhoun was stubborn. At more than 100 feet tall, removing the statue at the top of Charleston's most famous monument was never going to be simple, but what was supposed to be done in the dark of night took 17 hours instead. Before the statue could be lowered to the ground around 5:00 P.M., a diamond bandsaw was required to cut the statue off the column it had rested on since 1896. As someone who studies Jim Crow–era monuments and teaches at the College of Charleston, I wanted to witness the removal. I wasn't sure what I would feel. So I went to Charleston's Marion Square three times during a 24-hour period—my need to sleep, to walk my dog, and to do a TV interview meant I feared I would miss its coming down. Each time, I masked up, put hand sanitizer in my pocket, and dodged unmasked bystanders (it was in the midst of the COVID-19 pandemic). By my third trip downtown, I had figured out that I needed to bring snacks, a folding chair, and sunscreen, as this was going to be a long haul. As I sat with a colleague (careful to stay more than six feet apart) waiting in anticipation in the heat of the Charleston summer, I felt bad for the workers who hadn't slept for hours and were working in the sun.

When the statue finally came down, people cheered. No last-minute injunction had stopped the removal. No violent protests had broken out. A few yelling pro-monument defenders had made a scene the night before, but they had been ushered away from the larger crowd that was anxiously awaiting the monument's removal.

As a group of my colleagues stood around after Calhoun was lowered down, it seemed like we had made progress. In talking to various Charlestonians, it was clear they seemed excited about the changes going on around us. But how much progress had we made? And how long had it taken? After all, the monument had been there for almost a century and a quarter. And it was five years after the white supremacist terrorist attack at Mother Emanuel AME that killed nine

Figure 1. Calhoun Monument, Marion Square, Charleston, S.C., taken between 1890 and 1901. (Library of Congress Prints and Photographs Division, Washington, D.C.)

parishioners—within sight of the monument. It took nationwide protests in the aftermath of the murder of George Floyd to finally force the city to take action.

Charleston's commemorative landscape is a microcosm of the rest of the country, capable of illustrating the interplay between monuments, historic preservation, and community values, revealing a few key elements in understanding the summer of 2020. First, monuments do not teach history—in fact they are frequently inaccurate—but instead are about controlling public space and celebrating values. Arguments that monuments teach history are rarely made in good faith and are not supported by the monuments themselves. Second, from their conception, Confederate (and Confederate-adjacent) monuments in Charleston have been tied to white supremacy and efforts to disenfranchise African Americans. The movement to preserve them remains tied to anti-democratic movements today. Third, because race, politics, and memory are intrinsically tied together in the South, these monuments have always been controversial and political.

Not everyone celebrated Calhoun's removal. Someone, presumably upset over the monument's removal, lowered the American flag in Marion Square to half-mast, where it rested for much of the day as the workers prepared to remove the statue. Eventually, it was raised fully. The irony of having the American flag at half-mast for the intellectual father of secession was not lost on me.

Charleston remains a city that struggles to address race, racism, and its history. Carriage and plantation tours still frequently leave out or downplay slavery—instead focusing on a romanticized and whitewashed moonlight-and-magnolias depiction of the antebellum South. And the city remains racially segregated with white and Black neighborhoods easily distinguishable on census maps showing where people live. The announcement a few months after the Calhoun statue was removed of a planned highway expansion through an historically Black neighborhood made clear that the old power imbalances remained very much alive in the low country—and calls to preserve history still meant preserving the history of white South Carolinians.

As I packed up my stuff to leave Marion Square after Calhoun was lowered down, I looked around and my eyes fell upon another monument in the park. Located under some trees on the eastern edge of the park, the short thirty-five-foot-tall obelisk seemed unimpressive sitting in the shadow of the huge Calhoun monument (even with the statuary removed). Often overlooked, the Wade Hampton monument was erected in 1912. I could not help but think, Was this second monument any less problematic or devoted to white supremacy than Calhoun's?

At the dedication of the Hampton obelisk, Samuel Chiles Mitchell, president of the University of South Carolina, gave the keynote address. He felt that the monument's location was fitting and that it would serve cadets of The Citadel—which then resided upon Marion Square—as a "source of inspiration." But what did he think the monument would inspire the cadets to do? Hampton, Mitchell asserted, was worthy of remembrance not only for his military service to the Confederacy but also for his "civic" and "personal" attributes. Indeed, Mitchell wanted students to know that Hampton was "as great and noble in peace as in time of war." One might have expected he was focused on Hampton's twelve years as a senator, but instead, Mitchell claimed that "Hampton's character was shown in his leadership of his people in 1876 when he redeemed the State from the rule of the radicals and scalawags. He showed himself a great pacificator as he [had been] a military leader, and like Robert E. Lee, Hampton showed that he could lead his people in peace as in war."[1] Here was the key accomplishment that Mitchell felt students should know about: Hampton's success in winning the 1876 gubernatorial election was more important than his time as actual governor.

And what had that 1876 campaign looked like? A campaign of terror. Hampton won the governorship through violence, voter suppression, cheating, and appeals to white supremacy. Edgefield County had more than 2,000 more votes counted than there were eligible voters in the county. Acts of violence included the Hamburg Massacre, wherein six Black militiamen were killed by red-shirted rifle clubs.[2] The audience in Marion Square understood why Hampton was being celebrated—an undemocratic victory, the return of white southerners to power, and the subsequent disenfranchisements of Black South Carolinians. Like so many monuments of the era, this was a monument as much to the overturn of Reconstruction as it was to any Confederate veteran.

Ironically enough, the monument isn't even historically accurate in its short inscription, which notes it was erected in 1911. It wasn't. While the United Daughters of the Confederacy (UDC) had raised the funds for the monument, they had trouble getting approval for its erection. After rejecting a proposal to locate the monument at White Point Gardens, city officials also rejected proposals to locate the monument in Hampton Park as the cheap monument was deemed not "good enough" for such a prominent location.[3] Charleston's African Americans who opposed Confederate monuments' being erected were not alone in this case; some Confederate veterans opposed the Hampton monument, deeming the $2,000 in funds "too small for a fitting monument."[4] The delays in finding a location willing to allow the UDC to put the monument up meant it wasn't erected and dedicated until 1912. Additionally, the inscription claims that Hampton was "Governor of South Carolina / 1876–1878." In point of fact, he resigned as governor to take his US Senate seat in 1879, not 1878. While these are minor errors, advocates claiming that removing markers would erase history rarely call for corrections because monuments are not about teaching accurate history but about controlling public space.

Leaving Marion Square, I couldn't help wondering which Charleston monument would be the next to go. Would the next removal be by the city authorities or by protesters? South Carolina's Heritage Protection Act is a strange law that takes power out of communities' hands and by design provides no legal recourse for those seeking to remove a Confederate monument. The law forbids the removal of any Confederate monument from public property without the state legislature's approval.

These heritage laws are part of the fundamentally anti-democratic agenda of the modern Republican Party, which acknowledges that in an open democratic system they would lose. Not only does the law take decision making away from local communities, but legislators fearing the law might be modified in the future included a unique requirement of questionable legality mandating that two-thirds of the state legislature were needed to amend the law. It fits alongside voter ID laws, gerrymandering, felony disenfranchisement, the closure of polling places, and the undermining of the Post Office as policies that demonstrate Republican fears of mass participation in the democratic process.

The problem is that if all legal recourse to remedy a problem is removed, people will turn to extralegal solutions. When observers complain that protesters should seek to remove a monument in the "legal" way, they ignore the fact that in many states, conservative legislatures did everything in their power to assure that no legal way existed.

Ironically, laws meant to protect monuments are leading to their destruction. In neighboring North Carolina, the Heritage Protection Act, which bans the removal of most Confederate monuments, left a loophole for when a monument "poses a threat to public safety because of an unsafe or dangerous condition." Thus, once protesters pull down or damage a monument, creating a "dangerous condition," officials can remove it.[5] In the end, a law meant to protect monuments leads to their being intentionally damaged, as the presence of damage is the quickest way to provide a legal means to remove them.

The South Carolina law left loopholes for the removal of Calhoun because the statue was owned by the city but situated on private property—thus, the city could choose to remove it, but it wasn't protected by the law that protects monuments on public property. Additionally, the Calhoun statue, not being a war monument, was excluded from being protected by the law. Other monuments in Charleston, however, will be harder to remove legally.

So as I walked to my car, I wondered what would be next. Would a city challenge the constitutionality of the Heritage Act? Would protesters topple the Defenders of Charleston monument into the harbor? Or would students demand the removal of the College of Charleston's monuments at Fort Johnson in James Island? As a faculty member at the College of Charleston, I was troubled by the continued presence of this monument. While UNC has removed its Confederate monument—as a result of protesters' insisting on its removal—and the University of Alabama has now removed its, many people at the College of Charleston seem unaware they even have a Confederate monument on campus.

The College of Charleston's overlooked monument makes clear that these monuments were not intended to teach accurate history when they were erected.

Located at the college's marine lab, a Confederate monument claims to mark where the first shot of the Civil War was fired, although befitting a Charleston monument it isn't placed accurately. Even as the monument was being prepared for dedication on James Island, Elmer Puryear, a College of Charleston history professor, and as a fellow UNC alumnus my forerunner in many ways, admitted that he was not sure where the shot was actually fired from. Indeed, depending on how one reads the evidence, the monument should have been placed 400 feet away from its present location or potentially at a location now underwater. That wasn't the only historically questionable aspect of the monument. In the lead-up to the dedication, press reports noted that controversy remained as to whether George S. James really deserved the credit for firing the first shot, as the monument proclaimed he had.[6] And once again, as with the Hampton obelisk, the monument's dedication date is incorrectly listed on the James Island monument. The dedication occurred a day later than planned because of bad weather—including a tornado that destroyed four houses—but by then "Dedicated April 12, 1961" was already carved into stone.[7] None of this mattered because the monument was intended not to teach history but to celebrate the present.

At the dedication, Senator T. Allen Legare explained what he wanted "future generations" to take in when they "pause to read the words inscribed on" the marker; he declared, "[T]hey will know that on this spot our then divided people began the laborious process that gave birth to the greatest nation on earth," as if the very Confederates being commemorated for starting a war that divided the nation had fought for and not against the United States. His argument that the dedication ceremonies would "draw the healing curtain of time over the wounds" ignored the very real racial divisions playing out across the country at the very moment—or perhaps he just discounted their importance when considering what wounds mattered to him. Indeed, the US Civil War Centennial Commission had made national news a month earlier when the sole Black member of the commission was refused a room at the Frances Marion Hotel in downtown Charleston.[8] To Legare, it was the reconciling of northern and southern whites that mattered, a reunion premised on African Americans' losing the gains of Reconstruction. For those celebrating the Confederacy, the racial inequality still present 100 years after the war was a feature, not a bug. Thus a monument mismarking where South Carolinians started the Civil War presents both an inaccurate and a racist narrative of the past despite its being on a college campus—an institution devoted to education.[9]

While in 2020 conservative politicians complained that historians are rewriting history because of politics, this is nothing new. History and monuments have always been political. Indeed, before the dedication of the Fort Johnson Monument in 1961, Professor Puryear refused to be drawn into any historical debate about the accuracy of the monument's meaning, as a reporter noted that "he doesn't want to get mixed up in local history, which is the equivalent of local politics elsewhere."[10] Indeed, the monument was political and part of a second wave of monuments aimed at celebrating white supremacy. The first were erected during the Jim Crow era and served to celebrate the success of overturning Reconstruction.[11] The second wave of monuments were put up in the midst of the civil rights movement as the college resisted integration. The college would not begin to desegregate for another six years. Just as in 1961, decisions about monuments remain political, but perhaps removing the monument could also be historical—making a statement about the college's values and its history.

What does the future hold for Charleston? Will the city see more monuments or fewer? Charleston's commemorative landscape remains dominated by white men with the notable exception of the Denmark Vesey sculpture. Proposals to erect a monument to the United States Colored Troops on the Battery face political and design challenges. How does a monument to Black troops made up of men who escaped slavery and then fought to end the institution square with a narrative of history that glorifies the men who fought to keep them enslaved? How would the monument to the Confederate defenders of Charleston Harbor interact with this new proposed monument? This is not a battlefield marking where troops fought; no guns were fired in anger from the Battery during the war. Would one monument be larger than the other? If so, what would that imply about its relative importance? How would visitors interpret a commemorative landscape that insists both sides are worthy of celebration for what they fought for? Compromise between two narratives may not be an option when the two narratives are fundamentally opposed to each other. Even if politically possible, it certainly isn't a way to reach an accurate historical understanding.

Ultimately, changing our commemorative landscape isn't just about creating a more accurate history, although it can potentially do that. Nor does it signify tokenism or just a meaningless symbolic shift—although if Charlestonians are not careful and think the removal of Calhoun was the ends and not the means it could become that. It is a starting point that allows the citizens of Charleston to start having honest conversations, telling accurate histories of the underlying issues in the present. So long as a large number of Americans can look at the history of the United States and not see that history helps explain racial disparities, they can continue to believe that racism is a problem of the heart and not of societal structures. A more accurate understanding of the past can help Americans start having honest discussions about racial disparities in income, health, life expectancy, wealth, home ownership, arrest and imprisonment, and treatment by others. History helps explain why the lived experience of some Americans today is so different from that of others—even if they are walking down the same streets of Charleston.

Sadly, even some of those Charlestonians who have supported moving monuments of Confederates are not willing to keep working at addressing inequality in society. Nancy Mace, congresswoman for much of the city, was willing to remove problematic statues from the US Capitol in July 2021 but that same month attacked the supposed teaching of critical race theory in South Carolina elementary schools. It seems that misrepresentations are still being used to uphold oppressive systems in society.[12]

About two months after the Calhoun statue was removed, phase two of removal occurred. The column that Calhoun stood upon was brought down much more quickly; a chain was attached to a backhoe which then backed up. It came down in all of twenty-two seconds.[13] The third phase, removal of the base, took much longer. Brick-by-brick the base was taken apart as workers sought a "time capsule" in it. Not until early 2021 was the removal of the base finished, with little fanfare. Perhaps the fits and spurts of removal are an appropriate symbol of the work Charleston still has ahead if the city and its inhabitants intend to address race, racism, and the city's history.

Notes

1. "Shaft of Granite in Hero's Memory," *Charleston Evening Post*, March 29, 1912, 7.
2. Ronald F. King, "Counting the Votes: South Carolina's Stolen Election of 1876," *The Journal of Interdisciplinary History* 32, no. 2 (2001): 169–91; for more on this election, see Cappy Yarbrough, "'The Mark They Had in Sight': Black Women, Suffrage, and Politics in Reconstruction South Carolina" (Master's Thesis, College of Charleston, 2020), 51, 62, 64, 77–78; Mark Wahlgren Summers, *The Ordeal of the Reunion: A New History of Reconstruction* (UNC Press, 2014), 366–67.
3. "Hampton Shaft to Be Unveiled," *Charleston Evening Post*, March 26, 1912, 11; "Hampton Statue to Be Unveiled," *Charleston Evening Post*, March 13, 1912, 8.
4. "Veterans Enjoy Annual Meeting," *Charleston Evening Post*, April 22, 1911, 2, 9.
5. Protection of monuments, memorials, and works of art, G.S. § 100–2.1 accessible at https://www.ncleg.gov/EnactedLegislation/Statutes/HTML/BySection/Chapter_100/GS_100-2.1.html.
6. Tom Henshaw, "Who Fired First Shot Still Highly Controversial," *Charleston News and Courier*, April 9, 1961, 3-C. For more on the layout of the fort, see Michael B. Trinkley, Natalie P. Adams, and Debi Hacker, *The Property Nobody Wanted: Archaeological and*

Historical Investigations at Fort Johnson, S.C. (Columbia, SC: Chicora Foundation, Inc., June 1994), 4, 52, 70–71, 115.

7. "Dedication Today at Fort Johnson," *Charleston News and Courier,* April 13, 1961, 8–B; "Small, Vicious Tornado Left This Sort of Damage in Its Path," *Charleston News and Courier,* April 13, 1961, 8-B; John H. Moye, "Site of War's First Shot Is Marked by Monument," *Charleston News and Courier,* April 14, 1961, 1-A, 2-A.

8. For more on the centennial, see Robert J. Cook, *Troubled Commemoration: The American Civil War Centennial, 1961–1965* (Baton Rouge: LSU Press, 2007), esp. 88–115.

9. John H. Moye, "Site of War's First Shot Is Marked by Monument," *Charleston News and Courier,* April 14, 1961, 1-A, 2-A.

10. Tom Henshaw, "Attack on Ft. Sumter," *Richmond Times-Dispatch,* April 9, 1961, F-1.

11. For more on this first wave of monuments, see Adam H. Domby, *The False Cause: Fraud, Fabrication, and White Supremacy in Confederate Memory* (Charlottesville: University of Virginia Press, 2020), esp. 21–23.

12. Nancy Mace, "Mace: About those statues in the US Capitol," *Charleston Post and Courier,* July 20, 2021, https://www.postandcourier.com/opinion/commentary/mace-about-those-statues-in-the-us-capitol/article_0df002e6-e5b9-11eb-b716-7f1591eb1c75.html; "Rep. Mace: 'Marxist ideology' should not be taught in American schools," *Fox News,* July 8, 2021, https://www.foxnews.com/media/rep-mace-marxist-ideology-should-not-be-taught.

13. Mikaela Porter, "In 21 seconds, granite column that held John C. Calhoun above Charleston tumbled to ground," *Charleston Post and Courier,* August 26, 2020, https://www.postandcourier.com/news/in-21-seconds-granite-column-that-held-john-c-calhoun-above-charleston-tumbled-to-ground/article_ea5a9238-e712-11ea-a826-03d4603d02cf.html.

15

"Back at Bragg"

Civil War Memory and the US Army

Beau Cleland

Polk. Bragg. Benning. Hood. For historians of the American Civil War, these names immediately bring to mind Confederate general officers with a decidedly mixed battlefield record. For many present-day soldiers, these names are shorthand for installations and the institutional culture and memory that they and their associated garrison units have developed over the course of many decades. An infantry soldier who hears the name Benning almost certainly associates it with Sand Hill drill sergeants, heat, sweat, and earning their coveted blue cord signifying a qualified infantryman. Others will hear the name and think of airborne school, Ranger school, the Third Infantry Division, 3rd Ranger Battalion, and the seedy strip of Victory Drive. The Civil War probably never crosses their minds. I personally passed through Officer Candidate School at Fort Benning without an inkling that Henry Benning was a Confederate general or why that particular patch of Georgia pines and red dirt bore his name. I just wanted to get the hell out of there and on to my next duty station.

I should not have been in such a hurry. The Army, a nurturing institution, made sure I ended up at what many, me included, regard as the least-desirable post in the Army: Fort Polk, Louisiana. Fort Polk is in far western Louisiana, about halfway up the state and a relatively short drive from the Texas border. I may not have known who Henry Benning was while in Columbus, but I *had* heard of Leonidas Polk, the Episcopal bishop of Louisiana who became a Confederate general. I finally bothered to notice that I had spent a good chunk of my time in the Army at places named for people who tried to kill men in the same uniform—the same regiment even, by lineage—as mine.[1] This bothered me. I was not comforted by the fact that nearly everyone else seemed either not to notice it, or to feel too powerless to make a fuss about something they could not change. I brought the subject up once while waiting for a battalion training meeting to begin, casually remarking that I did not think we should name bases and other things after people who fought against the US Army. A few other officers expressed agreement. My battalion commander told me, in the florid language of

Figure 1. Lieutenant-General Leonidas Polk. A graduate of the United States Military Academy at West Point, Polk left the US Army to become an Episcopal clergyman. He was made bishop of Louisiana in 1841, a year after the census reported him as having more than 100 slaves. By the 1850s he owned several hundred slaves. In the spring of 1861 he accepted a commission in the Confederate Army to fight against the United States.

soldiers, that the names celebrated our military heritage and that I should refrain from opening my mouth about it again. I complied, as a battalion commander in a line unit is akin to God. My crusade against the Lost Cause memory of the Civil War was over for the sake of good order and discipline.

This incident has nagged at me ever since. My commander was, and is, a good and conscientious man. He was careful with our lives, and I admire his conduct toward the people of Iraq during our deployment there—he went out on a limb to try to protect them from more bloodthirsty elements of our own forces. His defense of Polk, Bragg, Benning, and other Confederate generals seemed wildly incongruous to me. He was not from the South. He was not commissioned

Figure 2. The author (*second from left*) and the other officers of B Co., 2nd Bn., 4th Infantry Regiment, 4th Brigade, 10th Mountain Division at the Shugart-Gordon training site, Ft. Polk, Lousiana, in 2005. (The George Washington Presidential Library at Mount Vernon.)

through the Citadel or similar institutions. He grew up in New Jersey and attended West Point. So why did he care enough about these names to rebuke me over a casual remark? The answer, I suspect, lies in the peculiar way the Army has embraced elements of the Lost Cause and Civil War memory over the preceding century—by emphasizing Confederate military valor as part of the Army's own heritage and ignoring the causes and politics of the war and its aftermath.[2] This seeping infiltration of Lost Cause symbolism goes far beyond installation names—even though they have been changed, it will take much more to shake loose Confederate veneration in the institutional memory and culture of the Army.

This question once again reared its head almost as a precursor to the events of the summer of 2020, when nationwide protests erupted against police brutality and racial injustice after the police murder of George Floyd in Minneapolis. Faced with increasing evidence of white supremacism in the ranks, in February 2020 the US Marine Corps banned the display of Confederate flags and similar paraphernalia.³ The other services immediately faced pressure to follow suit, and during the summer the US Department of Defense effectively banned them in the midst of the nationwide protests against police brutality and racism.⁴ Public attention also turned, not for the first time, to the fact that some of the largest and most prominent installations of the US Army were, in a way, Confederate monuments—what I have termed the Lost Cause installations. Eight Regular Army posts in the South bore Confederate names in 2020: Forts Polk, Benning, Bragg, Gordon, Lee, Hood, A. P. Hill, and Rucker, along with two major National Guard facilities, Fort Pickett and Camp Beauregard. Even more existed as temporary facilities during the mobilizations for the world wars, such as Camp Forrest, Tennessee, but did not persist after demobilization.⁵ These installations received their Confederate names at the apex of the reconciliationist era of Civil War memory, as the Army considered (but rarely consulted) local interests when choosing the names. This was not a politically neutral act, nor was the refusal in the decades to come to seriously consider renaming the posts, even as the racial and political fabric of the nation and the Army transformed around them. This is not the distant past, either: In 2017 the Army's own Center of Military History (CMH) conducted a study on the naming, and renaming, of these facilities but did not release it to the public, allegedly because the results were embarrassing. It came to light only as a reaction to a Freedom of Information Act request by journalists.⁶ Army historical studies are public domain and are virtually always released freely and immediately. Yet this one remained under wraps until October 2020, when the CMH quietly published it on its website.⁷ The Lost Cause installations got their names because the Army accepted Jim Crow. They have kept them because the institutional culture of the Army built its own associations around and on top of the original Confederate meanings. This has made it challenging to separate the two and made the effort to rename the posts fraught with the accumulated baggage of a century of history and memory, even though decades of Army doctrine and policy forswear racism and promote diversity.⁸

The Lost Cause installations all got their names during the height of the Jim Crow era, between roughly 1916 and 1942. The world wars and the rapid expansion of the Army required numerous new training facilities, and sites in the South were popular because the climate was more hospitable for year-round training. The Army's policy was to name the new camps and bases after distinguished individuals associated with either the base's region or the home regions of the soldiers assigned to train there.⁹ It was the Army itself, not local advocacy groups or politicians, that chose the names in most cases, although Army officers did entertain outside requests for those names.¹⁰ Of posts established during World

War I, only for Fort Benning is there evidence that an outside group, in this case the Columbus, Georgia, chapter of the United Daughters of the Confederacy, requested a Confederate name.[11] During World War II the Army abandoned an effort to name the new camp near Blackstone, Virginia, after Judge Roger A. Pryor on the opposition of Douglas Southall Freeman, and instead named it for Confederate General George Pickett, of Pickett's Charge notoriety.[12] The ready acquiescence of the Army in these instances suggests that *if* other locations had requested the base be named after their favorite local Confederate, there was a high likelihood of success. Nevertheless, the Army's leaders granted most of the Lost Cause installations their names with no outside prodding—the rebellion was forgotten in favor of reconciliation.

The presence of Confederate names and iconography in the military is not limited to base names. Everything from a West Point barracks and a Naval Academy hall, to armored vehicles and warships, to operational terms and graphics, has borne Confederate appellations.[13] I frequently saw Confederate names mixed in with others for things like phase lines, route names, and other minute features of battle planning that civilians never see and that are generally not preserved permanently. A number of National Guard units have Confederate battle streamers on their battalion or regimental colors as well—an honor that directly celebrates fighting the US Army.[14] These streamers, which commemorate a unit's participation in a prominent battle or campaign, are a point of pride within units, but also a prominent piece of their collective identity specifically governed by the Army. The Army's Institute of Heraldry and the CMH have to approve of their display—in other words, their existence means that the US Army itself has specifically approved of the display of items celebrating its own defeats and the deaths of its soldiers.[15] The display of these streamers, the acknowledgment of Confederate Army "lineage" in active unit histories, and the prevalence of Confederate iconography in places large and small all point to the broad acceptance within the Army's institutions of a stripped-down version of the Lost Cause that celebrated and studied Confederate military prowess but ignored the Confederacy itself.[16]

The evolution of Robert E. Lee's commemoration at West Point, where he was a cadet and later Superintendent, is a prime example of the changing style of Confederate memory in the Army. Lee was ignored in the Rebellion's aftermath but slowly returned to West Point veneration alongside the early-twentieth-century sectional reconciliation and was then aggressively promoted amid the battle for Black civil rights. West Point's current Lee Barracks, a cadet residence hall, was not named until 1970.[17] The persistence and ubiquity of Lee and his lieutenants demonstrate the peculiar version of the Lost Cause that has survived in the Army, one that has slowly lost much of its direct connection to the Confederacy itself. This anodyne version, in which Confederate officers are simply Americans with a "significant place in our military history," lets those who wish to glorify the Confederacy do so, while providing a convenient excuse for Army leaders' inaction.[18] General Maxwell Taylor, celebrated commander of the 101st Airborne Division during World War II, said in a speech dedicating a massive portrait of Lee (wearing his Confederate uniform) at the West Point sesquicentennial in 1952 that Confederates who had attended West Point "were intrepid, steadfast, honorable soldiers who brought world renown to American arms on many a hard-fought field of war. It is proper for West Point to take pride, not of necessity in the rightness of its Confederate graduates, but in their uprightness." To Taylor, Lee was "an immortal battle leader of the Confederacy, whose deeds will stir men's souls" and that "West Point has no right" to "[sit] in judgment upon General Lee's political opinions."[19] Lee returned to pride of place at West Point because the Army deliberately ignored those opinions in favor of stirring (white) souls. Little wonder, then, that names like Fort Bragg continued to exist.

If Confederate names and other iconography have been so prevalent in the modern Army, one could be forgiven for assuming there were regulatory barriers preventing them from being stamped out. This was not the case. One Confederate base *was* renamed during World War II: Camp Toombs, Georgia, but not because of Robert Toombs's Confederate service. Army leaders considered the name too similar to "tombs" and thus too macabre for a dangerous paratrooper-training facility. It was renamed Camp Toccoa, after the nearby town.[20] Amidst a renewed postwar push for integration and Black civil rights, the Army quickly realized that the Lost Cause installations held the potential for controversy and moved to mute it. The first formal regulations on memorialization made it more or less impossible for any future installations to be named for Confederates, but the Army made no attempt to rename the existing posts.[21] According to the current rules, the Assistant Secretary of the Army for Manpower and Reserve Affairs has the power to approve proposals to name, and rename, installations with very few stipulations, although renaming facilities is "strongly discouraged, and seldom appropriate."[22] This language is tailor-made to provide an easy excuse to reject proposals to rename Lost Cause installations, if Army leadership is reluctant to do so. Nothing prevented that from happening but the internal culture of the Army itself.

That culture has built its own body of references around post names that live largely independent of their Confederate origins. My fellow officers and I often threw around the mocking phrase "back at Bragg" about soldiers and officers who had come to our post from Fort Bragg, home of most of the Army's airborne and special operations units, who had a reputation for comparing everything around them unfavorably to conditions there. Other soldiers—mostly officers or senior enlisted men—I asked about the name Bragg almost universally responded with something related to the post itself or the units stationed there; the Confederate association was usually an afterthought or did not come up at all. One of my former commanders simply replied "Airborne!" to my query. These place names have sunk so deep into Army life that they are used reflexively and with little or no understanding by most of the provenance of those names and how they came to label these installations, and that this simultaneous familiarity and lack of awareness helps explain the long life and resistance to change of these base names, and the enduring pervasiveness of Confederate names and symbols in the Army.

Despite the events of the summer of 2020, there is reason to be skeptical that the Lost Cause will be ousted from the Army anytime soon. The Army's long-term institutional comfort with Confederate iconography and heritage, along with its implicit conservatism, has long made it unlikely to move without a push from above. That said, there is hope: The current generation of officers and soldiers is more openly supportive of renaming these bases, and skeptical of the Confederate connection in general.[23] Nothing in the regulations prohibits renaming installations—it simply requires the will to do so, and Congress has forced the Army's hand—provisions in the 2021 Department of Defense Appropriations Bill requires the Lost Cause installations be renamed, and a commission to rename them has recently released its report, which includes a recommendation to rename Fort Polk after US Army Sergeant William Henry Johnson, who earned the Medal of Honor and French Croix de Guerre for heroism in the Argonne Forest in 1918.[24] The vice-chair of that commission, retired Brigadier General Ty Seidule, told me recently that his new career is "killing dead Confederates." This veteran is entirely in sympathy with General Seidule's ambition to root out the Lost Cause, and I sincerely hope the Army will take this opportunity to honor those who stayed true to their oaths and live up to its self-image as a place where diversity is a strength and anyone can succeed on their own merits. Renaming posts will not excise the Lost Cause from the Army, but it's a good start. I hope future soldiers get to mockingly say, "back at Johnson" to their peers.

Notes

1. I served for a portion of my time at Polk in the 2nd Battalion, 4th Infantry Regiment, although I was in the 5th Battalion, 25th Field Artillery, at the time of this incident. The 4th Regiment fought as Regulars in the Civil War in the Virginia theater.

2. The Army's Gettysburg Staff Ride materials, for example, do not mention slavery at all, except in the brief biography of Lincoln. William Arthur and Ted Ballard, "Gettysburg Staff Ride: Briefing Book," unpublished manuscript, U.S. Army Center of Military History, Washington, D.C. Newer materials do tend to place greater emphasis on considerations beyond the immediate battlefield.

3. Jeff Schogol, "Marine Commandant Banishes Confederate Symbols from All Corps Installations," *Task & Purpose*, February 26, 2020, https://taskandpurpose.com/news/marine-corps-bans-confederate-symbols.

4. Mark Esper, Memorandum on Public Display or Depiction of Flags in the Department of Defense, July, 16, 2020, https://news.usni.org/2020/07/17/secdef-esper-memo-on-displaying-flags-on-u-s-bases (accessed October 28, 2020).

5. Brig. Gen. Joseph E. Kuhn, Memorandum for the Chief of Staff, with enclosure, 16 July 1917, Army Posts Documents, U.S. Army Center of Military History, https://history.army.mil/faq/army-posts-documents/005b-Names_for_cantonments_and_posts_with-policy_statement_1917_(memo_retyped).pdf (accessed October 26, 2020). Collection referred to hereinafter as Army Post Documents (APD).

6. Paul Szoldra, "The secret history of Confederate post names the Army never wanted you to see," *Task and Purpose*, October 14, 2020, https://taskandpurpose.com/news/army-confederate-post-study (accessed October 24, 2020).

7. "Naming of U.S. Army Posts," United States Army Center of Military History, https://history.army.mil/faq/naming-of-us-army-posts.htm (accessed October 26, 2020).

8. Department of the Army, "Diversity, Equity, and Inclusion Annex," in *Army People Strategy*, https://www.army.mil/e2/downloads/rv7/the_army_people_strategy_diversity_equity_and_inclusion_annex_2020_09_01_signed_final.pdf (accessed October 24, 2020).

9. Many of these camps hosted National Guard units that came from just one or two states, and the policy focused on choosing Union officers for those from northern states, and Confederate officers for those from southern states. The practice changed during World War II to consider only locally associated figures, with no special reservations for Confederates. See U.S. Army Center of Military History, "Naming of U.S. Army Posts," and associated documents, https://history.army.mil/faq/naming-of-us-army-posts.htm#Section02 (accessed October 25, 2020).

10. For one example, the widow of Confederate Gen. James Longstreet wrote, asking that a facility be named after her late husband, and Secretary of War Henry L. Stimson promised it was under consideration. Henry L. Stimson to Helen Dortch Longstreet, July 26, 1941, APD, https://history.army.mil/faq/army-posts-documents/295-Camp_Toombs_corresp_re_possible_renaming_1941-1942.pdf (accessed October 29, 2020).

11. Brig. Gen. Little Brown, Memorandum for the Chief of Staff, August 26, 1916, APD, https://history.army.mil/faq/army-posts-documents/035-Camp_Benning_1918.pdf (accessed October 28, 2020).

12. John W. Martyn to Rep. P. H. Drewry, January 27, 1942; Gen. George C. Marshall to D. S. Freeman, January 13, 1942, APD, https://history.army.mil/faq/army-posts-documents/270-Camp_Pickett_corresp_1942.pdf (accessed October 29, 2020).

Freeman was a staunch promoter of the Lost Cause and a biographer of Lee and his lieutenants.

13. Robert S. Cameron, *Mobility, Shock, and Firepower: The Emergence of the U.S. Army's Armor Branch, 1917–1945* (Washington: United States Army Center of Military History, 2008), 390–91.

14. Merle T. Cole, "Confederate Service Campaign Streamers," *Military Collector and Historian* 69 (Winter 2017): 371–74. Several southern university ROTC programs also carry Confederate battle streamers on their colors.

15. See, for example, Army Regulation 840-10, Heraldic Activities: Flags, Guidons, Streamers, Tabards, and Automobile and Aircraft Plates, June 15, 2017, section 9-11, 132. This regulation authorizes Confederate battle streamers and dictates their appearance, distinct from those for the US Army in the War of the Rebellion.

16. Cole, "Confederate Service Campaign Streamers," 371. An Army National Guard historian wrote that "the issue [of authorizing Confederate streamers] was never debated" within the War Department.

17. Jimmy Bryn and Gabe Royal, "What Should West Point Do About Its Robert E. Lee Problem?" Modern War Institute, https://mwi.usma.edu/west-point-robert-e-lee-problem/ (accessed June 22, 2020).

18. John Ismay, "The Army Was Open to Replacing Confederate Base Names. Then Trump Said No," *New York Times Magazine*, June 10, 2020, https://www.nytimes.com/2020/06/10/magazine/army-confederate-base-names.html (accessed October 25, 2020).

19. Eugene Jagust, ed., *The Sesquicentennial of the United States Military Academy; an Account of the Observance, January–June 1952* (Buffalo: Baker, Jones, Hausauer & Savage, Inc., 1952), 43.

20. Col. Emerick Kutschko to The Adjutant General, June 28, 1942, with enclosures, APD, https://history.army.mil/faq/army-posts-documents/295-Camp_Toombs_corresp_re_possible_renaming_1941-1942.pdf (accessed October 29, 2020).

21. Michael A. Hill, "A Question of Treason? Confederate Generals and U.S. Army Post Names" (Master's thesis, Adams State University, 2013), 81. Hill's thesis is the only at-length scholarly treatment of the issue at present.

22. Department of the Army, Army Regulation 1-33, The Army Memorial Program, 25 October 2018, section 2, paragraph 1–7, 1, and section 5, paragraph 2–13, 8. Hereinafter cited as AR 1–33, along with the effective date of that version of the regulation.

23. Leo Shane III, "Nearly Half of Troops Polled Support Changing Names of Bases Honoring Confederate Leaders," *Military Times*, September 3, 2020, https://www.militarytimes.com/news/pentagon-congress/2020/09/03/nearly-half-of-troops-polled-support-changing-names-of-bases-honoring-confederate-leaders/.

24. Joe Gould, "Defense authorization bill delayed until after election," *Defense News*, 9 September 2020, https://www.defensenews.com/congress/2020/09/09/no-defense-authorization-bill-before-election-says-thornberry/ (accessed October 24, 2020); The Naming Commission, "Final Report to Congress, Part 1: United States Army Bases" (August 2020), https://www.thenamingcommission.gov/report, 60–66.

16

There's still no balm in Gilead

The Fatal Costs of Traumatic Memory

Scott Hancock

Vietnam killed my father. Not right away. Not for almost thirty years. Vietnam got him in the end, though.

It wasn't Vietnam's fault. It was truth's fault, or rather, my nation's failure, the United States of America's failure, to deal truthfully with the past. In some ways, I repeat that failure by writing "Vietnam." Since you're reading this book that deals with an American war, you likely knew, without a second thought, that "Vietnam" = Vietnam War, despite the brutal reality that, as Viet Thanh Nguyen points out, it could be called the American War, which is also inadequate because it ignores how this war, a war that the US Congress dumped a trillion of today's dollars into despite never "declaring" it war, a war that, if one wishes to soften what shouldn't be softened, you might describe as a "conflict" that "spilled" into other countries and decades, even though it was a war that killed up to 3 million people from Vietnam, Laos, and Cambodia and lasted at least into the 1980s. The 58,318 names on the Vietnam Veterans Memorial in Washington should not be forgotten. Neither should the millions of veterans and civilians throughout Southeast Asia. These are the realities that my nation too often fails to grapple truthfully with.[1]

My father, like me, like his nation, failed to deal fully with the horrifically violent parts of our past. His failure was by no means entirely, or even mostly, his fault. American society, along with financially strapped veterans' associations, then and now, struggles to help veterans deal effectively with post-traumatic stress disorders. And like those of many veterans, my father's personality, shaped as the son of a Depression-era single mother, lent itself to a certain oddly optimistic stoicism. You fulfill your obligations, work hard, don't complain, and keep moving forward; no point dwelling on what's happened. There's a great deal to admire in that. My father, maybe the quickest wit I ever knew, and my mother, also a veteran and the child of a Depression-era single mother, are the hardest-working people I've ever known. But, in the long run, I'm not sure that nose-to-the-grindstone stoicism was the tool he needed most. And nobody handed him any other tools. There's strong evidence that, during his third tour in the American Vietnam Cambodia Laos Southeast Asia War, as a US Army warrant officer in military intelligence, he saw and experienced some things that left him with severe trauma. Something changed for him and in him. But he never talked about it much.

The Hebrew Bible prophet Jeremiah asked, "Is there no balm in Gilead?" In Jeremiah's Israel, Gilead was known as a place of healing. My father needed a Gilead. Instead, unresolved trauma, complicated further by other things that dog-piled on his life over the twenty-nine years after he left Vietnam for the last time, killed him.

Today, the American Civil War keeps killing us. When I started writing this in August 2020, amid our latest sweltering summer of legitimate discontent, once again our national failure to truthfully face the memory and experience of what historians rarely label a race war was still helping to replicate and protect structures of inequity, injustice, and violence. Over the past century and a half, our national failure has helped kill far more than the 750,000 soldiers and sailors who died during four years of combat.[2] Now, as I continue to write since 2020, after we have grieved and protested for Breonna Taylor, Ahmaud Arbery, and George Floyd, as we have watched COVID-19 devastate Black and Brown communities, Daunte Wright has been shot dead in the Minneapolis area by police after being stopped for having an air freshener hanging from his window; Ma'khia Bryant, sixteen years old, has been killed in Columbus, Ohio, by a police officer the same afternoon that a jury declared George Floyd's killer guilty; two days after that, Andrew Brown, parked in his car in Elizabeth City, North Carolina, has been shot by police with his hands on the steering wheel, and then again in the back of the head as he attempted to flee for his life. Every month, maybe every week, I could keep adding to this paragraph as the death count of our national failure marches on.

In October 2000, I spoke briefly at my father's sparsely attended memorial service at Fort Huachuca, Arizona. A month earlier, I had flown from Alabama to spend a few days with him after his first stroke. He was lonely. It was painful to leave him. But I had to go back to work. He had been lonely for a long, long time, but only once, in a rare moment of vulnerability, had he talked about his loneliness. We got along well, talked on the phone monthly, though deep conversations were rare. I suspect this was true with all of his relationships. He did the best with what he knew. What he didn't know was how to heal. After returning from that last year-long tour in Vietnam, he found ways to dodge, though not escape, the demons chasing him. But life just got lonelier, until, just a few weeks after that first stroke, a second stroke finally let him escape.

As Viet Thanh Nguyen wrote, "All wars are fought twice, the first time on the battlefield, the second time in memory."[3] So far, my father and our nation have lost both times. One critically important difference is that when my father lost, the death toll was exactly 1. But as his nation keeps losing, the toll keeps mounting.

In the decades after the Civil War, white veterans, and many white civilians, had trouble coming to terms with the troubling reality that the cruel war had been triggered by Black people who, simply by being enslaved and by resisting enslavement, caused white southern leaders to quick-step their states out of the Union.[4] Their new government refused countenancing any notion of future Black freedom, much less equality, and instead, as Alexander Stephens, vice president of the Confederacy, precisely stated, founded a nation "upon exactly the opposite idea; its foundations are laid, its cornerstone rests upon the great truth, that the negro is not equal to the white man; that slavery—subordination to the superior race—is his natural and normal condition. . . . This, our new government, is the first in the history of the world based upon this great physical, philosophical, and moral truth."[5] Confederate apologists who still attempt to cast Stephens as an outlier are drowned out by declarations of secession and a plethora of other sources from the war that echo Stephens's emphatic proclamation.[6]

The Civil War was a race war. Not always a war between races, but always about two races. For most white southerners it was about whether southern states would keep another race enslaved. For the vast majority of both white southerners and northerners before, during, and after the war, the war was about maintaining whiteness and white supremacy.[7]

White supremacy was one thing nearly all white Americans on either side of the Mason-Dixon line never disagreed about. Historians' debates about the pace and ease of reconciliation, which involved settling supposedly deep disagreements between white northerners and southerners about their past, present, and future, presume fundamental disagreement.[8] But we should presume agreement: White supremacy was such a norm, such a given, that it was like the air that white Americans breathed. They usually didn't think about it consciously; they just did it. Preserving it was a universally accepted and agreed-upon reality. Despite the USCT, the foot soldiers of the largest Black rebellion in the world outside of Haiti, and the emancipation they helped secure, the war never truly threatened white supremacy. There were no competing sectional views about white supremacy. One historian, summing up historians' debates, wrote that reconciliation "enabled the triumph of white supremacy."⁹ But there was no enabling. White supremacy had been triumphant all along.

The Grand Army of the Republic may seem an exception. Its many integrated posts appear to have made little distinction between Black and white veterans. However, even at the peak of the GAR's substantial national political power, white vets who "passionately embraced the Memory of black freedom" did virtually nothing about the savaging of Black freedom and rights beyond GAR posts, despite their Black comrades and Black leaders like William H. Day explicitly calling out the Grand Army of the Republic to "make it practical before the world." What may have seemed to us like a contradiction in 2020 was no contradiction for those white vets, because maintaining the mission of white supremacy was never questioned. Integration inside the controlled environment of a GAR post could be protected without giving up one inch of white supremacy's territory everywhere else.¹⁰

For USCT vets like George Jay, whose family and neighbors said that "the army experience did something to his head," the grim realities of fighting for the "won cause" initiated a lifetime of untreated mental illness until he died in 1911.¹¹ I wonder how much Jay's suffering was compounded by the failure of his white comrades to admit or even recognize the cost whiteness extracted from African Americans. In this regard, the interests of his former comrades differed little from the interests of his former opponents.

I do not dismiss the crucial role of the Union Army in ending slavery. Nor am I minimizing the incredibly high human cost. When the Pennsylvania 90th Regiment Infantry dedicated its monument at the first Pennsylvania Day in September of 1888, Colonel A. J. Sellers recalled the trauma of war for the soldiers "who gave up the best period of their life . . . marched under blazing suns, slept upon the ground, breathed the miasma of the swamps, racked with fevers, endured the horrors of the prison-pen, and amidst shot, shell, and saber-thrust." His memorializing was not simply dramatic embellishment. Those memories of what they endured and whom they lost may have made him waver briefly, emotions momentarily choking his voice, before reminding his audience of why their suffering mattered: They endured to keep "their colors aloft to eventual triumph, which secured for the people of the Republic and their descendants civil and religious rights and business opportunities unsurpassed."¹²

I want to keep the humanity of these soldiers—as well as those who fought for the Confederacy—always in the forefront. I would want the same for my father, who was part of an army fighting in a war that I do not think was ultimately a war for freedom and democracy and instead abetted some of Southeast Asia's homicidal authoritarianism in the following years. I wonder if he ever came to that conclusion, especially during his last tour. After he passed, I learned that he had talked once about going into Cambodia to count bodies. He was probably one of the "combat advisors" Nixon sent in 1970, reprising his first tour in 1964 as, according to his wry description, a noncombatant advisor, when his advising consisted mainly of firing at North Vietnamese troops from a helicopter gunship. During this last tour, he could have counted the people killed in demonstrations against the US-backed ouster of Prince Sihanouk, or the many more Vietnamese subsequently killed by the US-backed Khmer Republic, or the 800 Vietnamese workers massacred by Cambodian troops, or Cambodian and Vietnamese refugees, fleeing violence that the United States helped foment, dying from starvation and lack of access to basic medical care, or some of the hundreds of thousands of people killed by "the most atrocious aerial campaign waged against a country in the history of modern warfare," or other dying and dead people who too often get obliterated yet again when Western scholars and pundits elide America's role in the Khmer Republic's banquet of death that preceded an even more horrific feasting under the Khmer Rouge. The latter is the kind of atrocity we could enthusiastically condemn, because the Vietnam War was supposedly over and America was out. Not our fault.[13]

My father did not describe Vietnam as a justifiable war. Nor did he criticize the United States' stated purpose. He simply did not talk about any of it much. He'd tell a funny story about how he got his Purple Heart. He didn't talk about his Bronze Star. If he had had assistance in working through these conflicting and complicated memories, maybe he'd be alive now to talk more. And perhaps if my country had worked through its conflicted and complicated past with race, slavery, and war, millions more people would have lived through the difficult century and a half after the Civil War.

It would be easy to just blame the Confederacy, since it fought an immoral and unjust war to maintain slavery. But there is plenty of blame to share in how we have collectively remembered, or disremembered, race, slavery, and war. One place and time where much of this came into focus was during the dedication of Union monuments in 1888 and 1889 at Gettysburg.

On the second Wednesday of September 1889, the second official Pennsylvania Day on the Gettysburg battlefield, the Pennsylvania 84th Regiment Infantry dedicated a monument. The 84th, having been assigned to guard supply trains to the south of Gettysburg, did not see combat during the battle. Nonetheless, the monument stands just a few dozen yards north of the Pennsylvania state monument, the largest monument on the battlefield. Seeming especially sensitive to

Figure 1. 84th Pennsylvania Regiment Infantry Memorial at Gettysburg National Military Park, with Pennsylvania State Monument in the background. (Photo by Patricia Hancock.)

justify the 84th's importance, Captain Thomas Merchant insisted that the war "was not a conflict forced merely for the perpetuation of slavery."[14] Merchant's speech blamed southern elites—without ever calling them slaveowners—for forcing "states into rebellion, against the will of their people." By contrast, the northern "patriotic men of our country" would have done almost anything to avoid war, including adding to the Constitution an "amendment that would have fastened slavery upon the country forever."[15] That seems an implicit contradiction with his statement that the South did not secede over slavery. But Merchant was actually being consistent: Arguing that the North was willing to protect slavery was arguing that the war wasn't really about slavery.

Merchant's justification of the war distanced blackness. Most Union and Confederate veterans did likewise. Speeches mentioning slavery often moved past it as quickly as possible. During the previous year's dedication ceremonies, Colonel Sellers, acknowledging that slavery might still exist had the Union lost, skipped forward, emphasizing unity as "the blue and gray would merge wholly into the red, white and blue" and that "the Confederate soldier believed equally with us that he was fighting for the right."[16] Divisiveness, not slavery, was the primary villain. The lack of specification is significant, as it allowed audiences to detach the very real suffering of soldiers and civilians from the cause of the war: the presence of Black people as slaves.

Detaching suffering from anything or anybody Black avoided the risk of translating four years of white suffering, and the twenty-six years of recovering from that suffering, into a recognition of how the nation, including most white Union veterans, had abandoned the very people without whom there would have been no war. Instead, veterans like Colonel Sellers could reconstruct Reconstruction by emphasizing how the Confederacy's loss had been translated into the South's gain: "[T]he outgrowth of their failure has been the magnificent development of the South, and the hills and mountains are yielding up their treasures, to the founding and building of new Birminghams and Sheffields."[17] The suffering was worth it, but only if what caused the war was stifled. The sporadic mention of slavery was either cast against the purpose of the war or buried in the context of the good the war had wrought. And that good was certainly not racial equality.

Black southerners as fellow citizens in the 1880s vanish in battlefield memorialization. Sellers, like white GAR members, was likely aware of the processes of disenfranchisement and racial terrorism that were well under way in the South. Gettysburg residents almost certainly were. Local newspapers reported with some regularity on the suppression of the Black vote in the South, along with occasional references to the violence of white southerners' racial terrorism against African Americans. A few months before Sellers's speech, the *Gettysburg Star and Sentinel*'s front page summed up a recent Frederick Douglass speech in Connecticut, criticizing how "whites did not consider it necessary to keep faith with the poor, defenceless and powerless negro laborers," who had been "despoiled of all their political rights guaranteed by the blood of the Union armies and the Constitutional Amendments."[18] The very next day, though, the ugly past and bitter present dissipated during the 82nd Regiment's monument dedication. Speakers told attendees that even though "the Union was attacked during the late war on the pretext of the preservation of slavery," the "principle for which you fought was the 'Union of the States,'" and "the achievements of the soldiers of both armies . . . are the common heritage and glory of all the people of all sections of the country." Unaware of or ignoring Douglass's report, Colonel Wetherhill declared that "the men of the North fought for the Union, not for our section alone, but that its benefits and blessings should belong to and be the heritage of the whole country, South and North, as well for those who fought against it; and that the surrender at Appomattox established popular liberty for the whole country, as well for them as for us."[19] Hopefully a few listeners—probably all white—who had read Frederick Douglass's speech realized this most certainly did not apply to their fellow Black citizens. It is more likely, though, that for them the "us" connoted only white Americans.

The memorialization and resurrection of whiteness and white supremacy, after the brief threat of Black equality for nearly 4 million free Black people—now citizens—was due as much to Union veterans' recasting of the war as it was to white southerners' re-imaginings. Whiteness and white supremacy required a refusal to face whom that cruel war was over. And over the century and a half since, that refusal has morphed into denying or minimizing the costs of white supremacy and its impact on Black, Brown, and white people. Hundreds of thousands, if not millions, have been killed by discriminatory practices in health care, criminal justice, education, jobs, in almost every arena of this American life. We have not healed, and the festering wound keeps killing us.

At my father's memorial service, I repeated the prophet Jeremiah's lament "Is there no balm in Gilead? Is there no physician here? Why then is there no healing for the wound of my people?"[20] For Jeremiah and his people, there was none. And the fact that there was none was because of the people's sin, which included greed, deceit, and because their not having taken care of those they had harmed—"they heal the brokenness of the daughter of My people superficially, saying 'Peace, peace.' But there is no peace."[21]

My father never found a balm in Gilead. Our nation has yet to do so. And we won't if we don't deal with our past truthfully, accurately, and completely. If, someday we do, then we can sing, in the words of the old Negro spiritual,

There is a balm
In Gilead
To make the wounded whole
There is a balm
In Gilead
To save a sin-sick soul

Figure 2. Geoffrey Hancock Jr., circa 1998, outside Fort Huachuca, Arizona. (Photo by Patricia Hancock.)

Notes

1. Viet Thanh Nguyen, *Nothing Ever Dies: Vietnam and the Memory of War* (Cambridge, Mass.: Harvard University Press, 2016), 6–7. Nguyen also notes that ultimately "to argue over the Vietnam War or the American War is thus to argue over false choices. Each name obscures human losses, financial costs, and capital gains." Terms like "conflict" and "spilled" are not unusual in reliable, conscientious sources. See just a few examples, such as https://en.wikipedia.org/wiki/Vietnam_War; high school curriculum sites such as CK-12; William Lloyd-George, "The CIA's 'Secret War,'" *The Diplomat*, February 25, 2011. The number of US veterans' names on the Vietnam War Memorial is taken from the National Park Service; see https://www.nps.gov/vive/faqs.htm.

2. See J. David Hacker, "A Census-Based Count of the Civil War Dead," *Civil War History* 57 (December 2011): 307–48.

3. Viet Thanh Nguyen, "Just Memory: War and the Ethics of Remembrance," *American Literary History* 25, no. 1 (Spring 2013): 144.

4. To my knowledge, no scholarship has examined how Post-Traumatic Stress Disorder (PTSD) may have been exacerbated for those white soldiers on either side who accepted that the presence of African Americans as slaves was the central causal factor while simultaneously wanting to have little, if anything, to do with Black people. Dillon J. Carroll's fine work does argue that overall USCT veterans appear to have suffered less PTSD as a result of combat experience and also points out that historians have for the most part not sufficiently considered the ways in which some veterans did find ways to manage what they had experienced. Carroll does also document how many, many veterans tragically did not. See Carroll, *Invisible Wounds: Mental Illness and Civil War Soldiers* (Baton Rouge: Louisiana State University Press, 2021).

5. Alexander Stephens's infamous "Cornerstone speech" is widely available at reliable online sources. One source is Stanley Harrold, ed., *The Civil War and Reconstruction: A Documentary Reader* (Malden, Mass.: Blackwell Publishing, 2008), 61. Accessed August 14, 2020, http://nationalhumanitiescenter.org/ows/seminars/civilwarrecon/cwcause/Stephens%20Cornerstone%20Speech.pdf.

6. One of many excellent examples is Mississippi's secession declaration, which states emphatically that "Our position is thoroughly identified with the institution of slavery . . . none but the black race can bear exposure to the tropical sun. . . . a blow at slavery is a blow at commerce and civilization." See https://avalon.law.yale.edu/19th_century/csa_missec.asp and many other reliable online sources.

7. For examples of pre–Civil War Black challenges to white supremacy that center African Americans in emancipation efforts, see Manisha Sinha, *The Slave's Cause: A History of Abolition* (New Haven: Yale University Press, 2016); Richard Blackett, *The Captive's Quest for Freedom: Fugitive Slaves, the 1850 Fugitive Slave Law, and the Politics of Slavery* (New York: Cambridge University Press, 2018).

8. For an excellent survey and analysis of the historiographical discussion, see Nina Silber, "Reunion and Reconciliation, Reconsidered," *Journal of American History* 103 (June 2016): 59–83. David Blight's *Race and Reunion* pushed the debate into high gear, and others have provided invaluable responses that complicate his seminal work. See Blight, *Race and Reunion: The Civil War in American Memory* (Cambridge, Mass.:

The Belknap Press of Harvard University Press, 2001); Barbara A. Gannon, *The Won Cause: Black and White Comradeship in the Grand Army of the Republic* (Chapel Hill: University of North Carolina Press, 2011); Caroline E. Janney, *Remembering the Civil War: Reunion and the Limits of Reconciliation* (Chapel Hill: University of North Carolina Press, 2013); Gannon, *Americans Remember Their Civil War* (Santa Barbara: Praeger, 2017).

9. William A. Link, "The Civil War's Contested Past," *Reviews in American History* 42 (December 2014): 680.

10. Barbara Gannon, *The Won Cause*, 8, 162. Gannon astutely argues that white GAR members were part of a culture that was rejuvenating a past vision of America. I would argue that their reconstructed past vision had no room for challenging what other white men were doing to Black people in the South. For example, Sharon D. Kennedy-Nolle, in her analysis of Octave Thanet's novel, which was serialized in newspapers, notes that the novel was an example of "situating of vigilante violence at the postwar core of a rejuvenated white masculinity" in the 1890s. While there are no doubt exceptions, as a whole, white GAR membership seems to have been either unwilling or unequipped to mount a broad, sustained challenge to that rejuvenation. See Kennedy-Nolle, *Writing Reconstruction: Race, Gender, and Citizenship in the Postwar South* (Chapel Hill: University of North Carolina Press, 2015), 277.

11. Cheryl Renée Gooch, *Hinsonville's Heroes: Black Civil War Soldiers of Chester County, Pennsylvania* (Charleston: The History Press, 2018), 39. See Gooch's detailed recounting of the tragic life of Jay on pp. 38–48.

12. *Pennsylvania at Gettysburg: Ceremonies at the Dedication of the Monuments Erected by the Commonwealth of Pennsylvania*, v. 1 (1914), 497–98.

13. Bernard K. Gordon and Kathryn Young, "The Khmer Republic: That Was the Cambodia That Was," *Asian Survey* 11 (January 1971), 33–35; Sebastian Strangio, "Revisting Lon Nol's Cambodia," *The Phnom Penh Post*, 18 March 2010, https://www.phnompenhpost.com/national/revisiting-lon-nol's-cambodia ; James A. Tyner, *From Rice Fields to Killing Fields: Nature, Life, and Labor under the Khmer Rouge* (Syracuse, NY: Syracuse University Press, 2017), 60–62. For a brief overview and guide to other sources on US activity in Cambodia, see "Cambodia: U.S. bombing and civil war" at https://sites.tufts.edu/atrocityendings/2015/08/07/cambodia-u-s-bombing-civil-war-khmer-rouge/.

14. *Pennsylvania at Gettysburg*, 468.

15. *Pennsylvania at Gettysburg*, 477.

16. *Pennsylvania at Gettysburg* v. 1 (1914), 497.

17. *Pennsylvania at Gettysburg* v. 1 (1914), 497.

18. *Gettysburg Star and Sentinel*, June 12, 1888.

19. *Pennsylvania at Gettysburg* v. 1 (1914), 455–56.

20. Jeremiah 8:22, *New International Version*.

21. Jeremiah 8:11, *New American Standard Bible*.

Acknowledgments

We started discussing this book in June 2020, weeks after the murder of George Floyd. We naïvely thought that we could publish this book quickly, not expecting the disruptions and longevity of the global pandemic would have on so many, including us. We appreciate the patience of the contributors. The anonymous readers provided good suggestions to improve the manuscript. We thank Fredric Nachbaur and the entire team at Fordham University Press for the opportunity and support to create this important volume.

Hilary thanks her colleagues at Davidson College and Department of Gender and Race Studies at the University of Alabama who served as a sounding board, read drafts, and encouraged her in the entire process. She also would like to thank Holly Pinheiro, Adam Domby, Annie Merrill, Jessica Worl, and Rose Stemlau. She is thankful for the patience showed her as she transitioned to her new institutional home at Davidson College. Last, she wants to acknowledge her parents, brothers, friends, and the presidential cats who have supported without fail and helped her survive the worst effects of this global pandemic and the slow return to normalcy.

Andy appreciates the support of the History Department at East Tennessee State University for projects like this. He also thanks his family for discussing the project and offering advice, in particular Carl McCargo, Jackie Shanti, and Derek Slap. And of course, Andy knows that none of this would have been possible without Nicole Slap's taking care of two children during a pandemic while he spent countless hours in the office working on this book.

This book has been a journey for us as historians and people. We thank all of you who have accompanied and helped us on the journey.
    Hilary Green and Andy Slap

Contributors

John Bardes is an assistant professor of history at Louisiana State University. His work explores policing and incarceration in the context of slavery and emancipation. He is the author of *The Carceral City: Slavery and the Making of Mass Incarceration in New Orleans, 1803–1930* (Chapel Hill: University of North Carolina Press, 2024). His scholarship has appeared in many journals, including the *Journal of African American History*, *American Quarterly*, and *Journal of Southern History*.

Karen Cook Bell, an associate professor of history at Bowie State University, received her Ph.D. in history from Howard University. Her scholarship has appeared in the *Journal of African American History*, *Georgia Historical Quarterly*, *Passport; U.S. West-Africa: Interaction and Relations* (2008), *Before Obama: A Reappraisal of Black Reconstruction Era Politicians* (2012), *Converging Identities: Blackness in the Contemporary Diaspora* (2013), and *Slavery and Freedom in Savannah* (2014). She has published *Claiming Freedom: Race, Kinship, and Land in Nineteenth Century Georgia* (Columbia: University of South Carolina Press, 2018), which won the Georgia Board of Regents Excellence in Research Award. Her current book, *Running from Bondage: Enslaved Women and Their Remarkable Fight for Freedom in Revolutionary America*, is under contract with Cambridge University Press.

Daryl A. Carter is a professor of history in the Department of History and Associate Dean in the College of Arts and Sciences at East Tennessee State University. He is the author of *Brother Bill: President Clinton and the Politics of Race and Class* (Fayetteville: University of Arkansas Press, 2016).

Beau Cleland is an assistant professor at the University of Calgary. He is also a combat veteran of the US Army who served in Iraq and Afghanistan. His current research focuses on the ties between the Confederacy and the British Empire during the Civil War, and the importance of private citizens in creating and sustaining support for the rebellion in British America. His scholarship has appeared in *The Journal of Southern History*.

Emmanuel Dabney is a public historian based in Virginia. He holds a B.A. in Historic Preservation from the University of Mary Washington and an M.A. in History with a concentration in Public History from UNC-Greensboro. Emmanuel has given numerous presentations and written other essays and book reviews.

Adam H. Domby is an associate professor of history at Auburn University. He is the author of *The False Cause: Fraud, Fabrication, and White Supremacy in Confederate Memory* (Charlottesville: University of Virginia Press, 2020). He co-edited *Freedoms Gained and*

Lost: Reconstruction and Its Meanings 150 Years Later (New York: Fordham University Press, 2021). In 2018 he won the John T. Hubble Prize for the best article in *Civil War History*.

Myisha S. Eatmon, an assistant professor of African and African American Studies in the History Department at Harvard University, received her Ph.D. from Northwestern University. Her dissertation, "Public Wrongs, Private Rights: African Americans, Private Law, and White Violence during Jim Crow," traces the history of what Eatmon calls Black legal culture under Jim Crow, examining Black litigation strategies in response to white violence, Black newspapers' coverage of white violence, and Black newspapers and the NAACP's work as legal networkers. She was an ASLH Kathryn T. Preyer Scholar (2018), J. Willard Hurst Fellow (2019), and ACLS/Mellon DCF Fellow (2018–19).

Barbara A. Gannon is a professor of history at the University of Central Florida. She is the author of *The Won Cause: Black and White Comradeship in the Grand Army of the Republic* (Chapel Hill: University of North Carolina Press), which received the Wiley-Silver Prize for the best first book on the Civil War and an honorable mention by the Lincoln Prize Committee 2012, as well as being a finalist for the Jefferson Davis Prize. She has also published *Americans Remember Their Civil War* (Praeger) and numerous articles.

Hilary N. Green is James B. Duke Professor of Africana Studies, Africana Studies Department, Davidson College. She is the author of *Educational Reconstruction: African American Schools in the Urban South, 1865–1890* (New York: Fordham University Press, 2016), as well as numerous essays and articles. She is currently at work on two projects: a book manuscript examining how everyday African Americans remembered and commemorated the Civil War, and a digital humanities project on Black Civil War memory.

Scott Hancock is an associate professor of history and Africana Studies at Gettysburg College. After spending fourteen years working with teenagers in crisis, he switched careers and received a Ph.D. in Early American History in 1999 from the University of New Hampshire. This combination of careers fuels his desire to tell the stories of people whom society and history have tended to discount as troublesome and unimportant. Currently he is exploring how whiteness, white supremacy, and the systemic rejection of Blackness were the unifying features of white American identity and politics across the North–South divide, and how that unity was manifested during the creation of Civil War battlefields. Some of his scholarly work has appeared in the anthologies *Paths to Freedom*; *We Shall Independent Be*; *Slavery, Resistance, Freedom*; and in the journal *Civil War History*. As part of trying to continue being an activist scholar, he engages in dialogue with visitors to the Gettysburg battlefields and contributes to local and regional newspapers such as the *Gettysburg Times* and *Philadelphia Inquirer* or online publications such as CityLab.

William Horne is an Arthur J. Ennis Postdoctoral Fellow at Villanova University who writes about the relationship of race to labor, freedom, and capitalism in post–Civil War Louisiana. He holds a Ph.D. in history from The George Washington University and is co-founder and editor of *The Activist History Review*. His scholarship has appeared in the *Journal of Academic Freedom* and the *Journal of African American History*, along with contribution to numerous edited collections.

Andre E. Johnson is a professor of Communication Studies at the University of Memphis. He is the author of three national award-winning books, *The Forgotten Prophet: Bishop Henry McNeal Turner and the African American Prophetic Tradition* (2012), *The Struggle Over Black Lives Matter and All Lives Matter* (with Amanda Nell Edgar, Ph.D., 2018), and *No Future in This Country: The Prophetic Pessimism of Bishop Henry McNeal Turner* (2020). He is also the editor of the forthcoming *Speeches of Bishop Henry McNeal Turner: The Press, the Platform, and the Pulpit* (2023) and *Preaching During a Pandemic: The Rhetoric of the Black Preaching Tradition* (with Kimberly P. Johnson, Ph.D., and Wallis C. Baxter IV, Ph.D., 2023).

LeeAnna Keith teaches history at the Collegiate School for Boys in New York City. She is the author of *When It Was Grand: The Radical Republican History of the Civil War* (Hill & Wang) and *The Colfax Massacre: The Untold Story of Black Power, White Terror, and the Death of Reconstruction* (New York: Oxford University Press, 2009).

Jonathan Lande is an assistant professor of history at Purdue University. He earned his Ph.D. at Brown University in 2018 and won the Allan Nevins Dissertation Prize from the Society of American Historians and the Cromwell Dissertation Prize from the American Society for Legal History. He is currently completing a book exploring the desertions and mutinies of formerly enslaved men in the Union Army and their trials in the military justice system during the Civil War, which is under contract with Oxford University Press. Lande has published articles in the *Journal of American History*, *Journal of Social History*, *Journal of African American History*, *Journal of American Ethnic History*, *Civil War History*, and the *Washington Post*.

Anne E. Marshall is an associate professor of history at Mississippi State University. She is the author of *Creating a Confederate Kentucky: The Lost Cause and Civil War Memory in a Border State* (Chapel Hill: University of North Carolina Press, 2010). She is also the author of numerous articles in journals and collections, including *Slavery & Abolition*, *Agricultural History*, and *Master Narratives: Storytelling, History, and the Postmodern South* (Baton Rouge: Louisiana State University Press, 2013). In 2011 she won the George and Ann Richards Award for best article in *The Journal of the Civil War Era*.

Jaime Amanda Martinez is a professor of history at the University of North Carolina at Pembroke and the author of *Confederate Slave Impressment in the Upper South* (Chapel Hill: University of North Carolina Press, 2013).

Andrew L. Slap, a professor of history at East Tennessee State University, is the author of *The Doom of Reconstruction: The Liberal Republicans in the Civil War Era* (New York: Fordham University Press, 2006). He is also the editor or co-editor of three volumes on the Civil War era. His current book project is *African American Communities during Slavery, War, and Peace: Memphis in the Nineteenth Century.*

Nicole Myers Turner, an assistant professor at Princeton University, is the author of *Soul Liberty: The Evolution of Black Religious Politics in Post-Emancipation Virginia* (Chapel Hill: University of North Carolina Press, 2020).

Samuel Watts received his Ph.D. from The University of Melbourne, researching and writing about Black experiences of Reconstruction in the urban Deep South. He is the managing editor of ANZASA Online, writes for the *Australian Book Review*, and was recently awarded the Wyselaskie Scholarship for History award.

Index

Abbeville, SC, xiv
Aboriginal activists, 97, 99–100
Aboriginal communities, 3, 99–101
Aboriginal resistance, 97, 99–100
African American community, 3, 6, 41, 72n10, 117, 118
African American soldiers, xxi, 50–52, 57–60, 62–63 (see also USCT soldiers)
African American troops, 63n4, 110, 128 (see also specific regiments)
African American veterans, 50, 77, 143, (see also USCT veterans)
African Americans, xv–xvi, xxi, 1, 3, 4, 13, 16–17, 19–20, 22–23, 25, 29–31, 33, 40–44, 50, 53, 61, 66–70, 74–79, 91–94, 95n6, 100, 109, 111–112, 114, 116–118, 120, 123, 125, 127, 143, 146
African Methodist Episcopal (AME) Church, xv, 4, 117, 122
Ali, Muhammad, 2
Ambler, Javier, 97
American Revolution, 76
anti-Blackness, 35, 57, 62, 81, 84, 94
Anti-Defamation League, 17
ANTIFA, 13
AR-15 rifle, 4, 62
Arbery, Ahmaud, 3, 40, 41, 44, 60, 119, 141
Army of Northern Virginia (ANV), 13
assassinations, xvii, 2, 17, 74, 77
Aurora, CO, 3

Baldwin, James, 1, 62
Ball, Thomas, 77
Baptist Church, 23, 25, 29, 86
baseball, 66–68, 70–71
basketball, 66, 70, 71, 73n21
Battle of Liberty Place, 16, 18

Battle of Olustee, 59
Black Americans, (see African Americans)
Black bodies, xix, 6, 30, 35, 40, 50
Black communities, (see African American communities)
Black death, xiv, xviii
Black Lives Matter (BLM): BLM activists, 57, 60–63, 83, 99; BLM movement, 49, 83, 88, 93, 97, 99–101; BLM protesters, 2, 43, 62; BLM protests, 3, 62, 74, 98, 101; clothing and paraphernalia, 13, 50, 52–53; hashtag, 1, 49, 60
Black Louisianians, 39–40, 43
Black Power salute, 67
Black Twitter, 93
Blake, Jacob, 35, 61, 94
Bland, Sandra, 94
Brandenburg, KY, 117–120
Brooks, Rayshard, 35
Brown communities, 3, 7, 41, 68, 81–83, 141, 147
Brown, Andrew, 141
Brown, Michael, 49, 60, 94, 97
Bryant, Ma'khia, 141
Burford, Jr., Lawson, 90–91, 93–94
Burford, Sr., Lawson, 91–92
Burton, Andrea, 52–53
Bush, George W., 17, 68
Butler, Benjamin, 76

Castile, Philando, 94
Charleston, SC, 4, 30–31, 79, 83, 110, 117, 122–129
Charlottesville, VA, 18, 62, 112, 119
The Christian Recorder, xv, xvi, xviii, 57, 59
Civil Rights Movement, 17, 61, 68, 69, 83, 100, 111, 128

Civil War, 13, 16, 18, 20, 22, 25–26, 29, 31–32, 49–50, 54, 58–60, 67, 71, 74–79, 90, 98, 99, 107, 108, 110, 113, 115, 118, 127, 131, 137n1, 141–142, 144
Civil War centennial, 17, 127
Civil War historians, 5, 22, 25, 74, 75, 116, 131, 141
Cole, W. R., 90
Colfax Massacre, 107–110, 112
Colfax Riot marker, 107–110, 112
college campuses, 4, 127
College of Charleston, 122, 126–127
Columbia, SC, xiv, xvii
Confederacy, 20, 22, 24–25, 107, 119, 124, 127, 135–136, 142–144
Confederate flags, 117, 133
Confederate generals, 4, 5, 18, 20, 52, 84, 118, 131–132, 135
Confederate States of America, 15, 114
Confederate symbols, 113, 117, 137
Confederates, 99, 117, 118, 127, 129, 136, 137, 138n9
Constitution, U.S., 14, 18, 85, 86, 87, 91, 93, 145
constitutional conventions, state, xv, 33, 86, 87
contraband camps, 81, 85, 87
contrabands, 84
Corps d'Afrique, 76
COVID-19 pandemic, vii, xxii, 1– 3, 18, 53, 81–84, 88, 109, 122, 141, 151
Crawford, John, 94
Critical Race Theory (CRT), 5, 6, 129
Crutcher, Terence, 94
Cuomo, Andrew, 81

Democratic National Party (DNC), xviii, 16, 18, 22, 25, 111
Douglass, Frederick, 4–5, 49, 50, 58–59, 74, 77–79, 146–147
DuBois, W.E.B., 1, 6, 75
Dungay, Jr., David, 97, 101

East Tennessee State University (ETSU), 70–71, 151

Edmond, Alton, 53
emancipation, 75–76, 78–79
Emancipation Memorial (Boston), 74
Emancipation Memorial (Washington DC), 74, 77, 78, 79
Emancipation Proclamation, 49, 74, 75, 84, 85, 99
Emanuel AME Church, 4, 117, 122

Ferguson, MO, 49–50, 60, 94
Field Order No. 15, 84
Fifty-Fifth Massachusetts regiment, 57, 59–60
Fifty-Fourth Massachusetts regiment, 58
Floyd, George: cellphone footage, 1, 2, 23, 34; Chauvin, Derek, xiv, 1, 2, 35, 68, 74, 141; Frazier, Darnella, xxiii, 2, 68; international protests, 98, 101; Minneapolis Police Department, 35, 41, 43; murder, xiii, xxi, 1–3, 28, 34–35, 41, 43, 74, 81–82, 97–98, 107, 119, 133, 141, 151; racial reckoning, xxi, xxii, 1, 4, 5, 74, 78, 112; US protests, 50, 107, 123, 133
football, 60–61, 66, 70
Ford, Gerald, 69
Fort Fisher, 20–22
Fort Fisher State Historic Site, 25–26
Forty-Third United States Colored Infantry (USCI), 59
Fourth of July holiday, 4, 13, 58–59
Fourth United States Colored Infantry (USCI), 52
Freedmen's Bureau agents, xvi, 39, 42, 43
Freedom Park, 115–119
Freedom Rides, 49, 100
Freeman, Isaac, 51

Garner, Eric, 40, 44, 94, 97, 101
Gettysburg National Military Park, 4, 7, 144
Gettysburg, PA, 19, 49, 138n2, 144–146
Glynn County, GA, 3
Grand Army of the Republic (GAR), 143, 146, 150n10
Grant, Oscar, 94

INDEX

Grant, Shepard, 42–43
Grant, Ulysses S., 4, 84
Gray, Freddie, 94
Great Emancipator, 74, 77

Hamburg Massacre, 125
Hamer, Fannie Lou, 107
Hancock, Jr., Geoffrey, 140–143, 147–148
Hannah-Jones, Nikole, 5, 45n11
Harper, Frances Ellen Watkins, xviii
hashtag, #AllLivesMatter, 49
hashtag, #BlackLivesMatter, 49, 60
Hayes, Rutherford B., 5
Heyer, Heather, 18, 62
Hispanic Americans, 18–19
Historical Markers, xxi, 108, 115
Home Guards, 20– 22
Huntsville, AL, 107–108

Indigenous communities, 3, 4, 7, 15, 41, 98–101
Indigenous dispossession, 98–99

James, LeBron, 66
January 6, 2021 insurrection, 5
Jim Crow, xviii, 23, 33, 69, 88, 90–94, 111, 114, 122, 128, 134
Johnson, Andrew, 3, 4
Johnson, Lyndon B., 3

Kaepernick, Colin, 60, 61, 66, 70
Kennedy, Robert F., 2
Kerner Commission Report of 1968, 3
Khmer Rouge, 144, 150n13
King, Jr., Martin Luther, 1, 2, 17
King, Rodney, 68
Ku Klux Klan, xvii, 2, 13, 15–16, 22, 25, 108, 112

labor, 16, 17, 21–22, 26, 40, 43, 68, 75, 84, 98, 101, 111
labor contracts, 38–39
Latino communities, 34, 41, 68, 81, 82, 83, 141, 147
lawsuits, 91–94

Lee, Robert E., 5, 18, 84, 124, 135–136, 138–139n12
Lewis, John, 60, 85, 107
Lexington, KY, 119
LGBTQ communities, 18
Lincoln, Abraham, xv, 4, 5, 14, 49, 74, 77–79, 85, 99
Lost Cause, 6, 107, 114–115, 118–119, 132–137, 139n12
Louisville, KY, 3, 41, 53, 113–120
Lowry gang, 23
Lowry, Henry Berry, 20, 24
Lumbee communities, 20–25

Mace, Nancy, 129
Martin, Trayvon, 40, 44, 60, 69
Mason-Dixon line, 67, 142
McClain, Elijah, 3
memory, xiv, xxi, xxii, 4–5, 7, 14, 77, 110–112, 114, 123, 131–135, 141–143
Memphis, TN, 31, 33, 52, 66
Memphis Massacre of 1866, 33
militiamen, 14, 15, 18, 58, 107, 125
militias, 13–19, 21, 49, 30, 62
Miller, Abaline, 38–39, 41, 44
Mitchell, Samuel Chiles, 124–125
monuments/memorials: Christopher Columbus monuments, 4, 78; Confederate monuments, xxi, 6, 78, 107, 111, 113, 125–126, 134; contextualization, 116; Fort Johnson Monument, 126, 128; Gettysburg National Military Park monuments, 143–145; John C. Calhoun monument, 79, 122–124, 126, 129; Louisville Confederate monument, 113–114; removal, 79, 112, 119–120, 122, 124, 129; removal debates, 107, 116, 117, 119–120, 125–126, 128; Robert E. Lee statue, 18; Sons of Confederate Veterans, 110, 117; Wade Hampton monument, 124–125
Morrison, Scott, 97–99, 101–102

National Guard, 16–17, 120, 134, 135, 138n9, 139n16
Native American activism, 100

Native Americans, 14, 20–22, 24–26, 116
National Collegiate Athletic Association (NCAA), 66, 71n1
National Football League (NFL), 60–61
New Orleans, LA, xv, xviii, 16, 30, 32–33
New Orleans Massacre of 1866, 33
New York, NY, 30, 34, 67, 79, 81, 94, 108–109, 112
newspapers, xiv–xv, 31, 32, 57, 58, 59, 109, 110, 146, 150n10
1968 Summer Olympics, 2, 67
Nixon, Richard, 3, 144
North Charleston, SC, 94

Obama, Barack, 17, 18, 69, 109
Oklahoma City, OK, bombing, 17

patriotism, 57–59, 62–63
plantations, 22, 31, 33, 38–40, 49, 75, 76, 99, 108, 124
police brutality, xix, xxi, 3, 7, 71, 81, 101, 133–134
police harassment, 33, 50, 52, 93
police violence, vii, 2, 28, 43, 83, 90–91, 94, 98, 101
Polk, Leonidas, 131–133
Presidential Election of 1876, 5, 16, 107
Presidential Election of 2020, 1, 5
Pringle, John J., 38–40, 42–43
prison, xvi, 31, 41, 52, 83, 97, 98, 109, 143
Pulitzer Prize, 2, 5
Puryear, Elmer, 127–128

racial reckoning, xxi, 1, 4, 5, 74, 78, 112
racism, xxi, xxii, 3–4, 19, 45n11, 53, 59, 60, 62, 70, 71, 85, 87, 94, 98, 101, 124, 128–129, 134
Reagan, Ronald, 69
reconciliation, 5, 135, 142
Reconstruction, xvi, xix, 3–7, 13–14, 16, 18, 75, 81, 83–85, 89n6, 108–109, 125, 127–128, 146
repair and reparations, 7, 101
Republican National Party (RNC), xviii, 16, 18, 25, 68, 108, 125, 126

resistance, xxi, 7, 14, 18, 23, 62, 76, 83, 90–91, 93–94, 97–99, 100–101, 137
Rice, Tamir, 40, 44, 94
Richmond, VA, 28, 31, 33–34
Rittenhouse, Kyle, 2
Robeson County, NC, 20–25
Robinson, Jackie, 67
Rose, II, Antwon, 94
Roof, Dylann, 17, 83, 117
Ruby Ridge, ID, 17

Savannah, GA, 30
Scott, Charlotte, 77
Scott, Derrick, 97
Scott, Ned, 28–29
Scott, Virginia, 29
Scott, Walter, 94
Seidule, Ty, 137
self-determination, 99–100
self-emancipation, xxi, 31, 74–77, 84–85
self-ownership, 92
The 1776 Commission, 4–5
Sherman, William Tecumseh, 22, 84
Simpson, O.J., 66
The 1619 Project, xxi, 5
slave patrols, xxi, 14, 15, 30, 38, 40
slavery, xxi, 5, 13–14, 38– 40, 42–44, 49, 54, 57– 59, 67, 74–76, 78–79, 81, 84–88, 94, 98–99, 118, 124, 128, 138n22, 142–146, 149n6
Singleton, William Henry, 54
Smith, Tommie 2, 67
sports, 2, 66, 67, 68, 70, 71
Southern Claims Commission, 21
Southern Poverty Law Center, 17
Southern Strategy, 69
summer of 2020, vii, xxi, 3, 5–7, 20, 25–26, 68, 70, 107, 109, 123, 133, 137
surveillance, 38, 40, 42, 98
Sydney, Australia, 3, 100

Taylor, Breonna, 3, 35, 40–41, 44, 53, 60, 79, 91, 94, 107, 119–120, 141
Taylor, Maxwell, 136
terrorists, xix, 17, 62

Terry, O'Shae, 94
Terry, Capt. T.Z., 90, 91
Thirteenth Amendment, 38, 75
Tilden, Samuel, 5
Toombs, Robert, 136
trauma, 100–101, 140–141, 143
Truman, Harry S., 68
Trump, Donald, 3–5, 18, 24–25, 61–62
Turner, Henry McNeal, xiv–xix

Unite the Right rally, 18, 62, 112, 119
United Daughters of the Confederacy (UDC), 6, 110, 113, 125, 135
University of Louisville (U of L), 115, 117–118, 129
University of Memphis, 66
University of North Carolina, Chapel Hill, 126–127
University of North Carolina, Pembroke (UNCP), 20, 23
University of Virginia, 18
US Army, 57–61
USCT soldiers, xv, 50–52, 54, 59, 143
USCT veterans, 143
US Military installation renaming: Center of Military History self-study, 134; Lost Cause installations, 134–137; namesakes, bases/installations, 131, 134, 136; namesakes, National Guard installations, 134; 2021 Department of Defense Appropriation Bill, 137

Vesey, Denmark, 128
Vietnam War, 2, 17, 140–141, 144
violence: performative violence, 28, 35; police brutality, xix, xxi, 3, 7, 71, 81, 101, 133–134; racial incidents, xiii, 2, 43, 53; racial massacres, 107–112, 125; rhetorical, 62, 69; violence as spectacle, 28, 34–25
voter suppression, xix, 111, 125–126
voters, 25, 68, 125
voting rights, 33, 85, 88, 111–112

Waller County, TX, 94
Warriors of the Aboriginal Resistance (WAR), 99–101
West Point, 132–133, 135–136
white Christian nationalism, xix
White Leagues, 16, 18
white supremacy, xxi–xxii, 3, 13–19, 40, 43, 61, 62, 69, 71, 84, 91–94, 97–101, 107–108, 110–112, 116–117, 119, 122–125, 128, 133, 142–143, 147
whiteness, 109, 142–143, 147
Whitmer, Gretchen, 18
Wilson, Darren, 49
Woodson, Carter G., 60
Works Progress Administration (WPA), 21, 111

Reconstructing America
Andrew L. Slap, series editor

Hans L. Trefousse, *Impeachment of a President: Andrew Johnson, the Blacks, and Reconstruction.*

Richard Paul Fuke, *Imperfect Equality: African Americans and the Confines of White Ideology in Post-Emancipation Maryland.*

Ruth Currie-McDaniel, *Carpetbagger of Conscience: A Biography of John Emory Bryant.*

Paul A. Cimbala and Randall M. Miller, eds., *The Freedmen's Bureau and Reconstruction: Reconsiderations.*

Herman Belz, *A New Birth of Freedom: The Republican Party and Freedmen's Rights, 1861 to 1866.*

Robert Michael Goldman, *"A Free Ballot and a Fair Count": The Department of Justice and the Enforcement of Voting Rights in the South, 1877–1893.*

Ruth Douglas Currie, ed., *Emma Spaulding Bryant: Civil War Bride, Carpetbagger's Wife, Ardent Feminist—Letters, 1860–1900.*

Robert Francis Engs, *Freedom's First Generation: Black Hampton, Virginia, 1861–1890.*

Robert F. Kaczorowski, *The Politics of Judicial Interpretation: The Federal Courts, Department of Justice, and Civil Rights, 1866–1876.*

John Syrett, *The Civil War Confiscation Acts: Failing to Reconstruct the South.*

Michael Les Benedict, *Preserving the Constitution: Essays on Politics and the Constitution in the Reconstruction Era.*

Andrew L. Slap, *The Doom of Reconstruction: The Liberal Republicans in the Civil War Era.*

Edmund L. Drago, *Confederate Phoenix: Rebel Children and Their Families in South Carolina.*

Mary Farmer-Kaiser, *Freedwomen and the Freedmen's Bureau: Race, Gender, and Public Policy in the Age of Emancipation.*

Paul A. Cimbala and Randall Miller, eds., *The Great Task Remaining Before Us: Reconstruction as America's Continuing Civil War.*

John A. Casey Jr., *New Men: Reconstructing the Image of the Veteran in Late-Nineteenth-Century American Literature and Culture.*

Hilary Green, *Educational Reconstruction: African American Schools in the Urban South, 1865–1890.*

Christopher B. Bean, *Too Great a Burden to Bear: The Struggle and Failure of the Freedmen's Bureau in Texas.*

David E. Goldberg, *The Retreats of Reconstruction: Race, Leisure, and the Politics of Segregation at the New Jersey Shore, 1865–1920.*

David Prior, ed., *Reconstruction in a Globalizing World.*

Jewel L. Spangler and Frank Towers, eds., *Remaking North American Sovereignty: State Transformation in the 1860s.*

Adam H. Domby and Simon Lewis, eds., *Freedoms Gained and Lost: Reconstruction and Its Meanings 150 Years Later.*

David Prior, ed., *Reconstruction and Empire: The Legacies of Abolition and Union Victory for an Imperial Age.*

Sandra M. Gustafson and Robert S. Levine, eds., *Reimagining the Republic: Race, Citizenship, and Nation in the Literary Work of Albion W. Tourgée.* Foreword by Carolyn L. Karcher.

Brian Schoen, Jewel L. Spangler, and Frank Towers, eds., *Continent in Crisis: The U.S. Civil War in North America.*

Raymond James Krohn, *Abolitionist Twilights: History, Meaning, and the Fate of Racial Egalitarianism, 1865–1909.*

Hilary N. Green and Andrew L. Slap, eds., *The Civil War and the Summer of 2020.*

www.ingramcontent.com/pod-product-compliance
Lightning Source LLC
Chambersburg PA
CBHW020413080526
44584CB00014B/1304